James Morgan Hart

German universities: a narrative of personal experience, together with recent statistical information, practical suggestions, and a comparison of the German, English and American systems of higher education

James Morgan Hart

German universities: a narrative of personal experience, together with recent statistical information, practical suggestions, and a comparison of the German, English and American systems of higher education

ISBN/EAN: 9783337157302

Printed in Europe, USA, Canada, Australia, Japan

Cover: Foto ©Andreas Hilbeck / pixelio.de

More available books at **www.hansebooks.com**

GERMAN UNIVERSITIES:

A

NARRATIVE OF PERSONAL EXPERIENCE,

TOGETHER WITH

RECENT STATISTICAL INFORMATION, PRACTICAL SUGGESTIONS, AND A COMPARISON OF THE GERMAN, ENGLISH AND AMERICAN SYSTEMS OF HIGHER EDUCATION.

BY

JAMES MORGAN HART.

NEW YORK:
G. P. PUTNAM'S SONS,
FOURTH AVENUE AND TWENTY-THIRD STREET.
1874.

Entered, according to Act of Congress, in the year eighteen hundred and
seventy-four,

By G. P. PUTNAM'S SONS,

In the office of the Librarian of Congress, at Washington.

CONTENTS.

PART I. — PERSONAL NARRATIVE.

CHAPTER.		PAGE.
I.	First Impressions of Göttingen,	1
II.	Attacking German,	19
III.	Matriculation and Lectures,	35
IV.	*Auf der Mensur*,	65
V.	Daylight in German,	84
VI.	Idlesse,	100
VII.	Removal to Berlin — *Umsatteln*,	104
VIII.	Wiesbaden — The Institutes,	122
IX.	Anniversary of Battle of Leipsic — *Commers*,	137
X.	The Pandects,	149
XI.	The American Colony — Birthdays,	158
XII.	"Spurting,"	172
XIII.	The Final Agony of Preparation,	192
XIV.	Examination,	217

PART II. — GENERAL REMARKS.

I.	What is a University?	249
II.	Professors,	264
III.	*Privatdocenten*,	276
IV.	Students,	287
V.	Discipline,	313
VI.	Comparison with English Universities,	321
VII.	Comparison with American Colleges,	338
VIII.	Statistics of German Universities,	356
IX.	Practical Hints	383

TO

GEORGE HAVEN PUTNAM,

WHOSE STEADFAST WISH HAS BEEN FATHER TO THE AUTHOR'S
THOUGHT, THIS BOOK IS INSCRIBED, IN FRIENDLY
REMEMBRANCE OF THE

GEORGIA AUGUSTA, 1861–2.

PREFACE.

Much has been published in a fugitive form upon the fruitful topic of university life in Germany. One man has taken up the lecture-system, another the dueling, a third the manners and customs of the instructors or of the students. But no one, I believe, has told, in a plain, straightforward narrative, how he himself passed his time at the university, what he studied, and what he accomplished. It seemed to me, therefore, that I might do the cause of education in America some service, by offering my own experience as a sample of German student-life in the average. Had my career in Göttingen been an extraordinary one, full of exciting episodes, I should have hesitated to make it public. But precisely because it was so uneventful, so like the lives of my associates, I have deemed it fit to serve as a model for illustration, not imitation, and as a basis for digression. I have had throughout but one aim: to communicate facts and impressions from which the reader might draw his own inferences. Even those portions of the Personal Narrative which assume the form of argument are intended to remove prejudices, not to state final conclusions.

The General Remarks must abide the verdict as they stand. If they contain aught that is erroneous or distorted, the present is not the place for correction. I can only say that I have striven faithfully to make them both accurate and just. Should the reader be disposed to regard my estimate of the German Universities as extravagant, of the English as too unfavorable, I would refer him to an oration delivered by von Sybel, in 1868, upon "German and Foreign Universities." It forms part of a volume entitled *Vorträge und Aufsätze*, recently published under the auspices of the *Allgemeiner Verein für deutsche Literatur*. The renowned historian, who is certainly the last man to be taxed with blind, unreasoning patriotism, approaches the subject from a different side, yet his views bear such close resemblance, both in form and in spirit, to those set forth in the present work, that, to escape the imputation of unfair borrowing, I feel bound to state explicitly that I did not read the oration, in fact was not aware of its existence, until my own manuscript had passed entirely into the hands of the printer. After all, there can be but one opinion as to the merits of the several university systems of England, France and Germany.

It may not be superfluous to add that the present work is not an attack upon the American College. Although holding that the German method of

Higher Education is far above our own, I should be very sorry to see that method adopted at once, and in the lump. Before taking decided steps towards the expansion of our colleges into quasi universities, it will be advisable for us to consider thoroughly what a university really is, what it accomplishes, what it does not accomplish, the basis upon which it rests, the relations that it holds to the nation at large. Until we have formed clear and stable conceptions upon all these points, innovation, I fear, will be only tinkering, not reform. If I have succeeded in throwing any light upon the subject, my wish is abundantly realized.

J. M. H.

NEW YORK, *August*, 1874.

GERMAN UNIVERSITIES.

CHAPTER I.

First Impressions of Göttingen.

ON a quiet Saturday afternoon — the last, if I remember aright — in the month of August, 1861, I took my first stroll "around the wall" of the town of Göttingen. I little imagined that the quaint group of rather scraggy looking houses then unrolling itself before my eyes for the first time was to be my home for three long years. I had reached Göttingen late the preceding night, having traveled through by the day express from Basel, Switzerland. The journey had been, of course, a fatiguing one. It was midnight before I had been able to get to bed, and although a prolonged rest had done something in the way of refreshing me, I still felt disposed to take life easily. The weather was suited to my mood. The summer of 1861 was very hot and dry throughout Europe, causing the foliage to turn and fall much sooner than common; on that particular afternoon, a cool breeze rustled among the fast withering linden tops, and whispered already of autumn and early winter. The sober colors of the houses and garden walls, the general tameness of the North German landscape visible from the summit of the wall, the comparative insignificance of the surrounding hills, the entire atmosphere of the place to which I had been suddenly transplanted, disposed me to reflection. My sense of the picturesque was not wounded by the perception of positive ugliness, nor was there any thing in the state of my personal affairs to call forth a feeling of sadness; I was simply in a mood for revery. My first year abroad had been passed in Geneva, on the borders of the glorious lake, and in sight of the still more glorious Mont Blanc; I had just finished a pedestrian tour of many weeks through the Upper Alps, had seen all the beauties of Chamounix, the Bernese Oberland and Zermatt, had risked my neck more than once on glacier and *arête*. Small wonder, then, that the contrast was striking, not to say oppressive; I missed all that I was accustomed to feast my eyes upon, the rich, warm glow of Switzerland in its summer radiance, the rocks, and eternal snows, and blue waters.

I was to adjust my faculties of perception to novel surroundings, my habits of thought to a fresh phase of life. The very walk over which I directed my footsteps was something wholly strange and unexpected, something without an analogy in my previous experience. Göttingen was, in the Middle Ages, a town of some importance, and in consequence strongly fortified, for those days, by an earth wall. This wall, erected before the era of artillery, is nothing more than a rampart of earth completely encircling the town, deflecting here and there from the line of the circle because of inequalities in the ground, but without any of those salient and reentering angles which are the characteristic features of modern artillery walls. It is useless for the purposes of defense. The Hanoverian troops, on their retreat through from Hanover to Langensalza, in 1866, did not even make an attempt to hold the town, although it lay directly in the line of the Prussian advance from the north, and although checking that advance for only a few hours might have enabled them to break through the intercepting force on the south. The wall is simply a promenade, about twenty-five or thirty feet wide at the top, and averaging fifteen feet in height. There is a row of lindens on each side, the branches of which overarch so as to form a shaded avenue in summer; in winter, the wall, being high and exposed to the rays of the sun throughout its entire length, is always dry under foot. It is the walk by eminence of Göttingen; when one man asks another to take a walk, he means, as a matter of course, "around the wall," unless he specifies some excursion into the country. The wall has been broken through in five places for the entrance of the country roads. The quondam ditch or moat running around the wall outside is entirely dry, except for a short distance, where it has been enlarged into a sort of pond, and is used for vegetable and fruit gardens, or converted into a public park. The houses of the town do not abut against the wall, but stand back, generally at some distance; the intervening space is cut up into house gardens. The time occupied in making the circuit of the wall is forty-five minutes of average walking. Go when you will, morning, afternoon, or evening, by rain or by shine, in the nipping frost of winter or the oppressive heat of summer, you may be sure of meeting promenaders out for a stroll: grave professors snatching a few minutes of relaxation from their manuscripts, and looking as meek and helpless out in the open air as a policeman off duty; schoolboys tumbling one another down the sloping grassy sides of the wall; gay *Corps-studenten*, in knots of three or four, gaudy with top-boots and *Cerevis-mützen* (beer caps), each carrying the inevitable cane, with which he keeps himself in fencing practice by cutting graceful *Lufthiebe* (blows in the air) at an imaginary antagonist; maidens of the intensest German type, plain featured but erect and hearty, stepping briskly, and looking neither to right nor to left ; or, perhaps, an entire family *mit Kind und Kegel*, that is to say, "the dog and I and father and mother," escaped from the Philistia of rickety stairs and low-ceilinged shops to inhale the free breath of nature.

Although thirteen eventful years have since elapsed, I have still a vivid impression of my first walk around the wall There were very few strollers out, for it was the middle of the long vacation and all the students and many of the professors were away. My companion, the landlady to whom I was recommended by a kinsman who had recently left Göttingen to return home, chatted away volubly in the purest Hanoverian. Is there any thing, by the way, so exasperating as one's first attempt at conversation in a foreign language, the abortive, frantic efforts to convey one's own ideas, the utter inability to follow the thread of the simplest narrative? Is there any thing so humiliating as the consciousness that, although your companion is evidently using the shortest phrases and most every-day words, in fact a sort of baby talk adapted to your undeveloped mental capacities, you, in spite of all your book-learning and private lessons at so much an hour, cannot catch more than one idea in ten? Yet, tyro as I was in German conversation, I detected a difference; my teacher in Geneva had been a Saxon, and he had certainly not spoken as my landlady was then speaking, while the contrast to the jargon of Switzerland, and to the broad sing-song of the Rhine region through which I had hurried the day previous, was still more evident. The vowels were clear and full, the Umlauts pure, the consonants sharp; there was no apocope of letters and syllables, no running of words together; the general intonation of the voice was graciously modulated. I had no difficulty in distinguishing each word as it was uttered, although I might not have the faintest conception of its meaning.

I had gathered from various sources, that Hanover was the province in which to begin one's study of German to the best advantage. My very first day's experience only corroborated the belief, which has not been shaken by years of subsequent study and travel. The cultivated classes throughout Germany speak substantially the same language. Even in Vienna, the professors and men of letters do not differ much, either in their choice of words or in their accent, from their colleagues in Berlin or in Heidelberg. Still the difference exists, and is plainly perceptible to the trained ear. But among the uncultivated classes, the variations of speech and accent amount to dialects. Along the Rhine, in Suabia, Bavaria, and Austria, the folk speaks in a language that is almost unintelligible when first heard. The grounds upon which I base my preference for Hanover are briefly these. In the first place, the Hanoverian pronunciation conforms more closely than any other to the printed form of the word, it is more precise, it does not confound *e.g.*, *Feuer* with *Feier*, *Wörter* with *Wärter*, *Thür* with *Thier*. I do not pretend, of course, to settle in this off-hand way the competing claims of the various German dialects; there are grave reasons why we may, perhaps, regard the Saxon pronunciation as historically the most correct. This is a matter for the professed philologist; but the foreigner, who has to grope his way the best he can, who has to train both ear and throat to strange sounds, and to derive the greater part of his knowledge from books, will find it a decided advantage to begin his studies among a population that, more than any other, speaks as it writes and writes as it speaks.

In the next place, the Hanoverians generally use good grammar. There are, of course, uneducated persons who make an occasional slip; but in the main, the foreigner may take for granted that whatever he hears he can repeat with safety. We, of the English-speaking race, are apt to overlook the importance of this point; our own language is so bare of grammatical inflections, that we have really lost an adequate sense of their significance. A few very gross vulgarisms aside, such as *went* for *gone*, *done* for *did*, there is almost no bad grammar in English, however much we may be plagued with bad style. But in German, the importance of a correct knowledge of words, cases, government of prepositions, agreement of adjective and noun, is ten times as great. To the foreigner in Germany, then, who has to learn every thing at once, as it were, to struggle with dictionary and grammar, it makes a material difference whether or not he resides in a community whose utterances he may look upon, for practical purposes, as infallible, whether or not he has to unlearn in his room what he has learned on the street. It is a mistake to imagine that one's dealings in a foreign country are exclusively with the cultivated classes; one comes in contact with shopkeepers, waiters, servants of all kinds, and if their communications are corrupt, one's own manners will suffer. In Berlin, for instance, one often hears some such expression as, *Ich habe Ihnen nicht gesehen.* The advanced student of German will not be misled by such a gross blunder; but the tyro, who has not yet fully unraveled the perplexities of the dative and accusative cases, could scarcely escape bewilderment. In learning a language, one has need of every help; it is no small comfort, then, to converse with even a servant girl or a boot-black and feel a reasonable degree of assurance that one's grammar is not becoming infected at every other sentence. Taken all in all, there is no section of Germany where the foreigner can converse so safely with any and every body as he can in the kingdom (now province) of Hanover.

Mr. Bristed,* in his introductory chapter, entitled "First Impressions of Cambridge," has suggested rather than described the general features of an English university town. The reader can construct from them a tolerably clear picture of what Cambridge or Oxford must be, the grandiose character of its architecture, the half-monkish official garb of the students and dons, the pervading tone of scholasticism. Both Cambridge and Oxford are simply congeries or clusters of colleges, each college doing about the same work; neither is a university in the true sense of the term. But reserving the discussion of

---

* Five Years in an English University.

this point for another place, I shall deal for the present exclusively with externals, with buildings, if the reader prefer this expression.

No two institutions of the same species can be imagined more diverse than an English and a German university. Were I to push the antithesis to its extreme limits, I might say that the former was all body, all bricks and mortar; the latter, no body and all soul. The Englishman or American who visits a German university town for the first time will scarcely realize the fact that it is the seat of a great institution of learning. He can see nothing; there is no visible sign of the university, no chapel, no huge buildings, whether we call them dormitories or quadrangles, no campus. There is no rallying place of professors and students, where he can stand and, letting his eye sweep around on every side, say: This is the university. He may even pass his entire life in the town and never once see the body of professors and students assembled in one place.

I dwell upon this distinction, because it is an important one. The reader who wishes to get a just notion of the character of a German university must dismiss from his mind all prejudices, any expectation of finding what his early associations may have led him to consider as the conspicuous features in a seat of learning. As I walked around the wall of Göttingen for the first time, the predominating thought in my mind was: Where is the university? I could find no tangible evidences of its existence, its reality. Putting what questions I could in my imperfect German, and paying strict attention to the answers, I could make out that the dome to the left, near the starting-place of our walk, by the Geismar Gate, was an observatory; considerably farther on, in close proximity to the railway station, was a large building bearing the inscription "Theatrum Anatomicum," evidently the medical school; still further on, in the moat by the side of the wall, was an arrangement of glass-houses, that was no less evidently a botanical garden. This was all of the university that I could detect in my first tour of the great Göttingen promenade.

Having come to Germany without any definite plan beyond that of learning the language and familiarizing myself somewhat with the literature, I could afford to take things as I found them and await future explanations. The Americans at that time studying at Göttingen were all absent on one or another summer excursion, so that I was a stranger in a strange land. What with puzzling over German Grammar and taking short walks every afternoon in the county, time did not hang too heavy on my hands. Fortunately, in about a week an Englishman residing in the same house returned unexpectedly, having cut short his trip. Those who have never tried the experiment of settling in a foreign country and among utter strangers, with the most imperfect knowledge of the language and the ways of the people, can scarcely appreciate the discomforts of the first few days. My landlady was the most obliging and attentive one in the world, and had had more than one American in her friendly care. Still, she knew no English and I knew very little German, so that life for the first week was a half-amusing, half-provoking comedy of errors. The return of Mr. E——, then, was for me a bit of good luck; I had at last some one with whom to converse freely and from whom to get needful information. Having already passed four or five semesters in the place, he was thoroughly familiar with shops, and streets, and university life, and had leisure to pilot me around and tell me what to do. The university lectures, I learned, would not be resumed until the third week in October, so that I had fully a month and a half in which to get up my German. We worked together over the catalogue of lectures for the coming term, in the attempt to pick out one or more that it might be worth my while to attempt to hear. I learned a good many peculiarities of university language; for instance, that a professor never "instructs" or "lectures," he "reads;" the students do not "study," they "hear." I learned also that instruction in a German university runs in sharply defined channels. E—— was studying chemistry, consequently he could give me no information about lectures or professors in other departments; he did not even know half of them by name, and could not venture an opinion as to their respective merits. All that he could say was, "Wait until H—— gets back. He's a *Philolog*, and can perhaps tell you what you wish to know."

At all events, E——'s guidance enabled me to familiarize myself with the general aspects of the town and the location of the university buildings. Göttingen may serve as the type of the German university town. The population is about 12,000. The streets are neither very straight nor very crooked, and no one runs directly through the town; in general, they are tolerably wide. The houses are plain and poorly built. The frame work is of wood, the outer walls being filled in with a sort of mud that is mixed with a good deal of straw to give it consistency; after the mud has dried, it is painted. For a cheap mode of building, it is much better than might be supposed. The number of stone and brick buildings is small. The handsomest building in town is (or was in my day) the Laboratory, built under the supervision of Wöhler himself, since deceased. It is a large structure, built of light blue stone, and perfectly fire-proof. The *Aula* is the centre of the university, so far as it can be said to have a centre. It is a small but not inelegant looking building, somewhat after the Grecian order, standing on a small open place or square not far from the centre of the town. In this *Aula* new students are matriculated and the University Court holds its sessions; it also contains the general offices of the university, such as the treasurer's, and, last but not least, the *Carcer*, where unruly students are confined for a fortnight or less, for minor offenses; graver ones are punished by relegation or by expulsion.

Lectures on chemistry were delivered in the laboratory; those on medicine, in the Theatrum Anatomicum; all the others, including theology, law and philosophy, in the university sense of that term, were held in the so-called *Collegien-haus*, a short row of buildings that had once been private dwellings, but had been converted into lecture rooms.

In 1865 the new *Collegien-haus* was opened, a large and elegant building constructed for the especial purpose, just out of the Wende Gate, near the Botanical Garden. By the side of the old *Collegien-haus*, separated from it by an arched way, stands the celebrated university library, one of the best in Europe; the building is nothing more than an old church, adapted to secular uses and enlarged here and there by irregular extensions or wings. In the arched way between the lecture rooms and the library stood the *Schwarzes Brett* (black board), a long board painted black and having a wire screen in front. On this board were posted all announcements relating to university instruction, announcements of lectures or changes in lectures, of degrees conferred upon students, and the like.

Besides the buildings that I have described, there are other, minor ones scattered over the town; the headquarters of the agricultural department are even located about two miles out of town, on a model farm near the village of Wende.

It is needless to go deeper into details; I have said already enough to make it clear to the reader that a German university, as far as buildings and outward show are concerned, is made up of *disjecta membra*. There is a bond of vital union, a very strong one too, but it is wholly spiritual; it does not appeal to the senses. In architectural display, I am confident that the most unimportant college at Oxford or Cambridge will surpass any university in Germany.

The new life that I was leading dawned upon me very pleasantly. The weather continued fine for many weeks, permitting E—— and myself to take long walks every afternoon. Sometimes our landlady, Frau H——, accompanied us; sometimes, even, she made up a small party of her friends for our benefit. The Germans are very fond of walking, but look upon it much more sensibly than the English do; they regard it as a pleasure, a relaxation, not as so many miles to be covered, so many ditches to be leaped in an hour. Old and young, men and women, go out for a stroll whenever they can find the time and favorable weather. The roads in Germany are good, and the by-paths easy to follow. Around every town in the land, at distances varying from one mile to two or three, lie scattered here and there ten or a dozen villages or gardens where the pedestrian can sit down to rest and refresh himself with beer or coffee; in most of these places a warm supper even can be had. On any fine day in spring, summer, or autumn, one can see an entire German family, parents, grandparents perhaps, children, all wending their way to some *Garten* or *Mühle*, where they will meet other likeminded families and pass the afternoon and part of the evening in recreation; the men roll *Kegel* (ninepins), the women knit and gossip over their coffee, the children roam through the fields. Enjoyment is simple and unrestrained; there are no "roughs" in Germany. Now and then one reads in the newspapers of a murder or a robbery in the neighborhood of Berlin or Vienna; but such deeds are perpetrated only in very obscure, degraded localities. Such a thing as the breaking up of a pleasure party by wanton, malicious "roughs" is an unheard-of occurrence.

The scenery around Göttingen is not grand nor very beautiful, but it is pleasant. At first I thought it tame enough, coming as I did direct from the Alps. This feeling of disappointment, however, soon wore away, and I began to conceive a decided liking for my new home. Göttingen lies in a broad, fertile valley; the hill to the east, called the *Rhons* or the *Kehr* (both proper names of men who formerly lived there), stands quite near the town, and slopes away to a height of three or four hundred feet; the hill to the west, crossed in zig-zag by the railroad from Cassel, is much farther away and much higher. The little river Leine, a narrow, muddy stream, that would be called in America a creek, flows through the middle of the town, although it is so covered up by mills and other buildings that it is visible only in a few places.

The valley is uncommonly level, and, in the neighborhood of the town, rather marshy. A small branch of the Leine flows around the town in a detour. The water in this branch is a few feet higher than the land, and is allowed to overflow in winter, partly to fertilize the soil, partly to give the Göttingese an opportunity for skating. The land in the district of Göttingen is both *Grossgutsbesitz* and *Kleingut*, that is to say, there are both large estates and small peasant-holdings. The peasantry, *Bauern*, as a class, are industrious and wealthy, although by no means as wealthy as their famous brethren of Sachsen-Altenburg. In the immediate vicinity of the town, the land is given up to grass; farther out, there are immense fields of wheat, buckwheat, rye and barley. One feature of the German method of cultivation impressed me as being not only practical but as enhancing materially the beauty of the landscape; the same feature prevails also in France. I mean the total absence of fences, those wretched snake-like black trails that disfigure the face of the country in America. I have walked for miles in every direction from Göttingen, over meadows, through fields of wheat and rye, but I cannot remember once encountering a fence. Some of the gardens just outside of the town are surrounded by high walls; but after he has left them behind him, the pedestrian finds that he has an unobstructed sweep of vision. The boundary lines of farms and estates· are marked at the angles by stones sunk in the ground. In this way the Germans not only save themselves the trouble and expense of building fences, but they preserve the natural aspect of the *terrain*. Cattle, sheep and horses, when put out to graze, are not allowed to roam at will but are kept in herds by men and dogs, or else enclosed by a slight temporary fence. Not even along the great royal chaussée that follows the valley of the Leine from Witzenhausen through Göttingen and Nordheim to the city of Hanover, is there any thing to separate the road from the fields; only a small shallow ditch on each side, and two rows of monotonous Lombardy poplars blending into one in the dim distance.

The valley of the Leine has always been a thoroughfare between the region of the Weser and the region of central Germany, Franconia and Thuringia. During the Middle Ages, when the "fist-law" was in force, numerous castles raised their frowning battlements along the hills that line the valley, principally along the eastern ridge. The remains of two of these knightly burgs, or robber strongholds, still exist in the neighborhood of Göttingen, namely the Gleichen and the Plesse. The former is five or six miles to the south of the town; the latter, by far the more frequented of the two, is about four miles in the opposite direction, near the village of Wende.

The ruins are on a detached spur of the eastern ridge, and overlook the plain from an elevation of several hundred feet. The path leads up from the small concert garden at Mariæ Spring, through a charming grove of beeches and maples. The outer walls of the castle are, in most places, still standing, and the general ground-plan can be easily recognized. The old tower is almost intact. It was roofed-in with a stained-glass roof in 1862, if I remember rightly. The platform of the castle is a cosy retreat on a warm summer afternoon, and affords an extensive view of the smiling plains below and the long, high western ridge directly opposite.

CHAPTER II.

Attacking German.

I WAS now ready for the winter's work, namely, the formal investment of that Gibraltar ycleped the German language. On reaching Göttingen, I knew just enough of German to realize that I knew practically nothing. The three months' instruction, exclusively book-work, that I had received at Geneva was scattered to the winds during a long pedestrian tour through the Alps; scarcely any thing remained of the lessons but the uncertain remembrance of a few paradigms of nouns and verbs. The spirit of the language was wholly unknown to me; I was neither better nor worse off than the average American graduate who has been passed in Otto, Woodbury or Comfort, and has read an act or two of Wilhelm Tell.

As the opening of the fall term was still six or seven weeks off, I had a fair opportunity of trying what I could do in the way of preparation for understanding lectures. But before beginning the account, it will be advisable to say a few words about my novel abode.

Continuing the plan which had worked so well in Geneva, I determined to live, for the first few months at least, in a family where I should have the privilege of speaking and hearing German continually. The landlady, Frau H——, was the only one who pretended to give what we call "boarding." German students, be it observed, never board; each man lives by himself, in his own room, takes his breakfast, and generally his supper, there, but dines at the table d'hôte of a hotel or restaurant. The life, then, that I led during my first winter in Göttingen was not strictly that of a German student. My breakfast, merely rolls and coffee, was brought to my room by the servant; dinner and supper, we, *i.e.* myself and the other boarders, two Americans and an Englishman, had in the dining-room with our landlady. We paid so much a month for "full board," while the German student hires his room by the semester, and keeps a book-account for whatever he orders, paying up at the end of every week or month.

Yet the rooms that we had were like those of every other student. The one occupied by E —— being rather more typical than my own, I shall describe it in preference. It was a large square room, the two front windows facing on the street, the side window overlooking the wall as it sloped down to make an entrance for the Geismar road into the town. Off to one side was the sleeping-room, one half the size of the study. Neither room was carpeted. In one corner of the room, near the door, stood the inevitable *Ofen*, a big stove of porcelain reaching almost to the ceiling. The German theory of heating is to have a large stove of massive porcelain, in which your servant makes a rousing fire in the morning; after the blaze has died out, and nothing is left but the glimmering coals, the door and the clapper are made fast. The stove is then supposed to hold its heat and maintain a uniform temperature in the room. The fuel used is generally wood; even in Leipsic and Berlin, where wood is dear and coal comparatively cheap, the former is preferred for room and parlor stoves. This plan of heating has its advantages and its drawbacks. It is rather economical, and it secures a uniform temperature for a certain time; besides saving one the trouble of raking and adding fresh fuel every few hours, it dispenses with dust and ashes. The disadvantages are that the air in the room is not properly renewed, and also that the stove cools down so gradually that, before the inmate is aware, the temperature has dropped several degrees. On the whole, I prefer the American base-burner.

Another indispensable article of furniture in a student's room is the *Secretär*, or secretary. This consists of three parts: the lower, a set of drawers; in the middle, a sort of door that can be let down, disclosing a fascinating arrangement of pigeon-holes and very small drawers for storing away letters and papers and " traps " generally; up above, a cupboard.

The ceiling of E——'s room was scored in every direction. These marks, I was informed, were the scars of old sabre-wounds, that had been left there by the former inmate. As the ceiling was rather low, a tall man in reaching out for *Hochquart* would be apt to graze the top of the room with the point of his sabre or his *Schlä-*

ger. The former inmate, judged by the number of tokens of his existence that he had left, must have kept himself and his visitors in pretty thorough practice. Against the wall, in the corner opposite the stove, hung a pair of the instruments of destruction, with masks and gloves. In a third corner was the equally inevitable sofa, upon which the student lies off to enjoy his after-dinner pipe and coffee. Over the sofa hung a picture of the Brunswick *Corps*, representing, in lithograph, the members of the corps holding their annual *Commers* (celebration) at some place in the country, perhaps Mariæ Spring. Some are sitting around a table, others are grouped picturesquely on the grass, others again are standing; but every one has a long pipe in one hand, and a *Deckel-schoppen* (large beer-glass with a cover) in the other. E —— was not a member of the corps, but he had been for some time a *Conkneipant*, i. e., one who attends the weekly meetings when he feels disposed, and joins in the revelry; the picture, then, was a souvenir of his old friends. Around this large picture were grouped many smaller ones, all likenesses of German and American students. Scattered around the room were pipe-bowls, stems, ash-cups, "stoppers" (curious little arms and legs of porcelain for plugging the pipes), and the other paraphernalia of smoking. Nearly all these articles were gifts. The German plan of making presents, by the way, is a curious one. Jones and Smith, we will suppose, agree to dedicate (*dediciren*) to each other. They select two articles of exactly the same kind and value, say two porcelain pipe-bowls; each pays for the other, and has the inscription put on: Jones to his dear Smith, or Smith to his dear Jones (J. *sm.* — *ln.* S.) The advantage of the system is that you get a keepsake of your friend without feeling that you have put yourself under obligations. Each man gives as good as he gets.

What books E—— possessed were stacked up in a rather rickety set of shelves under the sabres. E—— was an industrious student, but, being a chemist, was not supposed to have need of a large library. His helps to study were in the laboratory, in the shape of apparatus.

Every student in a university town occupies a room like the one that I have described. The room may be larger or smaller, may be located front or back, its furniture may be more or less elegant, but the general features do not vary. The point to which I desire to call especial attention is this: every student, no matter how straitened in circumstances, has a study and a sleeping room exclusively to himself; "chumming" is unknown in Germany, except occasionally in the large cities, Berlin and Vienna, where the disproportionately high rents force a few of the poorer students to take apartments in common. But even in Berlin and Vienna, chumming is looked upon as a last resort. The superiority of the German system is incalculable; it is more manly, it conduces to independence of study and prevents much waste of time. One who shares his room with a chum is often at the mercy of bores; he can turn away his own visitors perhaps, but not his chum's. Besides, if two or more students wish at any time to work up a subject after the coöperative fashion, as the Germans frequently do, they can accomplish the object by simply meeting at each other's rooms. But really independent, thorough research, study that is to tell in after life, can be done only in the privacy of one's own sanctum.

There is no royal road to learning, at least to learning a living language. German, for instance, is a vast treasure-house from which each one carries off only so much as his shoulders will bear. A volume might easily be filled with all the schemes, some sensible, others absurd, for making the first approaches to German easier. The truth is that German never can be made easy, not even for the natives; there is a subtle, lurking spirit in the language that always baffles the vision and eludes the grasp. Speaking with the experience of thirteen years, I feel it my duty to warn the reader against all "easy courses" or works entitled "German in Thirty Lessons Without a Master." I doubt whether such a thing as a smattering of German is desirable or even possible. The man who thinks that he can "get up" German in a month or so, as he might French, will speedily discover his mistake. Permit me to quote, with reference to this very view of the case, one of Klopstock's Odes which is not so well known as it should be:

> Dass Keine, welche lebt, mit Deutschlands Sprache sich
> In den zu kühnen Wettstreit wage!
> Sie ist — damit ich's kurz, mit ihrer Kraft es sage,
> An mannigfalt'ger Uranlage.

Zu immer neuer und doch deutscher Wendung reich;
Ist, was wir selbst in jenen grauen Jahren,
Da Tacitus uns forschte, waren:
Gesondert, ungemischt, und nur sich selber gleich.

Nothing is farther from my purpose than to write a dissertation either upon the language or upon the best way of learning it. After all there is only one way, namely: to set about the work resolutely, to take plenty of time, and never to grow weary, especially of writing exercises. Scarcely one of the many Americans who were contemporary with myself in Göttingen seemed to devote enough time to the study of German grammar. The common belief was that one set of lessons in grammar was quite sufficient; after you had finished Otto or Woodbury, for instance, you might lay aside your grammar and trust to reading for further progress. Besides the general feeling of impatience, there is a practical motive that prompts to such a course; nine of every ten Americans who study in Germany regard a knowledge of the language as only the means to some ulterior object, generally a knowlege of chemistry or medicine. It is not surprising, then, that they reduce their preliminary study to a minimum, in order that they may begin what they consider their real work as soon as possible. They are satisfied with learning enough grammar to recognize the connection of words in a sentence; the technical words of their science, which are to them the all important ones, they know by actual practice; all others are relatively unimportant. They read a play or two of Schiller, some of Goethe's poems, perhaps a few of Uhland's or Heine's. Of the language as an entirety, of German literature as a body of thought, they have but a very inadequate conception.

It seems to me that this is to be regretted. The number of Americans who finish their studies in Germany is already large, and grows from year to year. Is it asking too much to expect from them, on their return, sound general notions of German literature and thought, some familiarity with the steps by which Germany has been conducted to her present pinnacle of greatness? At all events, is it not a shame that many a Ph. D., who has passed two or three years in the land of Lessing, should be beaten by his stay-at-home brother or sister in attempting to explain the mysteries of an easy play by Kotzebue or Benedix?

As for myself, I took a serious view of the question, and resolved to master the language as far as in me lay. In one respect, certainly, my plan differed from that of every one else. Knowing that there was at least a year before me, I decided to spend six months with the grammar, before venturing upon any course of reading. This may seem strange, if not paradoxical; how can one learn a language without reading its authors? Easily enough. Text-books of grammar, phrase-books give models of forms and sentences; the beginner, for whom the form is every thing, can learn more from a good grammar than from the best reading; that is to say, he will get, in a condensed and a more available shape, what lies scattered over many pages of an ordinary book. By writing exercises constructed for the express purpose, he can train himself in the use of the very modes of expression in which he may be weakest. Let me give an example or two. The most perplexing features of the German language are the so called passive voice, the government of the prepositions, the separable and inseparable verbs, the use of the particles of motion, *hin* and *her*. It is not so difficult to glide over these peculiarities as they arise in reading; the beginner can translate after a fashion, making out the meaning by the aid of the context. But it is a much more serious undertaking to master them so as to *use* them, and as it is impossible to put together five consecutive sentences in German in which they will not be involved, the shortest way out of the difficulty is to learn them once for all, by writing and committing to memory a great number of model sentences in which the same principles are applied again and again.

It is of little avail in German, or indeed in any language, to commit rules to memory, unless the student has an example for every rule and every modification of a rule at his tongue's end, ready for use at any moment and in every place. This result can be attained only through a generous outlay of time and patience, and incessant drill in certain standard forms, what a Frenchman might call *cadres* of expression. It is a common mistake to suppose that the beginner must acquire a large stock of words; fifteen hundred, perhaps even less, will answer for all ordinary conversation and writing. The first and chief thing is to learn how to put these fifteen hundred words together, to assign each one to its proper place in the sentence and to show its grammatical relations to other words. That done, but not sooner, the student may begin to enlarge his vocabulary.

Another point has been too much overlooked, namely, the importance, not to say the necessity, of translating copiously from the mother tongue into the foreign. There is probably no other means of seizing the spirit of a foreign language. The labor, I am aware, is immense, but it will be found to yield the largest returns. It is one thing to be able, grammar and dictionary in hand, to pick your way through a German book; it is quite another to read it off, looking out a word here and there perhaps, but feeling that all the idioms, the forms of thought, are familiar to you, that you yourself might have expressed your own ideas after very nearly the same fashion. It is the final stage of the student's progress, and when he has reached it he may well exult, for he is in possession of a new power. But this cheering result is not the work of a week or a month; it can be attained only by unremitting and well directed efforts. The way to it leads through composition and translation from the mother tongue. On many points composition and translation will coincide; they both have the advantage of breaking up one's habits of thinking and forcing them into new channels. By attempting to write as a German would write, we acquire the habit of using German words with the exactest knowledge of their meaning, we accustom ourselves to the use of particles of thought that do not exist in English, but which cannot be omitted from the German phrase, we are made to *feel* the importance of correct grammar, not as something foreign to ourselves, but as the only tolerable or even intelligible way of connecting single words. The advantage of translation over free composition is this. Each man's range of words and ideas is limited. When we compose, even in our mother tongue, we are liable to fall into a sort of rut. If we write in a foreign language, this natural tendency is only increased by the constant temptation to use the most familiar words and phrases; we are apt to say what we have to say in the shortest and easiest way possible, so as to avoid trouble. We fall into a school-boy style from which it is almost impossible to escape. But when we undertake to translate the writings of a stranger, we have before us work of a higher order; we are held to reproduce, to the best of our ability, words, ideas and sentiments that lie outside our own narrow sphere. Instead of merely working up old material, we enlarge our capacity of expression in both languages.

I trust that the reader does not take me to be better at preaching than at practising. The advice that I have just given him may sound strange and impracticable. But he can rest assured that it is sincerely meant, and is the fruit of my own personal experience. During the first six months of my stay in Göttingen, I read nothing that could be called a German book. It seemed to me

*3

profanation, as it were, to stumble through Goethe or Schiller, hunting up every other word in the dictionary, striving to seize the poetry of the original yet succumbing to every paltry irregular verb or preposition governing different cases. It was too much like parsing the "Paradise Lost." I felt persuaded that it would be better in the long run to wait until I had developed myself into somewhat of a German, before intruding into the sacred precincts of German art. The reader will have the opportunity, in a subsequent place, of judging whether the experiment succeeded.

So I settled down to an unmerciful "grind." For six long months I toiled over grammar and grammars. I wrote all the exercises in Woodbury and Otto, and a good many in Ollendorf, until this last grew insufferably tedious, and then mastered *Plate*. This work is not so well known in America as it should be; the author, principal of the Commercial Academy of Bremen, is thoroughly familiar with both languages, and has treated certain subjects, e. g., the separable verbs, the passive voice, and the German substitutes for the participial phrase, better and more fully than the other grammarians.* Woodbury I found chiefly valuable for the collection of idiomatic phrases illustrating the use of the German prepositions. Besides these English-German grammars, which I literally "swallowed" word for word, I also consulted incessantly *Heyse's Schulgrammatik der*

---

*It was not until my return that I became acquainted with Dr. Arnold's German Exercises. They are the best of the kind in existence.

deutschen Sprache, a book written for the use of pupils in the upper classes of the gymnasia. But my hardest work was in translating from English into German. Here I tried my hand at all sorts of books and styles, from Hawthorne's "Marble Faun" to leaders from the London *Times*. My plan was to translate a few passages from one book, enough to seize the peculiarities of the author's style and diction, and then pass to another. In looking over my old copy-books and manuscripts, blurred and corrected in places so as to be scarcely legible, it is easy for me now to see that, notwithstanding the help of grammar and teacher, I wrote a good deal of rubbish, clumsy, un-German sentences that no native would think of putting on paper. But with all their imperfections, these exercises answered their purpose; they gave me a better insight into the peculiarities of the language than I could have got in any other way. There was scarcely an English idiom that I did not attempt to "upset" into German after a fashion.

Permit me to narrate one amusing incident. In the English text that I happened to be working upon occurred the phrase "he said, by the way." The expression "by the way" I had left blank, not finding any equivalent in the dictionary. "But," said my teacher, "why don't you translate: *auf dem Wege?*" It was in vain I tried to convey the idea of the English, how the word "way" was not used in a literal sense, like "road," but in a figurative sense, to denote something thrown in, as it were, something incidental. What misled the teacher was the circumstance that the person speaking was actually in motion at the time described; of course, then, the phrase *must* be *auf dem Wege*. I felt instinctively that he was wrong; but how hit upon a word or an idiom that would convey the idea exactly? We talked to and fro, I exhausted my vocabulary and the teacher his patience, until we sat confronting each other as disconcerted as a bridal couple after their first quarrel. All at once a light, as the German students would say, a "tallow-light," dawned upon me. I bethought me of the French phrase *en passant*, and flourished it in triumph at my teacher. "*Ach so!* (with the delicate sneer that *so* can be made to suggest in German). *En passant! Na nun, natürlich;* BEILÄUFIG *wollen Sie sagen!*" I consulted my watch; we had spent ten minutes in finding one word. A liberal outlay of time, but then the word was there, and furthermore it had been got in such a way as insured its never being forgotten; there was no danger of my losing sight of *beiläufig*.

The teacher, "by the way," was not a particularly good English scholar. At that time in his third or fourth semester, he was a good philologist, but had read very little English and had never had an opportunity of hearing or of speaking the language. So far from regarding this as a disadvantage, I considered it then and still consider it a positive gain. It forced me into the position of talking German even in my lessons, of explaining all my wants in my own phraseology. Whenever any difficult passage or peculiar idiom occurred, as the above, I had to give the sense of the entire context by "beating around the bush," by stating what the thing was *not*, until the teacher could gather from my broken utterances what it really *was;* then, when the answer came, when the correct rendering was reached, it made its impression. It did not go in by one ear and out by the other, the mind was ready to receive and retain it. Judging from the experiences of my friends, I am disposed to look upon "crack" teachers in Germany with some mistrust. In the first place, they are apt to cultivate their own English at the expense of the pupil's German. In the next place, the pupil, finding the teacher thoroughly prepared on all points, lapses into a state altogether too passive; he is content to sit and listen to explanations, to take every thing for granted, to rely upon the teacher to do the thinking. After all, the chief result to be aimed at is to train and develop the faculties, to acquire the habit of expressing one's self in German, to get a German memory and turn of thought, as it were. This accomplished, the rest will follow as a matter of course, in due time and with patience; but whether a certain word is learned one week or the next, is a matter of comparative indifference. The more haste at first, the less speed at last.

The reader need not infer from the above account that I read absolutely no German during the first six months. I skimmed the papers every day for news from home — German leaders were too heavy for my taste, in fact they are so at the present day! — and read short pieces of poetry and an occasional story in the *Gartenlaube* or

Ueber Land und Meer. But I kept carefully in abeyance whatever looked like literature.

This plan of devoting one's self exclusively to grammar may seem to conflict with the opinions expressed by Matthew Arnold* upon the aim and methods of linguistic study, opinions moreover with which I heartily agree. Matthew Arnold says: "An immense development of grammatical studies, and an immense use of Latin and Greek composition, take so much of the pupil's time, that in nine cases out of ten he has not any sense at all of Greek and Latin literature as *literature*, and ends his studies without getting any. His verbal scholarship and his composition he is pretty sure in after life to drop, and then all his Greek and Latin is lost. Greek and Latin *literature*, if he had ever caught the notion of them, would have been far more likely to stick by him." But this conflict was apparent rather than real. I regarded my grammatical studies and translations strictly as a means to an end, and merely crowded them into a period of six months instead of letting them prolong themselves over a year and a half. It seemed to me, and still seems to me, that such a plan after all saves time. No sooner, however, did translation and grammar threaten to become a mere drudgery, a mere tread-mill round without progress, than I dropped them forever, as any thing more than incidental work, and took up reading, *literature* in Mr. Arnold's sense of the term, as the reader will learn in the sequel.

---

* *Higher Schools and Universities in Germany*, p. 183. (Edition of 1874.)

CHAPTER III.

Matriculation and Lectures.

Deeming it advisable to preserve a certain unity of subject, I have thrown all remarks upon the study of German grammar into the preceding chapter, in order to dispose of them, although thereby making that chapter overlap the present by several months. I was not through with my grammar-travail until early spring, but I was matriculated in October.

A German university is the one institution in the world that has for its motto: Time is NOT money. The university is a law unto itself, each professor is a law unto himself, each student revolves on his own axis and at his own rate of speed. English and Americans have formed not a few queer notions of university life in Germany. They picture to themselves a town like Göttingen, for instance, as a place where everybody is running a break-neck race for scholarly fame, where days are months and hours days, where minutes are emphatically the gold-dust of time. The truth is that no one hurries or gets into a feaze over any thing, the university itself setting a good example. The academic year is divided into two terms, called the winter and the summer semesters. The winter semester covers nominally five months, from October

15th to March 15th. In reality, both beginning and end are whittled off, so to speak, and there is a pause of two weeks at Christmas, so that the actual working time is little over four months. From March 15th to April 15th is the spring vacation. The summer semester then runs to August 15th, but practically the work is over by the first of that month.

Supposing yourself to be a tyro in such matters, and the 15th of October to be drawing near, you are naturally impatient to be matriculated and at work. But you will discover that the older students are not yet back, and, on consulting the "Black Board," you see no announcement of lectures. There is no hurry. A day or two after the 15th, perhaps, a general announcement is affixed, to the effect that candidates for matriculation may present themselves at the *Aula* on such and such days of the week, at certain hours. The ceremony is a simple one. In the first place, you proceed to the secretary's office and deposit there your "documents" entitling you to admission. For a German, this is a matter of some importance; he is not *admitted unless he is able to produce certain papers, the principal one of which is a certificate that he has attended a gymnasium or *Realschule* and has passed satisfactorily the final examination (*Abiturientenexamen*). As the university holds no extrance-examination, this is the only guarantee it can have that those seeking admission are properly qualified. But in the

---

* Or admitted only under very grave conditions and restrictions.

case of a foreigner, the utmost liberality is displayed. Ten years, ago, while Göttingen was a Hanoverian university, the only document required of a foreigner was his passport. It is the same to this day in Leipsic, Heidelberg, and the South German universities. The Prussian universities are a trifle stricter; in the case of Americans, they generally expect a diploma of Bachelor of Arts or the like, but they can scarcely be said to exact it. I doubt whether any German university would refuse to admit any foreign candidate who showed by his size and bearing that he was really a young man able to look after himself, and not a mere boy. Besides, it would be easy to evade the Prussian requirements, if they were strictly enforced, by first entering a non-Prussian university, say Leipsic, and after remaining there a semester or two, procuring an honorable dismissal (*Abgangszeugniss*) and then removing to Berlin or Bonn. By virtue of the parity existing among the universities of Germany, a student in good standing in one is entitled to admission to any other. But the Germans know perfectly well that they can afford to be liberal toward foreigners. They take it for granted that when a young man puts himself to the trouble and expense of a visit to Germany, the chances are that he means to do well. The mere fact of his coming is a compliment to them, which they reciprocate by making things easy for him. Foreigners do not interfere with the course of instruction, while they do lend *éclat* to the university and help to swell its income. There is nothing selfish or exclusive about the higher education in Germany; although intended for Germans, it is open to all who choose to avail themselves of it, capacious enough to accommodate every type of mind, and absolutely free from dwarfing restrictions. The newly matriculated student, the *Fuchs*, is made to feel from the start that he is his own master.*

But I am digressing. The next step in matriculation is to visit the treasurer (*Quaestor*) and pay the matriculation fees. These vary somewhat with the different universities, but are nowhere excessive. In Göttingen they amounted to about five dollars. In exchange for your fees you get two weighty documents, the *a b c* of student life: your *Anmeldungs-buch*, and your student card. The former varies in size and shape (in Berlin they used the *Anmeldungs-bogen* as distinguished from *buch*), but whether book or merely folded sheet, it answers the same purpose; it is to be your record of work done. Imagine to yourself a large, stout book, like a copy-book; each page is for a semester, and there are eight or ten pages in all, that being the estimated maximum number of semesters that you will remain; if you study longer, you can get a fresh book. The page is ruled in vertical columns, one for the names of the courses of lectures that you hear, another for the treasurer's certificate that you have paid the lecture-fees, a third and a fourth for the professor's certificates that you have attended the course, entered at the beginning and at the end of the semesters. The

---

* The applicant has also to sign a pledge that he will not become a member of any secret political society.

modus operandi is as follows. After deciding what lectures you will hear, you yourself write the official title in the left-hand column. You then get the *Quaestor* to affix his *teste* in the second column. This entitles you to a seat, and if the course happens to be a popular one, attended by large numbers, the sooner you secure your seat the better. After "hearing" a week or two, you make your visit upon the professor himself, selecting some hour in the forenoon when he has no official engagement. If you wish to conform rigorously to etiquette, you must appear in grand toilet, i. e., in dress coat and kid-gloves, although the chances are ninety-nine in a hundred that in so doing you will catch the professor himself in wrapper and slippers, unshaven and smoking a long pipe. Your appearance in grand toilet is an intimation that you not merely wish to have your attendance at lectures certified, but that you know "what is what" and take the liberty of presenting yourself to him, as gentleman to gentleman. Whether you remain to chat for a few minutes or simply present your book for certification, will depend upon the manner of the professor himself; some instructors make it a point to detain the student for about ten minutes, others regard the affair as something to be disposed of in the quickest manner possible, and scarcely even ask the student to sit down. With regard to the second certification, given at the close of the lecture course, there is no fixed rule; any time not too long before the end of the semester will do; you can even wait until the next semester or still later, in fact you need not go in person, but can send the book around by your servant-girl or your boot-black.

The certifying to attendance at lectures has lapsed into an empty form. Every now and then a professor, inspired with unwonted zeal for his vocation, tries to make it a means of enforcing attendance, of preventing "cutting." But such isolated attempts speedily die out and are forgotten; if you show yourself two or three times at the beginning and a dozen times at the end of the semester, your attendance is certified as a matter of course, although you may have "cut" the entire intervening time. As an item of my own personal experience, I can state that Professor Gneist of Berlin certified to my attendance at his lectures on the Institutes, (*fleissig besucht*), although he must have known, if he knew anything, that I had not been inside his lecture-room within a month. The real proof of a student's diligence is not the professor's certificate but ability to pass a searching examination.

In a large city, like Berlin, it is not even necessary to call upon your professor; the latter remains for a few minutes after every lecture during the first week or two, so as to give the students an opportunity of coming forward and presenting their *Anmeldungs-bücher*.

The student-card, like the *Anmeldungs-buch*, is a peculiarly German institution. When you are matriculated, not only is your name entered in the general university register, but you must be inscribed under some one of the four general faculties, viz.: theology, law, medicine, philosophy. You then receive a card, not much larger than an ordinary visiting card, of stout pasteboard. On the face of the card is placed your name, Herr N. N., *aus* (from) such and such a place, student in such a faculty. On the reverse is a printed announcement, couched in the knottiest of German sentences, that none but the accomplished scholar of both English and German can untie, to the effect that you are always to carry this card about you on your person, and produce it whenever it may be demanded by the university or town police, under penalty of a fine of twenty Silber Groschen (50 cents).

This simple card is your *Legitimation*. In a university that has a complete jurisdiction of its own, as Göttingen has, at least did have in the days of which I write, producing this card secures you against all municipal arrest. You are member of a special corporation, and as such are amenable only to the university court; neither civil nor criminal action can be brought against you in the ordinary courts, but must be laid before the university court in the first instance. If this body should find you guilty of a crime or a grave misdemeanor, it would then surrender you to the Supreme Court, Criminal Section, the German equivalent to our Circuit Court. You cannot be arrested or locked up by a town policeman; all he can do with you is to keep you for a few minutes in custody, until he finds a University *Pedell* (beadle) to take you in charge. I hope to be able to speak more at length in another place of this curious relic of mediaevalism.

Your card in your pocket and your *Anmeldungsbuch* in your hand, in company with ten or twelve other candidates, you are then ushered into the august presence of the *Rector magnificus*,* or Chancellor of the University. You will probably find him to be a man much as other men, only looking a trifle uncomfortable in his dress-coat. The rector makes a short harangue, of which, if you are in the backward condition that I was, you will probably understand one word in five, but the substance of which is that he is rejoiced to see so many promising young men aspirants to the higher culture imparted by the *Georgia Augusta* (the official name of the university), and that he hopes you will be good fellows and make the most of your time and opportunities. In token of which, each candidate in turn shakes hands with him. You are then ushered out, to make room for a fresh squad who have just got their books and cards.

The ceremony is over; you are a German student, or a student in Germany, at last, ready to absorb all the knowledge and *Bildung* that your Alma Mater deals out with lavish hand. If you happen to be of an amiable, convivial turn of mind, your spirits will be buoyant; you will consider it your privilege and duty to celebrate the occasion by "dedicating" a bowl of punch to your elder brethren and compatriots who have helped you through the ordeal by telling you where to go and what to do. You and they will then make an afternoon of it, driving out to the Gleichen or the Plesse to enjoy the scenery, and indulge in coffee in the open air, and on your return,

---

*Prorector, in universities where the sovereign is the nominal head of the corporation.

if still unsatisfied, you can make a night of it at Fritz's or the Universitatskneipe. Should you wake up the next morning with a headache, a *Jammer* or a *Kater*, you can derive consolation from two circumstances: first, that it is only what has happened to thousands before you and will happen to thousands after you; next, that you have fairly and honorably initiated yourself into student-life. You know now what it is to be a student, as Victor Hugo might felicitously express it, *avant d'avoir craché du latin dans la boutique d'un professeur.*

Having habituated yourself to the sense of your new dignity, the next step is to decide upon the professors with whom you are to "hear." This will not be so easy as you might suppose. Unless you have come to the university with a preconceived plan of study, you will find yourself embarrassed by the wealth from which you are to choose. Fortunately the professors give you ample time for making a suitable selection.

The university opens nominally, it may be assumed, on the 15th of October. One professor announces that he will begin to read on the 18th, another on the 20th, a third on the 25th; in fact, I have known one professor to begin his course on the 9th of November. Each professor, it has been already observed, is a law unto himself; the main point is that he read at least one course of lectures each semester, on a subject of his own selection, for which he has properly qualified himself, and that he cover about so much ground. Whether he begins late and stops early, is a matter in his own discretion. This is not indifference or sloth on the part of the professors, but rather a deliberate forecasting of time and labor. Where the work is heavy and the field wide, the professor will not waste an hour. Vangerow, for instance, in lecturing at Heidelberg on the Pandects, used to begin on the very first day after the nominal opening day, and continue, averaging three hours daily throughout the winter, until two weeks after the semester had nominally closed.

Each course of lectures is paid for separately, the prices varying with the number of hours occupied in the week. Thus a single course, as it is called, one taking four or five hours a week, is charged about $5; a double course, one of ten or twelve hours a week, would cost $10. The usual double courses are those on the Pandects, on Anatomy and Physiology, and on Chemistry. The highest number of courses (double and single) that I have taken in any one semester (my fifth) was four, aggregating twenty-five hours a week, for which I paid between $25 and $30, a small price, in view of the quantity and quality of the instruction.

Lecture-fees are paid to the *Quaestor*, and not to the professor direct, although this latter eventually receives them, or the greater part of them, from the *Quaestor*. The new-comer will be puzzled at the distinction between lectures *publice*, *privatim*, and *privatissime*. Public lectures are those held by a professor gratuitously, on some minor topic of general interest. In the Prussian universities each professor is held to announce at least one such lecture a term. The *privatim* lectures are the ordinary ones, for which fees are paid and which are regarded as the substance of university teaching. A lecture *privatissime* is nothing more than our private lesson, the terms and times for which are settled by agreement between the professor and the student. The fees for it are not paid to the quaestor, and the lecture or lesson, is not entered in the *Anmeldungsbuch*.

I have used more than once the expression " a course of lectures "; to guard against misapprehension, it may be advisable to stop and explain at length. By a course of lectures in a German university is meant a series of lectures on one subject, delivered by one man, during one semester. A German university has, strictly speaking, *no course of instruction;* there are no classes, the students are not arranged according to their standing by years, there are no recitations, there is no grading, until the candidate presents himself at the end of three or four years for his doctor's degree, when the quality of his attainments is briefly and roughly indicated by the wording of the diploma. More of this hereafter. For the present it will be sufficient to say that all students stand on a footing of perfect equality in the eye of university, and that theoretically each one is free to select such lectures in his faculty as he sees fit to hear. Practically, the case is somewhat different. While there is no curriculum, no routine of studies and hours, through which all students have to pass, as in our colleges and, to a less extent, in the English universities, still there are.

certain limitations to the freedom of "hearing," which are occasioned by the nature of all study. When a young man attends the university, he is supposed to have some definite object in view; he wishes to fit himself for becoming a theologian, or a lawyer, or a physician, or an historian, or a teacher in the public schools, or a chemist, or a mathematician. In other words, he is to get his professional outfit. But this of itself implies the pursuance of a certain routine or order in study. The primary or fundamental branches must be mastered first, before the student can take up the more advanced. In medicine, for instance, he cannot understand pathology, without having studied anatomy and physiology. So in chemistry, a knowledge of general organic and inorganic chemistry is required before passing to analysis. In law, the routine is to take up the Institutes and History of Roman Legislation (*Aeussere Rechtsgeschichte*), then the Pandects and Doctrine of Inheritance, then Criminal and Ecclesiastical Law, before venturing upon such matters as the *Practica* (practical exercises) and theories of Procedure. But this is something altogether different from a curriculum in which mathematics, classics, metaphysics, history, and the natural sciences are pursued simultaneously. It is nothing more or less than conformity to the organic law of development. Furthermore, it is not formally obligatory upon the student, but left to his own good sense. I do not say that a professor of pathology or of chemistry would not refuse to admit into his clinique or his analytical laboratory a student who had neglected to qualify himself in anatomy or in general chemistry. In all probability the professor would, and very properly. But in the philosophical and legal faculties, with which I am more familiar, I can assert confidently that the utmost freedom is allowed. One can "hear" the Pandects before the Institutes, Criminal Law before the Law of Inheritance, as I myself have done. Students generally follow a certain routine, but not so much because it is *octroyé*, as because they find it to be the easiest and best way to a right understanding of the subject.

Not having any inspirations after medical, theological, or legal attainments at that time, in fact not having any plan of study at all beyond mastering the language and literature, I had myself entered in the philosophical faculty, as being the one that offered the widest range of lectures from which to select. Under the pilotage of H—, a countryman who had been pursuing classical studies for two years, I went the rounds of what the German students call *hospitiren*, i. e., dropping into a lecture to see how you like the lecturer. This practice prevails to a considerable extent at the university, at least at the beginning of a semester. It is practically the only way that newly matriculated students have of deciding between rival lecturers or of selecting some lecture that is not embraced in the ordinary routine of study. On this, as on so many points, the Germans display a great deal of practical sense. The student is free to roam about for two or three weeks, but at the end of that time it is expected of him that he come to a decision and settle down either to steady work or to steady idleness. Consequently, if you should attend regularly a certain course of lectures, occupying a seat and taking notes, without presenting your *Anmeldungsbuch* to the professor, you would probably be waited upon by the beadle, at your room, and interrogated as to your studies, what you had paid for, what you intended to pay for, and the like. In other words, your freedom of *hospitiren* will not be suffered to amount to unmistakable "sponging."

I availed myself pretty thoroughly of the *hospitiren*-privilege, attending one or two lectures in every course delivered upon subjects connected in any way with letters. The philosophical faculty covers every thing that is not law, medicine, or theology. It embraces consequently the exact sciences, mathematics, physics, chemistry, and the like, the descriptive sciences, botany, physiology, geology, the historical sciences, political history, political economy, finance, the humanities, that is, Latin and Greek, *Alterthumswissenschaft*, Oriental and general philology, and the modern languages, as they are taught philologically and critically. The field, therefore, is immense, and often overlaps those of the other faculties. Thus the medical student, being held to a general knowledge of chemistry, botany, and comparative physiology and anatomy, has to pass at least three semesters under the philosophical faculty, although enrolled in the medical. Hebrew, as a study in linguistics, is not regarded as a part of theology proper, but the professor of Hebrew is a member of the philosophical faculty. Candidates for orders, by the way, are obliged to master the outlines of Hebrew grammar at the gymnasium, before entering the university. On the other hand, students who obtain the degree of Ph. D. for studies in history and political economy are examined in certain legal topics, viz.: Institutes, *römische Rechtsgechichte*, and *deutsche Rechts-und Verfassungsgeschichte*, that is, the history of Roman legislation and constitutional forms in Germany. This would cover nearly two semesters in the legal faculty. The German theory is that no one is qualified to become an historian or an office-holder of the higher grades, who has not an insight at least into the elements of jurisprudence.

In making my selection of lectures, I was determined by one simple consideration: which of the many distinguished men whom I heard would be likely to teach me the most German. I decided upon two, about as opposite in manner and substance as can well be imagined: Ernst Curtius, now professor in Berlin, who lectured on Greek Art, and Ritter, since deceased, who lectured on the History of Modern Philosophy. Curtius, then a comparatively young man, had an energetic and rapid, but very distinct enunciation. As his lectures were to a large extent the analysis and criticism of the remains of Greek art, such as temples, friezes, statues, intaglios, and the like, I judged that the subject itself would not only be interesting and profitable, but that the prints which were passed around the class during the lecture would give me at least a visible image of what the lecturer was speaking about. I made no attempt to take notes. In fact, had I been even a much better German scholar than I was, I could not have written fast enough. The auditors generally seemed to listen rather than to write, and to use their pens only for noting down leading principles and important facts. I contented myself with jotting down now and then a word or a phrase that I could arrest in the general flow of the language, with a view to studying over it at my rooms. The chief good that the lectures of Professor Curtius did me was to train my ear day by day to the flow of very rapid and very elegant German. This point, it seems to me, has not been sufficiently attended to. It is one thing to read a work in the privacy and quiet of your own room, but it is quite another to listen for an hour to the same author as the words come fast and warm from his lips. Even if you do not catch at first more than a thought or two here and there, and the body of the discourse sounds as the tangled maze of a symphony does to the uninitiated in music, still you are training your perceptive faculties far more than you are apt to suspect. Both ear and brain are on the stretch, you put forth your best efforts to seize and hold the fleeting breath; in short, you work under pressure, whereas in your room you are apt to dilly-dally over your books, to fall asleep, as it were, for want of outside stimulus. Hearing, of course, does not exclude reading; both are necessary, and the one supplements the other. But I take the liberty of calling especial attention to the importance of hearing German well delivered, in view of the fact that only too many English and Americans neglect this element of training.

Professor Ritter was, as I have intimated, the exact opposite of his colleague. He spoke very slowly and deliberately, from full notes, with a mild, almost droning intonation, so that it was possible, even for me, to write down every word. In his lectures, then, I used my pen industriously, and succeeded in making an exact reproduction of the professor's text. This it was my practice to take to my room immediately after the lecture hour, which was from four to five in the afternoon, spending the interval to tea time in going over it again, grammar and dictionary in hand, and writing the translations of words and phrases on the margin and between the lines. The reader may perhaps doubt the possibility of one's writing down correctly expressions which he does not understand at the time. But in a language where the pronunciation conforms so closely to the spelling, and the words are run together so little, as is the case in German, the feat is not at all difficult, provided the lecturer reads slowly enough to let each word strike the ear as a well rounded unit. Besides, German is emphatically a language of terminations and prefixes, which give the ear a chance to rest and the pen a chance to abbreviate. It will suffice to call the reader's attention to such syllables as *ei*, *heit*, *keit*, *schaft*, *ung*, *niss*, *ling*, *thum*, *ig*, *lich*, *isch*, *los*, *fach*, *falt*, *sam*, *bar*, and the entire group of the so called separable and inseparable prefixes. I can assure the reader that during the first two months certainly I wrote down, from dictation as it were, between one and two hundred pages by mere sound, generally unable to recognize the connection between two successive words, unless they happened to stand in the simplest grammatical relation, and nearly always unable to follow the transition from sentence to sentence. My feelings during the process were somewhat akin, I suppose, to those of the compositor who sets up "copy" in a foreign language.

Besides a general knowledge of German, I made one valuable acquisition through Professor Ritter's lectures, to wit, an acquaintance with the vocabulary of abstract and philosophical terms. This, it is well known, is the most difficult part of the language. Our abstract terms are taken from the Latin and Greek, as they are in French, so that the reader who is familiar with their meaning in one language can easily recognize them in the other. All that an

Englishman or an American needs to prepare himself for reading a French treatise on art, or science, or history is a slight knowledge of the pronouns and irregular verbs. It is only where concrete terms come in question, names of objects and things, such as *bread*, *house*, *dog* and the like, that the two languages diverge. These concrete terms in German coincide generally with the English. But the abstract terms have been developed by means of suffixes and prefixes from German root-forms, and cannot be comprehended without an insight into the genius of the language. I mean such words as *Einbildung* imagination, *Gedächtniss* memory, *Vernunft* reason, *Geschichte* history, *Begriff* conception. Furthermore, the German abstract terms are not always the exact equivalents of the English words employed to translate them in the dictionary. Thus the German word *Urtheil*, given in the vocabularies as denoting *judgment*, covers only that word as it may be used in the sense of *opinion*, the product of the faculty of judging; the faculty itself is designated by *Urtheilskraft*. This is only one example out of thousands. The beginner will find himself tripped up continually by these abstract terms; they are hard to understand and harder still to remember and apply. They really represent more of the genius of the language than any mere inflectional or syntactic peculiarities. These latter will become of themselves a matter of routine, but the derivation of words, especially of abstract terms, calls for the most delicate appreciation of the formative, what the Germans call the *building* elements of the language. As a means of acquiring this appreciation, I can heartily recommend a course of lectures on the history of philosophy. A course upon pure speculative philosophy would be altogether too difficult for the beginner. But a course something like the one delivered by Professor Ritter, beginning with Roger Bacon and coming down to Kant and Hegel, interspersed with short, easy biographical and historical notices, seems to me to blend sufficiently the abstract and the concrete. The hearer gets the proper play of abstract terms, while the very effort of writing them down one by one in ignorance of their meaning, or at least the exact shade of meaning, and afterward patiently educing the sense with the help of his dictionary or of his teacher, fixes them firmly in the memory. At all events, the lecturer should speak slowly and with the clearest articulation.

The lecture-system of Germany has been extolled and decried with equal injustice. Like every other system of man's invention, it is confessedly imperfect. One who attends lectures is not necessarily on the road to knowledge, one who lectures is not necessarily wiser or more interesting than a printed book. But taken all in all, I think that it works well. It gives the lecturer an opportunity of revising his own studies and incorporating fresh knowledge; every course of lectures can be made as it were a new edition, which is not usually practicable with a printed book. It gives the hearer the ripest fruits of research direct from the investigator himself, it quickens the faculties of apprehension and stimulates subsequent study and collateral reading. Say what they will, the devotees of the Socratic method will never succeed in arguing the *personal* element in the lecture-system out of existence. It is well enough to be made to feel that you are wrong, but it is a higher gain to be made to feel that some one else is right, and that you are catching from his lips the thoughts over which he has spent days and years of patient toil.

There are as many different styles of lecturing in Germany as there are different professors. They can all be reduced, however, under three general categories: the system of dictating everything, the system of dictating part and explaining part, the system of rapid delivery. By the first is meant that plan in pursuance of which the professor reads off the entire lecture at a uniform rate of speed, slow enough to allow his hearers, unless they should be very clumsy writers, to take down every or nearly every word. Under the second system, the professor dictates a paragraph at a time, reading so slowly that his hearers cannot help catching it, and even pausing and repeating, if he should see that any one in the audience is at fault, and then proceeds to comment rapidly and in a colloquial tone upon what has just been dictated. Under the third system, that of rapid delivery, the instructor speaks after the fashion of our public lecturers, aiming more to impress his students, to arouse and stimulate them, than to give them something that they can carry home "black on white." Many of the more popular lecturers on political history or on topics connected with literary history are delivered in this style, especially where the professor can take for granted that his hearers have some previous knowledge, so that his remarks are as it were the novel presentment of an old theme. But in general it may be safely asserted that wherever exact, positive information is to be conveyed, as for instance in law, or in the descriptive and exact sciences, there the only systems followed are the first and the second.

Lectures are usually delivered with what is called *tempus*, which is emphatically *not* "on time." *Tempus*, or the "academic quarter," as it is otherwise styled, denotes that a lecture announced, e. g., for ten o'clock, is not begun until ten or fifteen minutes after the hour. The reason for this apparent procrastination is a practical one. It not unfrequently happens that the lecturer, to save the time and trouble of going to and fro between his home and the *Collegien-haus*, will secure two successive hours for two lectures. Still, it is not desirable to read one hundred and twenty minutes on a stretch; the pause, then, is very opportune, giving the lecturer a chance to rest his voice. But the chief utility of the "academic quarter" is for the students themselves. As many of them have three or four lectures in succession, perhaps in different buildings, the pause enables them to make the transition without inconvenience. Besides, it is really a blessing in disguise to be able to idle ten minutes between each two hours. One who knows by actual trial what it is to attend lectures every day in the week, say from nine o'clock to one, or even from eight to one, as I was circumstanced on the Saturdays of my last winter semester (1863-1864), will appreciate the relief afforded by such brief respites. To fingers grown stiff and numb from constant writing, to brains become hot and confused, the "quarter" comes as a positive boon; you put on your hat and hasten into the open air for a short stroll, to meet your friends and acquaintances and have a little chat about every-day matters. Still, notwithstanding all its advantages, the academic quarter is not infrequently reduced to very narrow limits. The Pandects are considered the "heaviest" lecture in the legal faculty, that is to say, they never occupy less than twelve hours a week through the winter semester. Mommsen,* with whom I heard them in Göttingen, began at five minutes past nine, read without interruption until ten minutes past ten, then made a pause of five minutes only, and continued until five or ten minutes past eleven. As he read rapidly, it was all that one could do to keep up with him. From the moment he entered the room until he rose from his desk to leave, there was not a pause,

---

* A cousin of the celebrated historian in Berlin.

every pen traveled over the paper in feverish haste. But the worst "grind" was at Heidelberg, under Vangerow, since deceased. This celebrated lecturer was in the habit of reading — also on the Pandects — from nine to half past ten, then making a pause of fifteen minutes, and reading on until one o'clock, and even later.

Every lecture is opened with the stereotyped formula, *Meine Herren* (Gentlemen)! The professors have their private meeting-room, from which they proceed to the lecture-room. In my day, there was the utmost license at Göttingen with regard to smoking. The students smoked on the stairs and in the entries of the *Collegien-haus* at all times, and even in the lecture-rooms themselves until the entrance of the professor. In Berlin, the rule was different; smoking was not permitted any where within the University buildings.

As a rule, a university lecture is a simple, straightforward enunciation of fact or opinion, without any attempt at brilliancy of style. You are seated with a dozen or two or three dozen other young men like yourself, smoking, perhaps, and chatting with your neighbor. The bench on which you sit is hard and uncomfortable, the elevated bench before you is inscribed with all sorts of devices and names, the legacy of former generations. Your pen, ink and paper are spread out before you. The door opens softly, the form of the lecturer moves quietly across the room and ascends the rostrum. Without preamble, without prelude, the hour's work begins. *Meine Herren — Thomas von Aquina sah in der vernünftigen*

Seele den höchsten Grad der weltlichen Dinge (Thomas Aquinas regarded the rational soul as the climax of things earthly). The lecturer has simply resumed where he had broken off the day before. I have listened to lectures by many different professors in different universities, but I can not truthfully say that I have ever heard one that could be called brilliant. The aim of a German professor is not so much to arouse or interest or even persuade his hearers, as to teach them. The substance of his discourse is the unfolding of truth, grave, solid truth. The utmost that he permits himself is an occasional touch of humor, when the subject will bear it. Thus, Zachariae, in his lectures on Criminal Law, was rather fond of showing up certain infractions of the criminal code in their ludicrous aspects, and expatiating upon the comically quaint nomenclature of the Carolina, or Code of Criminal Procedure enacted by Charles V. in the sixteenth century. One phrase in particular he never grew weary of rolling out with gusto: *Idem, so ein Weibsbild.* Gneist, in Berlin, lectured to his students about as a New York lawyer argues a motion before a judge with whom he is on easy terms, feeling confident that he has the court already on his side. Mommsen was always intensely earnest, speaking energetically and almost sharply at times, in his anxiety to impress his meaning upon his hearers. But by far the ablest lecture that I have ever heard, in Germany or at home, was one delivered by Vangerow. Happening to be in Heidelberg on a visit in October, 1864, I profited by the occasion to *hospitiren* with the then most prominent jurist in Germany. The subject was thoroughly familiar to me, as I was at the time in full preparation for my examination at Göttingen, which came off a few weeks later. The auditorium was crowded,— there could not have been much less than two hundred students present,— but the silence and attention were profound. Seated on a small raised platform near the center of the room, the lecturer spoke for an hour and a half in an easy, clear, sustained voice, without pause and without break, on one of the most complicated points in Roman Law. He had no notes, not even a schedule, only a slip of paper, on which were written one or two references to passages to be cited from the Digest; yet the ideas and words came forth as clear and logical and well placed as if the lecturer were reading from a printed book. The subject was one which the German spirit delights to develop after the I, A, 1, a α, β. γ.... style, in all sorts of main and subsidiary paragraphs, with minor and modifying clauses, exceptions, qualifications, and reservations, references to foot notes, and the like. But the lecturer had such an insight into and such a grasp of his subject that his discourse seemed to be nothing less than the easy, spontaneous process of organic evolution; it seemed to grow of itself out of his brain. There was no brilliancy, no flight of eloquence, no outburst of humor or sarcasm; the lecture would scarcely have been intelligible to one not familiar with the study. But it was a masterly didactic statement of the clear, crystalline truths of the law, introducing nothing superfluous, omitting nothing necessary, and putting everything in the right place. Only the best arguments of men like Webster and O'Conor could equal it for sustained power and absolute logical coherency. I heard from Heidelberg students that Vangerow lectured in this fashion from three to four hours daily through the winter, and from two to three hours through the summer term. If we add to this his duties as dean of the legal faculty and president of the *Collegium* for government references, his unremitting activity as an author, and — I regret to say — domestic troubles of the most painful kind, we need not wonder that one of such prodigious powers should sink into the grave while still in the prime of life.

The paper used for taking notes is of a peculiar kind. A German student rarely if ever has what we call a note-book or a copy-book. He uses the so called *Pandecten* or *Collegienpapier*, plain, white writing-paper, unruled; the page varies in size, but is generally what book-publishers designate as lexicon-octavo untrimmed. Six or eight sheets (twelve or sixteen pages) are stitched together at the back, making a *Heft*. The *Heft*, before it is sold, is put under a press of which the face is smaller than the face of the page. This blocks out by indentation a sort of inner page, leaving a wide margin. The inner page alone is used for writing in the lecture-hour; the margin is reserved for subsequent corrections and additions. At the end of the semester, the *Hefte* of any one course can be bound up in a volume for preservation.

The advantages of this paper are that it enables the student to dispense with an armful of cumbersome note-books — he has only to carry as many *Hefte* at a time as he has separate lectures to attend — and prevents the waste of paper. In buying a note-book, the student runs the risk of getting one either too small or too large; but with the *Pandectenpapier*, he has only to add a *Heft* from time to time, and he can also intercalate as long as the *Hefte* are unbound. It has always been a matter of surprise to me that the *Pandectenpapier* has not been introduced into our American colleges. It is by far the most practical method of taking notes. The *Hefte* are carried in a small black leather portfolio (*Mappe*), just large enough to hold three or four at a time, and flexible enough to be rolled up and carried conveniently under the arm. The notes are always written in ink. The inkstand generally used is not flat-bottomed, as with us, but terminates in a sharp point of iron, which can be thrust into the desk. When carried in the pocket, the point is protected by a capsule of horn that screws over it. A stranger visiting a university lecture-room for the first time would be puzzled to account for the innumerable round holes punched in the desks; a naturalist might call them fossil foot-prints of the *Bubo maximus*.

The conduct of the students during the lecture-hour is propriety itself. One might attend hundreds of lectures in different universities, without witnessing any disorder or whispering. The first attempt to create such disturbances as disgrace the halls of our colleges would be punished by the summary expulsion of all the offenders. To an American faculty, the discipline in the German universities will appear lax in more than one respect. There are no chapel-services, no marks, no tutorial supervision. The student is free to live where and as he pleases, his movements are unfettered. But whatever else the university may wink at, it never tolerates disrespect and disorder in the lecture-room. The student is treated as a man having a sense of propriety and duty. If he does not like a particular professor, he can hear another; if he does not like a particular university, he can go elsewhere. If he does not feel disposed to attend on a particular day, he can stay away. But if he attends, he is expected to conduct himself as in all respects a man. There have been, I admit, disturbances in some of the German universities. But they were not mere boyish freaks, but political demonstrations instituted for some special purpose and usually backed up by a clique in the faculty itself and by outside sympathy. The most notable instances were the Anti-German, Bohemian demonstrations at Prague, ten or fifteen years ago, which brought about the appointment of two sets of professors in all the departments, one for the German, the other for the Czechish students.

The German student, however, has one privilege which the American has not; he can manifest his wishes by scraping his feet on the floor. If a professor lectures too fast, or fails to explain a point to the complete satisfaction of his hearers, or if he lectures over the hour, instantly you will hear three or four pairs of shoes at work. This hint is always taken by the professor in good part. With regard to lecturing over the hour, the practice varies. Where the students know that the course is a heavy one, in which the professor has need of all the time he can get, they are not so apt to interrupt, unless the time of "grace" should exceed five minutes. More than once I have heard Mommsen say: "Gentlemen, excuse me for detaining you one moment longer, but I must finish this subject to-day." But where the professor is merely indulging in explanatory "talk," he is usually cut short without much grace.

The lecture-rooms, in their general appearance, are unattractive, not to say cheerless. Even in Berlin and Leipsic, they are much inferior to our recently constructed halls, while in places like Halle, Tübingen, Marburg — and Göttingen ten years ago — the want of ventilation is shocking. Still, one soon becomes used to the minor discomforts of dingy windows, hard benches, and close air, and learns to take comfort in the world of ideas.

CHAPTER IV.

Auf der Mensur.

ONE day T——, of New York, dropped into my room before dinner, saying: Don't you wish to see a first-class *Mensur* this afternoon? As a graduate of a respectable American college, there was the presumption that I must recognize the obvious connection between *Mensur* and mensuration; yet my rushlight of mathematical experience was insufficient to illuminate the German term, which, it is perhaps needless to state, had not come up in the round of my grammatical studies. Did it mean a surveying party, or a mathematical orgie, a concourse of "delicious triangles?" I had to call upon my better initiated countryman for an explanation, and learned that *Mensur* was the student-word for the dueling ground, that is to say, the area measured off, and hence — by extension — for the duel itself. Naturally desirous to get a practical insight into the *modus operandi* of this peculiar act of student life in Germany, concerning which I had heard so much, I accepted the invitation as unceremoniously as it was given. T—— himself was not a member of a *Corps* or *Verbindung*, but having spent three or four semesters in Göttingen, was on terms of easy acquaintance with many corps-students.

We arranged to meet in his room immediately after dinner, when I should be presented to S——, of the "Hanoverians," who was to conduct us to the *Mensur*. So T—— went his way to the Laboratory, and I resumed work on my translations.

From the windows of E——'s room, which faced on the street leading out through the Geismar Gate, I had watched almost every other day students in numbers flocking past with *Schl ger* and gloves, even in broad daylight, and learned that they were on their way to the dueling ground. The openness of their movements surprised me, as I had seen more than one picture of the arrest of dueling parties by University beadles, and supposed, before coming to Göttingen, that encounters of the kind were kept as secret as possible. The winter of 1861–2 was what might be called a star-season. There has always been a good deal of fighting in Göttingen, perhaps more than at any other university in proportion to the number of students. But this my first winter in the place was a remarkable one. There was an unusual number of veterans, big, heavy, scarred fighting-cocks, among all the corps, and especially among the Westphalians. The chief *casus belli*, however, was the establishment of a new corps, the Normans, by some new comers, among whom were two brothers from Heidelberg, named Mendelssohn, relatives, I believe, of the celebrated composer. The bantling, as might have been expected, had to undergo a baptism of "blood and iron." The rowing at one time was prodigious. Whenever the

Normans returned from their *Kneipe* in the evening, they were beset by the students of the other corps, chaffed and huffed, and challenged right and left. But as they were all fighting men, in fact, in Western parlance, "spoiling for a fight," this was no great hardship. The elder Mendelssohn was their leader, their *Haupthahn*, and, to his credit be it said, performed his duties manfully. After fighting two or three duels a week throughout the winter, and escaping without a scratch, he got the *consilium abeundi* from the University Court and had to retire to the shades of private life, leaving twenty or thirty slight "unpleasantnesses" still pending. Others of the Normans were also relegated, and the corps in consequence was broken up. There were grounds for suspecting that it became too great an eye-sore to the University judge.

But all through the winter months the *Paukerei* was kept up, and one could see dozens of students going about with bandaged cheeks and noses. On the particular day of which I now write, the event was to be a duel between Mendelssohn and Von H——, the leader of the Bremensians.

At two o'clock I made my appearance at T.'s room, and found him and his friend S. quietly discussing coffee and cigars after the approved German fashion. S., by the way, was a tall, good-looking, bespectacled young man, anything but a "rower," to judge by his manners and actions. I had the pleasure of meeting him by the merest chance in Vienna, during the summer of 1872, and learned that he had become a manufacturer. At the university he was a student of chemistry.

When the cigars and coffee were at an end, we strolled up the Kurze Geismar street and out of the gate along the chaussée. We were preceded and followed by other students in knots of three or four, at wide intervals, to avoid the appearance of a crowd. After issuing from the gate, I observed younger students, *Füchse*, stationed on each side of the road every hundred feet, acting as scouts or sentries to give warning in case of the approach of a *Pedell** or other suspicious looking person. Having S. as our escort, we passed without exciting comment. Under ordinary circumstances, a duel is, for the outside world, a private affair; no one but the immediate backers of the duelists is permitted to attend. But a duel fought under the sanction of the S. C., the Senioren Convent, *i. e.*, under the auspices of the corps as a body, and according to their rules, and upon the corps *Mensur*, is open to all corps-students, and to the friends and acquaintances whom they may bring with them. The corps resemble, in more than one respect, the secret societies of our American colleges. Not that there is any element of secrecy about them; on the contrary, their statutes of organization and by-laws must be submitted for the approval of the university, and their meeting-rooms, *Kneipen*, are not screened from the public gaze. Outsiders are often invited to their reunions, which are

---

* The orthodox student term for the beadle is *poodle*.

nothing more than social gatherings held twice a week, generally on Wednesday and Saturday evening. The *Corps-kneipe* is merely a sort of club-room, and not a "lodge." Furthermore, a corps has no existence outside of its own university; it has no affiliations, no "chapters." There exists, however, a so-called *Cartel-verbindung* between corps of different universities, so that a member of the Heidelberg Vandals, for instance, in coming to Göttingen, becomes the *Conkneipant* without further ceremony of the Göttingen Bremensians, but continues to wear his colors as a Vandal. Each corps regulates its own affairs; all general rules are drawn up and promulgated by the Senioren Convent, or heads of the corps of All Germany, who meet once a year in solemn conclave. There were, and still are, I believe, seven corps at Göttingen: the Bremensians, Saxon-Borussians, Westphalians, Hanoverians, Brunswickians, Luneburgs and Teutons. These names have lost nearly all their geographical signification. Each corps has its set of colors; thus the Saxon-Borussians wore dark blue, white, light blue, and the Westphalians, dark green, white, light green, etc.

After the *Corps* come the *Burschenschaften* and *Verbindungen*. The origin of the *Burschenschaften* is to me obscure; I believe that they were at one time identical with the *Landsmannschaften*, started as a political club in the last century and broken up by governmental interference. The *Verbindungen* are of comparatively recent origin; they are mere social clubs, each existing by and for itself, and not subject to rules common to all. Moreover, many of them are professedly hostile to dueling, and aim at its suppression. Such *Verbindungen* at Göttingen were the Hercynians and New-Hanoverians, irreverently nicknamed the "tea-boys." The corps-students, it is perhaps superfluous to remark, regard themselves as the students by eminence, looking down upon the others and lumping them under the convenient designation of *Wilden,* wild-men. The distinction resembles that which exists at Yale, for instance, between "society-men" and "neutrals." The corps-students at Göttingen numbered scarcely more than one hundred and thirty in a total of seven hundred; but being well organized, and comprising nearly all the stirring, aggressive elements, they shaped things pretty much to suit themselves. It was the old story of the advantage of discipline and organization over mere numbers.

Each corps has its own *Fecht-boden,* or fencing-room, where its members meet every day for practice among themselves. The dueling comes off on the *Mensur,* which is selected by agreement; it is generally a room in some tavern outside the city, and is changed from time to time, to baffle the police. If a *Wilder* wishes to duel with a corps-student, he must fight on the *Mensur* and according to the rules of the S. C.; he must also furnish his own seconds. The corps, I believe, supplies the weapons. But, as an outsider, I cannot speak on these points very confidently.

To resume the narrative. About a third of a mile

outside the town, on the right hand of the chaussée, stands the well known tavern and concert-room *Zum deutschen Hause.* By the side of it is a smaller tavern. Here we entered, and, passing through the public rooms below, ascended a narrow rickety stairway in the rear to the upper story. In the first room that we entered, a small one, was a stand holding a barrel of beer, from which one or two waiters were busily filling *Schoppen* for the thirsty souls in the room beyond This, the *Mensur* itself, was a room about twenty-five feet by forty, rather low-ceilinged, and lighted by two windows at each end. The atmosphere was dim and heavy with smoke; groups of students stood around, puffing, drinking, boisterously talking. One or two were practicing "cuts" in the corners of the room, to the imminent peril of the ears and nose of any who might happen to stray into their vicinity. A duel was going on between two *Füchse* (Freshmen). The combatants wore caps in addition to the general defensive armor,— of which more hereafter,— and each had his second by his left side, whose business it was to parry the dangerous blows. The two combatants did their best, only to be ridiculed for their pains. Like all beginners, they tried to make up in rude force what they lacked in address. The swords got entangled every minute or two, and nearly every blow fell *flach*, i. e., with the flat of the sword instead of with the edge. The utmost that the better of the two did was to saw off a lock of hair from his antagonist's head and scratch his cheek enough to draw blood. The by-standing veterans indulged in various cheering remarks, such as: "Well hit," "Try it again," or, when a blow fell *flacher* than usual, "Where did you learn that?" "Here's a bumper to your royal good health." The affair was evidently a farce to all but those immediately involved.

The duel came to an end soon after we entered the room. The rule is that the duelists must fight either fifteen minutes (stops not included), or until one of them is *abgeführt*, literally led away, i. e., receives a wound that reaches to the bone or is pronounced dangerous by the surgeon in attendance. If no *Abfuhr* is declared, the umpire pronounces the duel over at the end of fifteen minutes. The two "foxes," accordingly, fought out their time and were released, greatly to their own satisfaction. Preparations were then made for the affair of the day, the duel between M—— and Von H——.

Mensur duels, as a matter of course, are fought with the *Schläger*, a long, thin, and narrow sword with a basket-hilt. One edge is left perfectly dull; the other is sharpened for about twenty inches from the end, which is not a round point but blunt. The guard, or position, does not resemble in the least that of the *sabreur* or the small-swordsman; it is something peculiar to itself. I can scarcely describe it better than by asking the reader to hold his right arm, curved, above and in front of his head, and let his cane hang perfectly loose from his hand. It should be observed that the only object of attack and defense is the head and face. The chest is protected by a thick, long pad of buckskin; around the neck, to protect the jugular vein, the carotid artery and the other important bloodvessels, is wrapped a very heavy silk cravat, that comes up to the point of the chin. The eyes are guarded by massive iron goggles without glasses. Attached to the rear of the buckskin pad, at the small of the back, is a short tag or loose projecting strip of leather; the object of this is to give the unemployed hand, during the round, something to hold on by and thus keep it out of harm's way. The sword-arm is protected by a heavy buckskin glove reaching from the shoulder to the sword-hilt. The guard, which would be useless for sabre or fleuret fighting, will be found to be a perfectly natural one for defending the face and head. The cut of the *Schläger* is not the heavy, down-bearing blow of the sabre, still less the thrust of the fleuret; it is a short, quick, whipping motion, whereby the swordsman, keeping his arm in the same general position, lets the sword revolve with the hand on a free wrist, as it is called, and tries to cut over or under his adversary's guard. This peculiar whipping movement is not to be described, and can be acquired only by long and incessant practice. In the hand of an experienced fencer, the *Schläger*, although of course inflexible in the line of its edge, seems actually to coil over one's guard, like the snapper of a whip.

Bloodshed aside, the general appearance of the duelists is very comical. The pad and cravat and spectacles make them look somewhat like a pair of submarine divers in their armor. Then, it is interesting to watch the left hand pulling on the tag in convulsive sympathy with the movements of the right hand. Whenever the swords become entangled, or a wound or what seems to be a wound is given, the umpire cries, Halt! The seconds then separate their principals, and the doctor makes his examination. This constitutes a round. As the hanging guard is a fatiguing one, and as lowering the sword-arm would be tantamount either to a signal of defeat or an evidence of cowardice, the principal is allowed to rest his arm on the shoulder of his second in the intervals between the rounds. I doubt whether the civilized world can afford an odder sight than that of a student in full panoply pacing up and down the *Mensur* and leaning his sword-arm confidingly on his corps-brother's shoulder, while the surgeon gravely inspects his adversary's head.

The duel between M—— and Von H—— was to be, in technical phrase, *ohne ohne*, that is, without caps and without seconds. The principals had their seconds, it is true, but these did not stand by during the round and ward off *Tief-quart* or other dangerous blows; they kept back, and only advanced to part the principals when the umpire cried, Halt. Nor did the principals wear the corps-cap; head and face, with the exception of the eyes, were entirely exposed.

Whatever else it may or may not do, the German *Mensur* certainly gives the observer a good field for studying diversity of character. M—— and Von H—— were placed face to face, seven or eight paces apart.

Every body became breathless with attention. The second of one party cried, *Legt aus*, lay out, i. e., get ready, get on guard; the other responded, *Sie liegen aus*, they are ready. The umpire called out, *Los!* The combatants took each three steps in advance and came up to position; the duel had begun.

Von H———, a swordsman of good standing, very popular and very plucky, was tall, slender but vigorous, and attractive in his mien and manners; his face bore the marks of one or two previous encounters. M———, on the other hand, was rather undersized, almost burly in appearance, but with keen dark eyes and a resolute, one might say an "ugly" set to the mouth. Although his face was as smooth and full of color as that of a girl, his action and expression made it evident that he was a dangerous man. In addition to quickness and coolness, he had the great advantage of being left-handed.

Von H———, who had apparently studied his antagonist's style, was bent upon giving him plenty to do. Being taller by several inches, he sought to improve the advantage by making a furious attack, striking four or five *Hochquart* in rapid succession, in the attempt to beat down M———'s guard or to reach over it and cut the back of his head. But for this M——— was altogether too cool and firm. Parrying each attack with his arm, which he kept in perfect position, he merely made an occasional upward feint, an easy flirt of the sword, rather than a decided cut. It was evident that he acted strictly on the defensive, and bided his opportunity. In this way three rounds were fought in about as many minutes. Von H——'s chin was slightly grazed, M—— had not been touched at all. In the fourth round, Von H—— made a more furious onslaught than usual, reaching very far over, and it seemed as if he had at last succeeded in cutting the back of M——'s head. The umpire cried, Halt, and M—— had to submit to the doctor's inspection; he did so with a bad grace, smiling ironically, as if to say: What nonsense. The surgeon could not find any wound, and round number five was called. As M—— came to position, I noticed that he thrust his forward foot a trifle farther out than usual, gave his head a slight shake and his lips a slight curl. I felt instinctively that this time he meant mischief. As usual, Von H—— led off, but this time with a rattling *Hochterz* that almost broke both blades. M—— parried, and replied with a quick, strong upward cut. Von H—— had barely time to recover guard and parry. He did so, however, but unfortunately in the movement suffered his wrist to drop an inch or two. In a twinkling, apparently as if it were the same motion, M——'s upward cut was reversed to *Hochterz* (what would have been *Hoch-quart* for one right-handed). With a dull gleam and an inexpressibly rapid swish, his *Schläger* swooped upon his antagonist's exposed forehead. A subdued hum thrilled through the assembly. A stream of bright red blood spirted on the floor, and it needed no doctor's examination to pronounce the duel over. It had lasted five or six minutes, and the victor had struck only one real blow. One may attend many a duel without witnessing a like display of tactics. The successful duellant had simply kept his guard and struck in the nick of time.

The reader is doubtless ready with his comments: What a shocking display of brutality, what a senseless mutilation of the human countenance! I agree with him fully. In fact, many a German corps-student will do the same. Yet it is only fair that we should look upon the matter from every point of view, and avoid judging it by our own standards exclusively. Were the students the only class of duelists in Germany, or in Europe, the practice would soon be put down. But such is not the case. In England, and in the older States of our Union, the appeal to arms as a satisfaction for wounded honor has gone out of fashion. Popular opinion is against it. But in France, Germany, Italy, Russia, duels occur continually. I need only cite, among recent instances, the deplorable encounter between Armand Carrel and Emile de Girardin, the one between the Duc de Montpensier and Henri de Bourbon, or the one that occurred but a few months ago between two Roumanian noblemen residing in Paris.* One who reads the European press regularly will find mention made of a duel every month or two. The truth is that public opinion on the continent sustains the practice, and, in such matters, public opinion is irresistible. German students duel for the same reasons that lead German officers,

---

* Even as I write, the world of Paris is agog with the duel in which Prince Metternich has figured.

*7

journalists, noblemen, and others of the *genus irritabile* to resort to arms, namely, because they regard it as the only dignified and *gentlemanly* way of resenting an insult. In this respect, they are in accordance with the general tone of feeling in the community, they are neither better nor worse than the other upper classes. But they are to be condemned, even on their own theory, for converting what should be the exception into a *modus vivendi*, as it were, making student-honor a matter of conventionalism and converting a final resort into an every-day pastime. They duel so much, and on such frivolous pretexts, that the impartial observer must accuse them of fighting simply because they like to fight. Furthermore, by their paddings and goggles (to say nothing of caps and seconds), and by their peculiar mode of fighting, they eliminate the element of danger almost completely, and make the *Mensur* encounter a mere display of address. The wounds inflicted by the *Schläger* are rarely serious, being clean cuts with a sharp edge, and generally heal in a fortnight. If properly cared for, they do not leave a bad scar. Occasionally one hears of a grave disfigurement, possibly a fatal termination to a *Schläger* duel; but such results come from what might be called an accident, as the breaking of a sword-blade. In ninety-nine instances out of the hundred, a student-duel is like the two that I have described : either a harmless and almost farcical set-to between men who cannot do each other much harm, or a scientific trial of skill between veterans who know how to give and take. I once asked a friend of mine, a corps-student at the time and a splendid *Schläger*,* what he really thought of the *Mensur*. "O," said he, "it is an abominable piece of nonsense (*ein grässlicher Unsinn*), but at any rate it is better than street-fighting."

It is a notorious fact that nine tenths of the duels are fought without any real provocation; one student happens to bump against the other in the street, or one chaffs the other a trifle too sharply. The students have a code of honor of their own, namely, a list of expressions which one can not himself use without rendering himself liable to a challenge and which one must always resent. Prominent among these is the word *dumm* (stupid), especially in the connection: *dummer Junge*. It is a direct provocation to call your colleague a *dummer Junge*; it is not, to tell him that he lies! The German word "lie" does not suggest such a degree of moral obliquity as does the English.

The reader must not imagine, however, that *Mensur* duels are the only ones. From time to time there is an encounter with sabres or even with pistols. These are rare, but they do occur, and are kept very secret; generally they are fought outside the limits of the University jurisdiction. They are real duels, the supposed satisfaction for some gross insult.

The reader will probably wish to learn why it is that the university as a rule treats *Mensur* duels so lightly, scarcely interfering to prevent them, and, when the

---

* He is now professor in a neighboring university.

beadles have made an arrest, punishing the offenders with a mere nominal imprisonment of a few days or a fortnight. Permit me to meet the interrogatory with the following imaginary counter-question from the university court. Here are hundreds of young men from various quarters of the country, all more or less imbued with the notion that it is right and honorable to resent an insult, all at that age in life when passion runs highest, sustained and even urged on by the general opinion of the community, that looks upon a *Mensur* as a venial youthful escapade, and a *Schläger* scar as something to be boasted of in after-life. What would you have us do? Suppress the duel and punish rigorously the duelist? We can not do the one, we dare not do the other. Our students *will* fight, because the quarrel is in them and must come out. Our colleagues of the Heidelberg faculty tried once, years ago, to put an end to the practice, but *outside pressure was too strong for them and they were forced to abandon the attempt.* All that is in our power, we do; we discourage utterly pistol and sabre duels, by ferreting out the real offender and punishing him to the full extent of our authority; we leave *Mensur* duels to the general good sense of the students; if they become too numerous, or if they threaten to assume an aggravated shape, we check them for a while by relegating the elements of discord. But there is one thing that we can do, and always do; we prevent *bullying*. We suffer no one to be overridden and dragged into a duel against his own judgment, either by threats or by abuse. If a man chooses to fight, he can take his chance. If he does not choose to fight, we protect him.

These are not idle words. The reader may rest assured that there is no more scrupulous defender of the inviolability of a man's person and feelings than the court of a German university. In 1863, at a time when diplomatic relations between Prussia and Hanover were rapidly becoming delicate in the extreme, the University of Göttingen did not hesitate to banish for two years the nephew of one of the most notorious and influential generals in the Prussian service, merely because he insulted verbally but grossly a fellow-student in the street. I feel no hesitation in affirming that the student who should presume to strike, either with his cane or with his hand, another student, and should decline to make public apology and amends, if demanded, would be cashiered within a week. He would have the pleasure of reading his name placarded in big staring letters on the Black Board, and knowing that he was excluded from every seat of learning between the Rhine and the Vistula. American though I am, I feel bound to state explicitly that, on this point at least, we have much to learn from Germany. Dueling, it must be admitted, is an evil. But there are others equally great and much meaner. I refer to "hazing," "rushing," "nagging," and "smoking-out." These are outrages upon all that makes life worth living. They not only invade the sanctity of a private room, but they humiliate the victim at a time when the character is forming and impressions are assuming their final set. Having myself escaped all these trials of American college life, I can speak my mind freely and without resentment. To one who has lived under both systems, our own will appear a mixture of childishness and tyranny, a system of terrorism administered by beardless youths who were better at home conning their geography and grammar. It is not my purpose to defend German practices, still less to commit the absurdity of arguing for their adoption in America. Both countries are in need of reform. But this much surely the sober-minded thinker can say: that the German system, rough and brutal though it may be, is at least manly. It holds the student to the strictest accountability for all that he does and says. He can not play the Hector one day, and the meek and lowly minded the next. By insulting in any way his fellow, he places himself before the inexorable alternative: apologize or fight! If a student wishes to lead a quiet, secluded life, devoting himself exclusively to study, he can do so with the assurance that his intentions will be respected, his person unmolested. He has only to manifest his disposition, to let the world know that he means peace. But then he must carefully observe the golden rule, he must not fail to do unto others as he would have others do unto him. He must never provoke abuse. If, on the other hand, his wish is to fight and row with congenial spirits, it is easily gratified. Time will never hang heavy on his hands. He will always find men by the score ready to quarrel with him over the color of the Prophet's beard and meet him steel to steel.

The fault of the American system is that, under it, the student who is in the least degree odd in appearance or manners may be subjected to annoyance and persecution from which there is no escape and for which there is no redress. The fault of the German is that it tolerates bloodshed, and makes student-honor, to a large extent, conventional. On the other hand, it confines personal altercation to those who choose to indulge in it of their own accord.

CHAPTER V.

Daylight in German.

THE fall and winter passed uneventfully. The season was a cold one, giving us plenty of skating on the Upper Meadows, outside of the Grone Gate. Skating and an occasional visit to the theater were my only relaxations; otherwise I kept close to my books and lectures. Had the theater troupe and stage repertory been better, I might have paid perhaps more frequent attentions to the muse. But it seemed to me that the evenings could be spent more profitably and agreeably in talking poor German to my landlady, and listening to her capitally told stories of German life. It has often been a matter of astonishment to me how much language one can learn in conversation with intelligent and cultivated women. The solid framework of knowledge one has to construct for one's self, slowly and painfully, but ease and grace of discourse, the mastery of those charming little words and phrases that make conversation a continuous flow, rather than a clumsy chain of detached propositions, can be obtained only through intercourse with the other sex. In this respect, German women are not equal to the French; they have less style; less finish, and also less animation. On the other hand, they have more heartiness, by nature a kinder disposition. They are devoted friends, always obliging, thoroughly unselfish, and easily pleased.

Perhaps the reader is familiar with the expression attributed to Dr. Johnson on landing at Dieppe: "Good Heavens! Even the little children speak French!" On arriving at Göttingen, I found, in like manner, that all the boys and girls spoke German! What was even more surprising and humiliating, they spoke a good deal faster and better than I could. Can there be anything more absurd than to find yourself, who have obtained your legal majority, beaten completely by a child not yet in its teens, to see that all your book-learning is as nothing by the side of prattle imbibed, as it were, with the mother's milk, picked up unconsciously and without an effort in the nursery-room? Although not offering my experience on this point as anything novel or extraordinary, I desire to make an application of it that has not yet received the attention which it deserves. It is this, that whoever seeks to learn a language well and completely must, in a measure, learn it even as a little child, must approach it in a humble, we might say a reverent spirit, and let it work upon him before he attempts to work upon it. Language is a mode of expression for the widest range of ideas and feelings; unless we essay it in all its stages, from its lispings and stammerings to its most exalted utterances, we shall never fully enter into its character. Furthermore, the beginner can learn very much from children's talk. The more I reflect upon the numbers of those who exert themselves from year to year to acquire a practical knowledge of foreign languages, the greater is my surprise that no one of our professed teachers has given to this fact special prominence. It would be going out of my way to attempt to give an explanation of all the causes. Let me call attention to one or two. The besetting sin of the beginner in language is *mauvaise honte ;* he is tongue-tied, helpless, embarrassed in the presence of his equals. He is ashamed to speak, for fear of making a mistake; it seems to him at times as though everybody were watching him and waiting for a blunder. Of course this is a delusion, but, like other unreasonable delusions, it cannot be reasoned away. In speaking with children, however, this *mauvaise honte* vanishes of itself; the young man who is ashamed to open his lips before other young men, will converse freely with a boy, as if it were his own brother; he loses the morbid dread of being watched and corrected, and blunders on the best he can. This, it is to be observed, is half the battle in learning to talk. But there is another point equally important. Children are great tyrants; they are not exacting in the matter of grammar; they tolerate all sorts of mistakes, without even suspecting one of talking queerly, that is, as a foreigner; but, in one respect, they are inexorable. They will have easy words and phrases, and they will have the right word for the right thing. No amount of circumlocution, of general platitudes and second-hand knowledge will answer; one must call a kettle a kettle, a saw a saw, or the child will not understand. Experience will teach us that in conversing with children we must always reconstruct our knowledge, so to speak ; must put our ideas into the clearest and most compact shape ; keep the sharpest watch over nouns, adjectives and verbs, and drop all conventionalisms. In listening to children's talk, we can almost imagine ourselves " hearing the grass grow;" we surprise the human spirit in its healthful, spontaneous evolution.

It is not in my power to dwell upon this subject. I can only assure the reader that, having lived in both French and German families, and tried the experiment thoroughly, I attribute whatever conversational ability I may possess quite as much to the children as to the parents. My landlady in Göttingen had but one child living with her, a mere girl just in her teens, but very affable, intelligent, and devoted to her lessons with an assiduity that would put to shame the typical American miss who has begun already to dream of balls and valentines. For three years we were the best of friends, and the German that I learned from her will stand me in good stead for a life-time.

Yet, notwithstanding the advantages of the home-circle that I was enjoying, I determined in early spring to make a change of quarters. To come to a German university and not live just as a student, seemed like visiting Rome without getting a look at the Pope. Besides, I was somewhat cramped and uncomfortable, the best rooms in the house being occupied by the older boarders. I selected, therefore, a student-room on the Wende street, the principal street of the town, and had my books and "traps" transferred. It was a pleasant abode. The main room had three windows in front, and one on the side; the sleeping-room, facing on a side street, had two windows. The furniture was altogether new. For all this comfort I paid the moderate sum of five and a half *louis d'or* per semester, i. e., from Easter to Michaelmas, or vice versa. In university towns, this is the habitual way of renting rooms. Reckoning the *louis d'or* at five thalers and a half, my rental for six months was a fraction over thirty thalers, say twenty-two dollars. I had really more room than I needed.

Meals and fuel were of course extra. I had to make a slight outlay for table-furniture, buying some knives and forks, plates, cups and saucers, napkins, and table-cloths. This was my bachelor outfit. The slight expense was more than balanced by the luxurious sense of being my own master, of being able to give a bachelor supper to my friends, whenever so disposed. I continued to take my dinner with Frau H——, but breakfast and supper were in my own room. Short of being in one's own family, I doubt whether there is a more enjoyable state than that of living by one's self in hired lodgings in Germany. It is possible in New York, to say nothing of London and Paris; but in New York, the expense is ruinous, and even in England and France one will miss that peculiar institution, the *Dienstmädchen*. The German *Dienstmädchen* is no more the *domestique* of France, or the "Bridget" of America, than Göttingen is Oxford or Harvard. She is an institution by herself, and therefore deserves especial mention. In fact, life in Germany would be scarcely what it is without her. If you wish an extra supper in the evening, you consult your *Dienstmädchen;* if you merely wish to send out for a glass of beer, you employ her services. She will bring home a basketful of books from the university library, make your fires, go on all your thousand and one errands, and do everything for you but blacken your boots. That is the perquisite of the *Stiefelfuchs.* Her capacity for work and her general cheerfulness border on the marvelous. One such servant girl will wait upon six or seven students and do the family-work in addition. She brings the dinner for those who take that meal in their rooms; she makes the beds and sweeps the rooms (when they are swept); in the autumn, she is sent to the family-estate outside the city walls to dig potatoes by way of variety. Yet she is able and ready to dance every Sunday night from seven o'clock to two, and go about her work on Monday morning as fresh as a June rose. Her only fault is a slight shade of impertinence; not the surly, mutinous impertinence of "Bridget," but the pert forwardness of a good-natured, spoiled child. Like all privileged servants, she thinks that she knows everything much better than her master.

Students commonly take their dinner at a hotel or restaurant, paying a fixed price per month. Some few, either on account of ill health or because they wish to economize time, dine in their rooms. This is unquestionably a pernicious habit; no one can really enjoy the principal meal of the day in solitude. But the basket used for bringing meals into the house is so practical and so peculiar that I cannot refrain from describing it. It is round, small in diameter, and very deep; a wide slit runs down one side to the bottom. Into this basket the dishes, generally four in number, are dropped one upon the other. The bottom of the first dish fits upon and into the second, the third upon the second, and so on, after the fashion of the rings used in moulding for long vertical castings. Each of the dishes has a knob that slips down the slit and is used as a handle in pulling the dish out. When the dishes are all in place and the cover is on, the whole can be easily carried quite a distance, by means of an arched handle over the top, without spilling or cooling the contents.

The reader may imagine me, then, as lodged in very comfortable sunshiny rooms on the principal street in town, nearly opposite the church of St. James. This venerable edifice, the stones of which have grown gray-black with the lapse of centuries, is not beautiful; its outlines are too bald, its solitary tower too stiff and awkward. Still it is an attractive building; my chief pleasure in connection with it was to watch the going and coming and listen to the incessant cawing of the rooks that had built them nests under the eaves and in the chinks of the tower. Every fair day, about sunset, they flew around the tower again and again in a flock, evidently settling the affairs of the day and wishing each other good night before retiring.

The first four months passed in my new abode were a period of unmixed delight. I was in the spring-time of life, unfettered, free to follow the promptings of fancy, and, above all, stimulated by the consciousness that daylight had at last dawned upon my studies. The patient toil of preparation through the fall and winter blossomed and put forth leaves, as it were, in company with the trees on the old city wall. For six long months I had slaved through grammar and translations; about the beginning of March, as near as I can remember, I said to myself: "Somewhat too much of this." Bidding grammars, copy-books and exercises a lasting farewell, I read! I gave myself up without restraint to the fit, let the appetite that had been fasting so long gorge itself without stint. The preparatory work having trained my memory and perceptions, it was an easy thing then to digest and assimilate whatever I might take up. My reading was as immethodical as possible; nothing was too easy and simple, nothing too exalted. In the language of Voltaire, *je permettais tous les genres hors le genre ennuyeux.* The first literary work that I read was the *Faust.* A strange selection, yet perhaps the best. The copy that I used is still in my possession, with all the notes and explanations inserted in pencil at the time. It surprises me to see how few words I was obliged to look up in the dictionary. It would be presumptuous to say that I understood *Faust* thoroughly; to do that, one must be mature in years and make it a subject of special study. But so far as sentiment and diction were concerned, I understood and enjoyed the poem with an intensity that rather unsettled me for the time. It haunted me day and night, the rhymes and the play of words rang in my ears. I read and re-read, until the lyrical and descriptive passages were firmly lodged in the memory. Besides *Faust*, I read *Egmont*, *Tasso*, in fact nearly all the dramas and all the minor poems of Goethe, committing many of them to memory. It seemed as though I could never weary of Goethe. As to Schiller, I cannot speak with like accuracy. I read much, but it did not make such an impression upon me as to keep the recollection distinct from reading done in subsequent years. My favorite author after Goethe was Lessing; I read all his dramatical works and poetical pieces, and many of his essays, but not the *Laocoon*. I also skimmed through the minor poets and romancers, Klopstock, Uhland, Wieland, Heine, and the like. But the book that impressed me most strongly, the *Faust* excepted, was one that I almost hesitate to mention. The name will sound so unfamiliar to the reader, and the subject so far-fetched and unattractive. It was Vilmar's *Geschichte der deutschen Nationalliteratur*, a history of the national literature of Germany from the earliest times down to and including Goethe and Schiller. The remembrance of the first reading is as distinct as though it were but yesterday. I began at seven in the evening and did not knock off until my eyes gave out at three in the morning. No sensational romance, I am confident, was ever devoured more eagerly. The book came upon me as the revelation of a new world. Kriemhild, Hagen, Gudrun, Parzival, Tristan and Isolt, now familiar apparitions, I then met for the first time face to face and recognized in their beauty and their grandeur. The entire field of German mediæval poetry, depicted so glowingly by the artist-critic, swept before me in a majestic panorama. Subsequently, when increased familiarity with the subject had brought me to look upon mediæval German and its literature with more critical eyes, I was often at a loss to account for the enthusiasm which the first perusal of Vilmar's work had called forth. His views seemed exaggerated, his judgments too sanguine. It was only in the fall of 1872 that I obtained the clue to the puzzle, and learned that my earliest impressions were after all justified. A pupil and warm admirer of Vilmar, Professor Grein of Marburg, with whom I was then privately reading Anglo-Saxon, informed me that Vilmar had written his *History* from a full heart, so to speak. He was invited to deliver a special course of lectures on German literature at Cassel. Although already very familiar with the ground, he went over it anew, going back directly to the authors or originals themselves, eschewing intermediate works of criticism, and reading *in extenso*. His tone and his views, accordingly, have something about them indescribably fresh and genial. As Professor Grein observed, the composition bears evident tokens of the "powerful impression got directly from the sources themselves."

It is not surprising, then, that Vilmar should have succeeded in portraying so artistically and vividly the growth of the German mind. His work contains errors, not a few of them grave ones. For minuteness and accuracy it is surpassed by the works of Gervinus, Koberstein, Kurz, and others. But taken all in all, as a genial, animated and animating, continuous flow of description and reflection, it is still unsurpassed. By the side of it, the other treatises are as dry as dust. It is a work that might be introduced with profit in the most advanced German classes of our colleges.

But interest in a novel subject, and the fascination exerted by Vilmar's style, were not the only ties that attached me to the *History*. More than any other work, more than *Faust* itself, it awakened me to the full sense of the mastery that I had gained — hitherto unconsciously — over the German language. Vilmar's style is difficult, that is to say, while the range of words is not large and the words themselves are graphic and easily understood, the sentences are complicated in the extreme. It is the German style $κατ'\ ἐξοχην$. I cannot recall another author who uses habitually such long sentences, who detaches the separable particle from the verb by such daring flights of direct and indirect object, adverbs, qualifying, explanatory, parenthetical clauses. One who can read Vilmar's *History* rapidly, say eight or ten pages an hour, taking in at a glance the grammatical relations of all the words in the complete sentence, seizing unerringly the separable particle two, or four, or even eight lines below the verb to which it belongs, retaining the sense of the whole and its parts while looking out an occasional word in the dictionary, not baffled by length or variety of expression, but seeing through it as through a transparent tissue: one who can do this is absolved from his apprenticeship. He is henceforth a master-workman; he has many things still to learn, but he can learn them one by one for himself; the drudgery is over. It was this sense of mastery, then, that gave me such pleasure. I had at last the satisfaction for many an hour of dry study. From that time on, grammar and dictionary were merely books of reference, not daily chains.* The work that gave me most trouble to read was, strange to say, the one in which the style is the simplest, Freytag's *Pictures of the German Past*. The vocabulary is very rich, and the numerous citations from old authors, although modernized in spelling, give the work an archaic tinge.

In this way, occupying myself exclusively with the master-pieces of German thought, I passed the spring and summer. My mode of life was very simple. At the

---

* As a specimen of Vilmar's style, permit me to cite untranslated the following passage from the analysis of Gottfried v. Strassburg's *Tristan und Isolt:* "*So* FLICHT *er* (the poet) *bei der Stelle, wo er erzählt, dass endlich dem betrogenen Gatten Marke die Augen aufgegangen seien, und er* (Mark, the husband) *der ungetreuen Isolde künftig besser zu hüten beschlossen, aber ihre Schönheit ihn dennoch blind gemacht habe, und Isolde auch der strengen Hut zu spotten verstanden habe, und zwar um so besser, je strenger die Hut wurde— eine Betrachtung* EIN *über die bei der Minne* (love) *übel angewandte Hut, in welcher er an den spitzigsten Tadel das zarteste Lob der Frauen auf die geschickteste Weise anknüpft.*" (p. 146, ed. of 1862.)

The entire passage turns on FLICHT, line 3, and EIN, line 8, which, together, form the compound verb *einflechten,* to interweave, insert.

beginning of the summer semester I took, *pro forma*,* a course of lectures by Professor Lotze, on *Natur-Philosophie*. This is anything but our natural philosophy; it is rather the philosophy of nature, a general speculative discussion of the laws of the material world in their relations to the human spirit, something between physics and psychology. I feel bound to confess that, although the professor was interesting, I cut him rather shabbily. Goethe and Lessing were still more interesting. The weather being fine, I spent nearly all my afternoons in the open air, exploring the vicinity of Göttingen, until every village and by-path and *Garten* became a familiar haunt. Usually unaccompanied on these excursions, I always made provision for spiritual diversion by having a book or two in my pocket to read whenever the inclination came over me and a pleasant resting-place offered itself. It was not my practice to carry a pocket-dictionary. When an unfamiliar word occurred in reading, I simply underscored it, tried to think out its meaning, and then consulted the dictionary after returning to my room. It has always seemed to me that pocket-dictionaries are a hindrance rather than a help. Being necessarily small, they are also necessarily incomplete, are not seldom inaccurate, and have the provoking trick of omitting the precise word or idiom that one wishes to find. Besides, it is no loss, but a gain, to carry a word or an idiom for a few hours in the mind without knowing its exact mean-

---

* Every student is compelled to take at least one course of lectures per semester.

ing. It seems to lodge itself better in the memory, and the mind turns it over and over in the effort to find an explanation, so that the explanation, when it comes at last, takes root in soil well prepared. Whereas words looked up as fast as they occur are apt to resemble seed scattered by the wayside. So far as my observation extends, those who go through life abroad with a dictionary in one pocket and a phrase-book in the other, are invariably slipshod conversationists.

I trust that the reader will not regard this digression upon the subject of German literature as superfluous. My personal experience is not offered as a model for imitation, but rather as a hint for reflection, and also in the hope of aiding in the correction of what seem to me certain grave errors in the accepted plan of learning foreign languages. In language more than in any other study, the tone-giving element, to borrow a Germanism, is *quantity*. One must read not by tens of pages, but by hundreds, must read rapidly, and above all must read authors entire. Permit me to cite one or two authorities. Matthew Arnold says: "Ask a good Greek scholar in the ordinary English acceptation of that term, who at the same time knows a modern literature — let us say the French literature — well, whether he feels himself to have most seized the spirit and power of French literature, or of Greek literature. Undoubtedly he has most seized the spirit and power of French literature, simply because he has read so very much more of it. But if, instead of reading work after work of French literature, he had read only a few works or parts of works in it, and had given the rest of his time to the sedulous practice of French composition and to minutely learning the structure and laws of the French language, then he would know the French literature much as he knows the Greek; he might write very creditable French verse, but he would have seized the power and spirit of the French literature not half so much as he has seized them at present."*

The other quotation is this: "During those secluded years, before the call to the New York University, he (i. e., Professor Tayler Lewis) read the Hebrew Bible through *annually*, for fourteen years; the Iliad and Odyssey, entire, almost as often; the whole of the Greek drama, forty-five extant plays, twice over, and many of them oftener; all the dialogues of Plato, some of them frequently; nearly all of Aristotle — his Physica, Metaphysica, and his more special physical treatises, and also his ethical and political writings; a large part of the lesser hexameter poets, such as Apollonius Rhodius and Aratus; also Pindar and the pastoral poets; all of Thucydides; all of Herodotus; all of Xenophon; nearly all of Plutarch, Longinus, Lucian, Diodorus Siculus, and the Gnomic and Epic poetry; all of Virgil, Horace and Ovid; and all of Cicero, except his orations."†

These citations will make my position clear and warrant me in asserting that there is only one way

---
* Higher Schools and Universities of Germany. Ed. of 1874, p. 181.
† Hart's Manual of American Literature, p. 578.

of learning a language, for literary purposes, and that way consists in *reading*. After the student has mastered the forms so that he is no longer under their thraldom, he has only to approach the master-minds and listen to all that they have to say; he will thus, as Matthew Arnold expresses it, seize the power and spirit of the literature.

Our collegiate and school instruction in French and German is faulty both in conception and in execution. The schools attempt nothing more than a superficial glibness of conversation and composition, which is rarely acquired and, when acquired, is never retained, and the colleges, which should exact a knowledge of French and German grammar for admission, make the course in modern languages little more than a tedious additional drill in paradigms and exercises; they overlook the real object of learning a language, namely the ability to read a book fluently and understand it both in itself and in its relations to kindred books. As for French literature and German literature, as representing the body of thought of those nations, the historic growth of the spirit of each, they never seem to have occurred to the minds of those who frame our college curriculum.

CHAPTER VI.

Idlesse.

THE spring and summer of 1862 were spent as I have described, pleasantly and profitably. Not so the following winter. For want of a better term, I have entitled the present chapter as above. It treats of the most dreary and discouraging part of my life in Germany, a period of many months spent in forced inactivity. I shall be as brief as possible.

The early summer was warm and agreeable. But in August the weather changed, and we had a succession of cold rain-storms. Not having succeeded in finding a traveling companion, I remained in Göttingen through the long vacation, and kept up my reading. In the early part of September, ill luck came upon me in the shape of a violent cold, that seemed to be satisfied with nothing short of running through the entire system. Every organ was affected more or less, the head, eyes, ears, stomach. By the end of the month, after suffering in every conceivable way and congratulating myself on the prospect of recovery, symptoms of rheumatism showed themselves. I became lame and unable to walk, and the right knee was badly swollen. The disease finally took the form of water in the knee.* It was an obstinate case, not yielding for weeks and months to the most persistent treatment. The disease itself did not occasion much pain, but the cure was extremely disagreeable. I was obliged to keep the leg stretched out on the sofa, to wear a heavy linen bandage wrapped tightly around the knee, and to paint the knee three or four times a day with a solution of iodine. The attack kept me a prisoner in my room from September until the first week in January. This close confinement became toward the last very depressing. The bandage was at times an almost insupportable burden, I lost my appetite, sleep came only fitfully and was seldom refreshing. So far as study, or even reading was concerned, I may admit that I did none. There was no energy, no "brains" for anything of a higher order than the average *Roman* or *Novelle*. The only literary works that I remember reading during this period were Schiller's short stories in prose and his *Thirty Years' War*. This last was a doleful infliction, it must be confessed, but then it tallied with the invalid's mood.

Fortunately kind friends stood by me patiently. Thanks to their unselfish devotion, I succeeded in weathering the trial without more serious loss than that of time. There were not many Americans in Göttingen during the winter, only five besides myself, and four of the five were new comers from over the water and con-

---

* The foundation for the trouble was probably laid the year before, by excessive indulgence in Alpine climbing and other violent exercises.

sequently had to look after themselves. Still, they did what they could. My German friends also visited me regularly. But my chief comforters were John I. Harvey (from Virginia), David Swan (from Scotland), and Paul Christofle, the son of the founder and at present head of the well known house of Christofle & Cie., in Paris. Harvey dropped in at my rooms regularly every morning and afternoon; the other two, who were generally busy in the laboratory during the day, came in the evening. As I had nothing to do but let myself be entertained in the best way possible, my room became a sort of headquarters for any one who might have an idle hour, and was ready to take a smoke or a hand at *écarté* or "sixty-six."

From beginning to end, the winter of 1862-3 was for me a strange episode. Thousands of miles from home, without a single person who was directly responsible for my welfare, in a foreign land, practically helpless, I nevertheless succeeded in outliving the trial uninjured. Everybody who came in contact with me seemed to take an interest in me, the owner of the house and the servants were obliging and good-natured, and my friends, especially the three whom I have mentioned, left literally no wish ungratified. Should these lines ever reach them, I hope that they will not be displeased at such a public acknowledgment. It is the only way that I can find of expressing the sense of gratitude still undimmed for valuable hours spent and services paid at the altar of friendship.

Soon after New Year, the surgeon pronounced me cured, and gave me permission to go out to dinner. The prospect of escaping from the confinement of four walls, even if only for an hour a day, was enchanting; but the permission, when I attempted to act upon it, was almost a mockery. The long continued bandaging had relaxed the muscles so much that I could scarcely stand. For the first day or two it seemed as if all my time and energy were consumed in limping up and down the two flights of stairs between the room and the street.

Thus the winter passed in slow recuperation, and spring came once again. I met it with feelings very different from those of the year before. Seven months had gone for nothing, or almost nothing. I had of course learned some additional German, but the gain was slight in proportion to the time. My reading had been broken up, and the plans of study that I had formed in the summer were not even begun. Everything in a university goes by semesters; to lose half a semester is to lose all. Even had my health permitted, I could not have begun any course of study after New Year. There was nothing left but to wait for the next semester, and in the meanwhile recover all the strength possible.

CHAPTER VII.

Removal to Berlin — Umsatteln.

BY the close of the winter semester (the middle of March, 1863), my health and spirits were restored. One or two friends kept me company in a visit of a fortnight in Berlin. I had seen the capital of Prussia before, for a few days in the summer of 1862, while making a sort of flying trip through a part of North Germany. But it had been then the *saison morte*, and the city presented anything but an inviting aspect. It was hot, deserted, and dusty as only Berlin in July can be. During the present visit, on the contrary, the city was all life and bustle. For three or four days there was incessant parading and flying of flags. It was the occasion of the dedication of Blücher's monument and the commemoration of Prussia's uprising fifty years before, in 1813, against the first Napoleon. The display of troops, especially of cavalry, was very handsome, but the most interesting event in the ceremonies was the parade of the veterans of '13. The survivors of the German War of Independence, wearers of the Iron Cross, had been invited to Berlin at the express request of the King, and many thousands had responded to the call. Every veteran had been declared by special orders to rank as officer for the while and to be entitled to an officer's salute. The sentries on guard at the gates and other prominent points in the city had consequently little rest; it was one incessant presenting arms. In the grand parade *unter den Linden*, the veterans marched in a body, by companies, in between the dismounted *Gardes du Corps*, and, as well as I can remember, the *Garde-Füsiliere*. It was an impressive sight, to contrast the feeble, tottering gait, the old, battered and outlandish looking uniforms, the broken ranks of the men of 1813 with the solid tread and massive forms of the Body-Guard, or the quick, lithe swing of the Fusiliers. On that occasion and during my subsequent stay in Berlin, I received an impression of Prussia's military power that later events have only confirmed. Even the best troops of France, the Paris garrison, which I had seen some time before, were far from being the powerful, well disciplined men of the Prussian Guard. Any one who visited Berlin in 1863 and 1864, at the inauguration of the Army Reform, could not fail to be struck as I was with the energy, I might say the agony of preparation. Yet no one could have predicted what it meant or what it was to accomplish only three years later. The air was full of military bustle, and the city resembled a huge camp even more than it does now.

For various reasons I decided to remove to Berlin for the coming summer-semester. As the reader can readily understand, Göttingen, once pleasant and inviting, had become associated with disagreeable remembrances of, illness and confinement. A change of air might do my health good; besides, being about to alter my plan of studies, or rather to adopt a plan where none had previously existed, I deemed it only proper to start *de novo*, by changing as well my place of residence.

After some hesitation, I had resolved to study law with a view of obtaining, if possible, the degree of doctor. Three semesters had already gone, one in learning the language, one in studying its literature, the third in enforced idleness. It was now time to settle upon something definite in the way of study. A German university, I had discovered, did not pretend to give a so called general education. There were lectures on every conceivable subject, on theology, medicine, the natural sciences, philology, history, but there was no general curriculum; the university evidently expected each student to take up one particular line of study and follow it to the end. I selected the law, as being the one most suited to my taste and disposition.

I obtained from the University-secretary the necessary *Abgangszeugniss* (honorable dismissal), and removed to Berlin about the middle of April. The ceremony of re-matriculation was very simple. Coming as a regular student from another German university, I had only to deposit the *Abgangszeugniss* with the Berlin secretary, pay a small fee, and give the customary pledge, the handshake, to the Rector. I then matriculated in the legal faculty. This transferring one's self from one faculty to another is called expressively by the students *Umsatteln*, changing saddles. One can meet students who have performed the operation three or four times; failing in every attempt at a degree, they are content to drift along from semester to semester and bear the sarcastic title of *bemooste Häupter*, moss-grown heads.

The Berlin university at that time was in its glory. The medical faculty was uncommonly strong. In theology there were such men as Dorner, Hengstenberg, Niedner, and Twesten, in philosophy Trendelenburg, Helfferich, Michelet, in the natural sciences Dove, Rose, Braun, in political economy Helwing and Hanssen, in history Droysen, Ranke, Jaffé, Köpke, Kiepert, in philology Steinthal, Bopp, Böckh, Bekker, Haupt, Weber. Many of these illustrious men have been called to their rest; their places have been taken, we can scarcely say filled, by their successors. In law there were Bruns, Gneist, Holtzendorff, Rudorff, Richter, Beseler, Homeyer, Heffter, and many others; I have named only the most illustrious. Gneist is the well known politician and leading debater in the Prussian Parliament and the Imperial Diet. Holtzendorff is now professor in Munich; Rudorff, and, I believe, Homeyer and Richter are deceased. The brightest stars of the Berlin legal faculty — Savigny and Puchta — had already set; in fact, as I afterward discovered, I might have done better for the first semester or two by going to Heidelberg, where Vangerow was then in his prime. Yet the loss was not great. In fact I may say, once for all, that a student cannot go very far out of his way in selecting any one of the leading univer sities. Two of the most delightful and most profitable months of my life were once passed in even a very small university, the name and fame of which have scarcely reached America. I mean Marburg, about half way between Frankfort and Cassel. The number of students, all told, did not exceed four hundred, and the professors were correspondingly few. Yet I was surprised at the comparatively large number of eminent men and the general breadth of culture. The reader may be assured that the smaller universities, such as Marburg, Rostock, Greifswald, Tübingen, differ from the larger ones in extent, in quantity, rather than in quality. Unless the student be engaged in the pursuit of some very limited specialty, he can do well almost anywhere.

To decide upon the study of the law is one thing; to carry out the decision is another. By consulting the list — still in my possession — of Berlin lectures for the summer of 1863, I find that there were announced no less than 59 courses of lectures on legal topics, covering 183 hours per week! That the reader, if of a legal turn of mind, may form some idea of what a legal faculty in Germany is and what it accomplishes, I give the list entire:

Encyclopædy and Methodology of the Science of Law, by Professors Heydemann and Holtzendorff and Dr. Schmidt.

Naturrecht, or Philosophy of Law, by Professor Heydemann.

Institutes, by Professors Bruns and Gneist.

History and Archæology of the Roman Law, the same.

History of Civil Procedure among the Romans, the same.

Institutes, by Drs. Rivier and Degenkolb.

Select Cases in Roman Law, explained by Dr. Degenkolb.

Pandects, by Professor Rudorff.

Erbrecht (Doctrine of Inheritance), by Dr. Baron.

Pandects and Erbrecht, by Dr. Witte.

Select Passages from the Pandects, explained by Professor Rudorff and Dr. Witte.

De Solutionibus (D. xlvi, 3), explained by Dr. Schmidt.

Practical Exercises in Roman Law (a sort of Moot Court), by Dr. Baron.

Ecclesiastical Law, Catholic and Protestant, by Professor Richter and Drs. Friedberg and Hinschius.

Law of Matrimony, by Dr. Friedberg.

Practical Exercises in Ecclesiastical Law, by Professor Richter and Drs. Friedberg and Hinschius.

History of German Constitutional Law, by Professors Beseler and Daniels and Dr. Kühns.

History of the Decline of the Roman-German Empire, by Professor Lancizolle.

German Common Law, by Professor Homeyer.

Law of Promissory Notes, by Dr. Kühns.

Practical Exercises in German Law, by Professor Beseler.

Public and Private Rights of German Sovereigns, by Professors Beseler and Holtzendorff.

German Constitutional Law, by Professor Daniels.

Church and State, by Dr. Friedberg.

Practical Exercises in State Law, by Professor Holtzendorff.

International Law, by Professors Heffter and Holtzendorff.

Civil Procedure, according to the Common Law of Germany and the Prussian Code, by Professors Heffter and Bruns.

The same, including also the Code Napoléon (for the Rhine provinces), by Dr. Hinschius.

Practical Exercises in Procedure, by Dr. Hinschius.

Criminal Law, by Professors Gneist and Berner.

Criminal Procedure, by Professors Heffter, Gneist and Berner.

Practical Exercises in Criminal Law, by Professor Berner.

The Death-Penalty, by Professor Holtzendorff.

Penitentiary System, the same.

Prussian Code, by Professors Daniels and Heydemann.

Special Questions under the Prussian Code, by Professor Heydemann.

Doctrine of Inheritance in Prussia, by Dr. Bornemann.

History of the Code Napoléon, by Dr. Rivier.

Franco-Rhenish Rights of Real Property between Husband and Wife, by Professor Daniels.

English Constitutional History, by Professor Gneist.

The total number of professors and doctors (*Privat-docenten*) on the list is twenty-one.

A few qualifying and explanatory remarks will not be superfluous. In the first place, not all the lectures announced, especially at a university like Berlin, are actually read. The professor, or *Privat-docent*, upon whom has been conferred the *venias docendi*, the privilege of lecturing, is held to announce at least one *publice* each semester. But if auditors fail to present themselves in sufficient numbers, as not infrequently happens, the course is not delivered, the lecturer is exonerated. This may seem an odd procedure, but the explanation is not remote. A German university faculty consists of professors (either regular or extraordinary), and *Privat-docenten*, who are nothing more than candidates for professorships. The university looks to its professors for bearing the burden of instruction; the *Privat-docenten* keep the professors up to the mark by competing with them. A *Privat-docent* is free to lecture on any topic connected with his department, even although a course of lectures on that same topic may have been announced by a professor. The reader will observe that the above list contains several instances of such direct competition. But ordinarily the *Privat-docent* prefers to compete indirectly, as it were, by reading on some special topic that is not taken up by any of the professors. These special-topic lectures are the germs of future essays and monographs; after the *Privat-docent* has worked his lectures into the proper shape by repeated readings, he publishes them in book-form with a view to wider reputation and a "call." But if the topic is too remote, too special, the lecturer will not find hearers. In fact, a professor, or even a *Privat-docent*, whose reputation is already established, and whose time is occupied with *privatim* lectures, will purposely select a very special topic, so as not to attract hearers and yet comply with the regulations.* On general principles, then, I should say that twenty per cent of the lectures announced in the above list were not read. On the other hand, the reader should bear in mind that it was the summer semester, which is always and everywhere "lighter" than the winter. I am inclined to believe that we should get the actual amount of winter work by restoring the twenty per cent.

The study of law in Germany is treated seriously. No one is admitted to the bar or to the bench who has not been through the full university course. This of itself presupposes the gymnasial course. The consequence is that every practitioner and every judge down to the humblest justice of the peace has had a *thorough classical and legal education.* Can we wonder, then, at the pride with which Germany points to her judicial system, and the scarcely concealed disdain with which she looks down upon the uncertainty and circumlocution of the English and the American? It is not my purpose to draw invidious comparisons. It must be admitted that our *best* judges and our *best* lawyers will compare favorably with those of any land. But the world is not made up of best men. Allowances are to be made for respectable mediocrity. Here it is that the superiority of the German system, as a system, over our want of system becomes manifest. That system is briefly as follows. A young German wishing to fit himself for the profession

---

* The terms *publice, privatim* and *privatissime* have been explained in Chapter III.

must first acquire the broad general culture of the gymnasium. In the next place, he must attend the university at least three full years, six half-years, and hear certain prescribed lectures, say eighteen or twenty in all. He need not hear them in any prescribed order, but he must hear them at some time. He need not pass the university examination, but he must pass the *Staats-examen*, which is a serious matter. This state-examination is conducted after a peculiarly German fashion. The candidate presents himself to the Court of Appeals of the state or province, bringing with him his gymnasial and university certificates. The court assigns to him two *schriftliche Arbeiten*, that is, two cases which have actually come up on appeal, and upon which he must give a reference. He gets facsimiles of all the papers in each case, from the original summons down to the final appeal in error, and also all the evidence. In his reference he must review every point taken on both sides, whether of law or of fact, whether controverted or not. In short, he must subject each case to an exhaustive theoretical analysis, and submit his reports in writing. This is a labor of several months. After the *schriftliche Arbeiten* have been read and approved by the Court, the candidate is admitted to an oral examination, which lasts from two to three hours. This second ordeal over, he becomes an *Auditor*. That is to say, he is assigned to some one of the higher courts (*Obergerichte*) as a compulsory listener to all the proceedings for two years. At the end of the two years, he has his choice either to pass his *second*
*10

examination then and be admitted to practice, or to wait two years longer as *Assessor*, that is, as one who sits on the bench with the judges but has no vote, and pass a final examination as a candidate for judicial appointment.

A German state, it is evident, does not regard either the practice or the administration of the law as something to be "picked up." While it is perfectly true that no amount of teaching and examining will make a lawyer of a man whom nature intended for something else, yet it can scarcely be doubted that the German system works admirably in suppressing shysters, pettifogers, and low-lived individuals of all sorts. One can not take the first step toward entering the profession without having acquired some substantial knowledge, some elements of culture and breeding. The law itself in Germany has its defects, obvious and grave ones; but these spring from the political and social organization of the country, and are not due especially to the bench or the bar. The whole tendency of the German system is to develop a body of enlightened, upright jurists, and to make the course of justice prompt and inexpensive. The judges, holding their office by royal appointment and utterly indifferent to so called public opinion, watch the lawyers very sharply and compel them to expedite matters. Besides, they regard themselves more as equitable umpires than as judges in our sense. They try as much as possible to bring about compromises and go far more than our judges into the real merits of the case. A judge, according to the English or American system, contents himself with passing his opinion on points that have been expressly raised; in Germany he will often take cognizance of points that have not been raised. In other words, he regards the equitable rights of the client as the main thing, and is not disposed to let them be sacrificed through the laches or ignorance of the attorney.*

Having thus given a brief outline of the way in which law is studied in Germany, I must say a few words about the substance of the instruction, reserving a fuller discussion of it for a subsequent chapter. The law of Germany has a threefold origin: it is either Roman, or German, or the product of recent legislation. By Roman law is meant that set of rules and principles which is contained in the *Corpus juris civilis*, the codification made at Constantinople in the sixth century by order of the emperor Justinian. To explain how the *corpus juris* came to be adopted in Germany would lead me too far out of my way. The adoption grew out of the intimate political relations existing between Germany and Italy, where the old Roman Law, as Savigny has shown, had never gone out of use. It was begun under the Hohenstaufen or Swabian dynasty, but proceeded very slowly, and was not thoroughly completed even at the advent of the Reformation. Its career was a prolonged struggle between the "illiterate" law of the folk and the subtleties of the clerks and doctors at the seats of learn-

---

* It should be borne in mind that, in civil suits, the judges exercise the functions of the jury.

ing. A somewhat similar phenomenon, but attended with very different results, may be observed in the course of English Common Law. The Canonists and Civilians of Oxford tried to introduce the *corpus juris* into England, and came nearer to success than is commonly known. In Germany, the passages of the *corpus juris* not annotated by the Glossators of the Italian school are not regarded as received. But these are few in number. Practically, the *corpus juris* may be said to have been adopted entire by the common consent and common practice of the German mediæval courts, so that the presumption is in its favor. Whoever attempts to controvert the applicability of any one annotated passage must show either that it has been specifically rejected or that it has been altered or abrogated. Even in countries that have a modern code of civil law, a thorough knowledge of the Roman law is regarded as indispensable, inasmuch as that law is still applicable in cases not provided for by the code.* The German law, i. e., the law of German origin, has chiefly to do with marital and domestic relations, and the rights and obligations of real property, more exactly, entailed and peasant estates. But all general ideas on legal topics, the entire legal nomenclature, the theory of contracts, payment, time, conditions, everything in short that is not limited or local is derived from the Roman law. A complete and accurate understanding of the principles

---

* The older parts of Prussia, e. g., are administered according to the code introduced in the last century ; the Rhine provinces have the Code Napoleon.

embodied in the *corpus juris* is therefore justly considered as the basis of the lawyer's education. The Canon Law, i. e., the principles and rulings embodied in the *corpus juris canonici*, or body of mediæval Roman Catholic law, has not been adopted to the same extent as the *corpus juris civilis*. Although the university title of LL. D. is *doctor juris utrinsque* (*sc. tam romani quam canonici*), the Canon Law as such is no longer taught in Germany. The *corpus juris canonici* embodies the rules that governed the mediæval ecclesiastical courts during their existence. As those courts had cognizance of everything relating to the church and church property, to marriage and divorce, crimes committed by or against the clergy, the sanctity of the oath, etc., their jurisdiction covered many cases that modern usage has vindicated for the secular courts exclusively. The terms Canon Law and Modern Ecclesiastical Law, therefore, do not coincide; the former is the law, whether spiritual or secular in its nature, administered by the old spiritual courts; the latter is the law now applicable to spiritual matters exclusively, whether that law be derived from the *corpus juris canonici* or from modern statutes and concordates, whether it be Roman Catholic or Protestant law. The universities of Germany teach at the present time only Ecclesiastical Law. The Canon Law made its influence upon Roman and German law felt chiefly in practice and procedure, and most especially in the theory of evidence. All these matters, however, have been thoroughly revised and put upon a new basis by the modern codes of procedure.

As regards the Roman law more particularly, the course of instruction embraces ordinarily four sets of lectures, which I give by their German names: *Institutionen, Rechtsgeschichte, Pandecten, Erbrecht.* The *Institutionen* are a condensed exposition of the outlines of the Roman law. The order followed is usually that of the Institutes of Justinian, and the object of the course is, not the exhaustive statement of all the principles in all their details, but rather the historic development of the leading principles, from the earliest times of the Republic, through the Empire, to the age of Justinian. In other words, the organic growth of the Roman law during seven or eight centuries forms the substance of the course called *Institutionen.* The *Rechtsgeschichte*, or *Aeussere Rechtsgeschichte*, as it is more exactly called, is a history of Roman legislation rather than of Roman law. It treats of the various phases of the Roman constitution, the growth of the *plebs*, the power of the Senate, the scope of the *senatus consulta*, the functions of the prætor and the prætorian edict, the rescripts and decrees of the emperors, the *responsa prudentium*, the history of Justinian's codification. The *Rechtsgeschichte*, then, aims at acquainting the student with the various agents and means at work in producing the body of the law. The *Pandecten* are in one sense merely the *Institutionen* expanded; in another sense, they are quite different. The professor who lectures on the Pandects, taking for granted that his hearers are already familiar with the *Institutionen* and *Rechtsgeschichte*, develops the Roman law as a matter of scientific theory. He does not follow the order adopted by Justinian in his *Liber Digestorum*. He seeks to define law in general, to define persons, things, the rights of persons, family relations, the rights of things, modes of acquiring and losing property, modes of entering into, suspending, and annulling contracts, and the like, fortifying each position as he goes by citations from the *corpus juris*. The treatment of *Erbrecht* (the doctrine of inheritance) as a separate course is purely arbitrary; it belongs rightfully to the *Pandecten*. But inasmuch as it is the most complicated and difficult part of the whole, it is more conveniently treated by itself. Vangerow, however, read it in his course on the Pandects.

I cannot revert to my semester in Berlin with much satisfaction. The fault was not with the university or the professors, but lay in myself. I committed the mistake of attempting to begin a new study in a large city. One who has advanced beyond the rudiments and has a clear idea of what he really needs and what he can dispense with, will derive benefit from the concourse of intellect and character in a capital like Berlin. But the beginner, I am persuaded, cannot do better than by remaining in a small town for a term or two at least. He loses less time in finding out things, in making acquaintances among those who are pursuing the same study, and in catching the spirit of that study.

After pondering over the distracting list of lectures given above, and getting the advice of one or two acquaintances to whom I had letters of introduction, I made the following selection of lectures: *Institutionen* and *Rechtsgeschichte*, by Professor Gneist, and *Encyclopædie und Methodologie der Rechtswissenschaft*, by Professor Holtzendorff. As the reader will readily understand, the lectures were "all Greek" to me. The German was not difficult, and both lecturers spoke slowly and clearly enough to let me take full notes. But the subject itself was a strange world of terms and ideas. I forced myself to write down paragraph after paragraph without being able to see into the connection or practical bearings of the whole. Fortunately I caught up a hint thrown out by Professor Gneist in one of his lectures, and purchased a copy of Mommsen's Roman History. Here at least was something that I could understand. Although my recollections of early Roman history, the fabulous dynasty of kings, the law of the Twelve Tables, the centurial constitutions and the like were as shadowy and imperfect as those of the average American graduate, still it was scarcely possible not to learn much from a master like Mommsen. I read through the two large volumes of the original with great interest and care. Then it was that something like light began to shine upon me, that I caught something like an insight into the growth of that wonderful organism called the Roman Constitution and the Roman State. Using Mommsen as a running commentary, I succeeded in understanding my lectures after a fashion. I purchased also Gneist's edition of the Institutes of Gaius and Justinian, but could make little out of the book. The Latin was easy enough, but I had no appreciation of the technical terms and no friend to whom to go for enlightenment.

The term was drawing to its close. I was threatened with a return of my ailment of the previous winter, and was generally discouraged. In view of the many old friends still left in Göttingen, I thought it best to spend at least the long vacation there and obtain advice for the future. I thereupon left Berlin before the end of the semester. This was the turning point in my university course.

CHAPTER VIII.

Wiesbaden — The Institutes.

By the advice of the physician who had attended me during the winter, I was induced to try the baths at Wiesbaden. The climate, the waters, the easy, quiet life at this celebrated watering-place, wrought in three weeks a perfect cure. Were the present a book on German life in general, I should take the liberty of describing fully the baths of Wiesbaden; for they deserve their reputation as the Mecca of rheumatic pilgrims, and the town and neighborhood are, upon the whole, the most agreeable of German *Curorte*. But I do not consider myself authorized to transgress the strict limits of the subject, which is the description of *university* life.

After a brief but most delightful trip down the Rhine to Cologne and back, and a run over to Heidelberg and Munich, I returned to Göttingen about the end of August. There were six weeks left in which to make ready for the coming winter semester. But to what should I turn my attention, and how should I make the most of the time? While in this quandary, good fortune led me to make the acquaintance of a man who was to become my steadfast friend and ready counselor for the next eighteen months. To him more than to any one else am I indebted for success at last. One afternoon, at a garden-concert, I was presented to Dr. Maxen, *Privat-docent* in the legal faculty, a stout, bluff, but genial and intelligent man in the thirties. Our conversation soon shook off all idle formality. Emboldened by the signs of friendly interest on his part, I told him my story; how I had made an attempt in Berlin and failed; how much, or rather how little, I had done; what a maze of doubt and ignorance I was in, even as to the best books to read. At all of which he laughed good-naturedly. " Well, said he, I do not think that you have done much worse than other students in their first semester. Rome, you know, was not built in a day. What you need is to read certain books well, and especially to go at the *Quellen*.* Let me draw up a scheme of work for you. In the first place, read through Marezoll's *Institutionen*. The book is not worth much, but it will familiarize you with terms and definitions, and the general groundplan of the law. Then, after reading Marezoll, take up Puchta's three volumes of *Institutionen*. This will give you everything you want to know in a clear, logical, thoroughly scientific shape. But, above all else, you must read the Institutes of Gaius and Justinian in the original. This study of modern text-books is all very well, but it cannot absolve you from the knowledge of the *Quellen*." I replied that I had Gneist's edition of the Institutes already in my possession, and had tried to read it, but without success. "Of course you can't

---

* The German word *Quellen* is the technical term to denote the primary sources of information on any topic, the *originals*.

understand it alone. You must have Heumann's *Hand-lexicon to the Corpus juris*, and you must read in company with some advanced student who can explain things to you step by step. Call at my room to-morrow or the day after, and by that time perhaps I shall have some one for you." I felt that a load had been rolled off my mind. These words of sympathy and advice, few, but to the point, had at least pointed out to me the way of knowledge. Henceforth it rested only with myself to follow up the clew.

I have dwelt at length upon this incident, because it will reveal in the brightest light the part played in a German university by the *Privat-docent*. The professors are, of course, very learned men, but they are not always amiable, at least not always communicative. Standing on the isolated pinnacles of science, they are rather cut off from the world below, and the student feels reluctant to approach them. But the *Privat-docent*, still a young man in the prime of physical life, fast growing in greatness, but not so far beyond the recollection of his own student days as to be unable to enter fully into the trials of his younger brethren beneath him, is the *Vermittler*, the mediator, in the university organism. With one hand he urges on the professor to renewed research, with the other he raises up and cheers the student. A university without *Privat-docenten* would be like a regiment without corporals, a ship without a boatswain; with them, it is the most powerful and yet the most flexible organization for spiritual purposes in the world. The student who knows one or more *Privat-docenten* can post himself readily on the literature of every topic as fast as it may come up, can get the latest ideas, pick up any amount of odds and ends of information such as books never give, and always be sure of friendly advice. The relation between *Privat-docent* and student is purely one of friendship, characterized on one part by elder-brotherly interest, on the other by respect unrestrained by ceremonial awe.

Within twenty-four hours all the books mentioned by Dr. Maxen were in my possession. A brief examination of Marezoll's *Institutionen* showed me that the Dr.'s estimate of the book had not been too unfavorable. But Puchta's work was something altogether different. Although entitled *Institutionen*, it was really a *Pandecten* treatise, but with a large infusion of the historical element. It gave me precisely the help that I had long sought after, a clear, concise exposition of legal ideas and doctrines, and a pretty complete genesis, so to speak, of the body of Roman law. The first volume is a discussion of Roman constitutional history and *Rechtsgeschichte*. The third volume, unfortunately, was left unfinished in consequence of the author's death, the last half being edited by Professor Rudorff from posthumous notes. For six weeks Puchta was scarcely out of my hand. I not only read through the entire three volumes (nearly 2,000 pages), but committed many of the definitions and distinctions to memory, and reviewed incessantly. In this way I obtained a tolerably clear idea of what law in general is, the difference between statute law and common law, the theory of suspending, abrogating, and retroactive conditions, the distinction between a condition and a *dies ad quem* or *a quo*, the Roman notions as to natural persons and juristic persons, as to *hereditas, patria potestas, in manu*, and the like, the more common kinds of contracts and of real property. Puchta's work is an eminently useful one for the beginner. It gives a good deal of law, but gives it in such a logical shape and in such a luminous style that it captivates the reader. It is much to be regretted that there is no similar work in English for the study of our English common law, in place of the antiquated method and jejune, eighteenth-century philosophy called Blackstone's Commentaries. If the reader can imagine Sharswood's Blackstone, Parsons on Contracts, Washburne on Real Property, and Willard's Equity condensed into three volumes, infused with the spirit of modern philosophic inquiry and couched in language as fresh and limpid throughout as that of Chancellor Kent, he will form some idea of Puchta as a jurist. With this exception, that no English or American writer goes after the fashion of the Germans into the history of the law. There are no such works in English as Savigny's *History of Roman Law in the Middle Ages*, Keller's *History of Roman Procedure by Formulæ*, Rudorff's *Rechtsgeschichte*, and a dozen others that I might mention, where advantage is taken of all the results of modern philology and modern historic inquiry. In England and in America, law is regarded as a practice, a mode of earning one's livelihood, a sort of blind swearing *in verba magistrorum*. In Germany, it is treated as an historic science, in fact, as the twin brother of history. Nearly every German jurist is somewhat of an historian, every historian is a jurist. Indeed, the student in history cannot obtain his Ph. D. without passing an examination in the rudiments of Roman and German law. We wonder at the firm grasp, the unerring insight of such men as Niebuhr and Mommsen, but we overlook the circumstance that they were jurists as well as historians. Mommsen in particular was for many years full professor in law. Germany has been for half a century under the influence of the so called "historic school," that is to say, a set of principles which have been advocated by such men as Thibaut, Savigny, Puchta, Goeschen, Vangerow, and which may be reduced to one fundamental idea: that law is a growth and not a product, and that it can be neither comprehended, amended, expanded, nor expounded properly without a full and scientific study of it from its beginnings.

Puchta was to me at that time a sort of condensed student-library, it contained nearly everything that I needed for preliminary instruction. But Puchta did not make me overlook the *Quellen* upon which my friend had laid such stress. Thanks to Dr. Maxen's co-operation, I was put in the way of becoming one of a trio to read the Institutes of Gaius. Fifty years before, the thing would have been impossible, for the work was reckoned among the lost treasures of antiquity, like the Comedies of

Menander. To explain this point fully, I must go into details which, I trust, will not prove uninteresting. The codification of Justinian was made in the early part of the sixth century. The Roman law had undergone so many and so radical changes, the legal literature had accumulated to such an enormous extent that the emperor, thinking to simplify matters, appointed a commission, of which the jurist Tribonian was the chief, to elaborate a reform by classifying and simplifying things. The work done by this commission was subdivided into three parts: 1. the *Institutiones*, a short, easy text-book for beginners; 2. the *Digesta seu Pandecten*, a vast compilation of principles and opinions taken from the leading jurists of the classic era of the Roman law (under the empire before the partition) and arranged in fifty books under appropriate headings; and, 3. the *Codex*, a similar collection of imperial statutes down to the reign of Justinian himself. These three parts, as one work, were declared to be of equal authority, and to be the sole legal guide and standard in the realm of Justinian. Everything else was expressly abrogated. The codification thus prepared was to be regarded as self-explanatory. After it had been published, the emperor enacted from time to time a number of subsequent statutes, many of them very important ones, which were collected under the title of *Novellæ*, or new laws. These four works, then, the Institutes, Digest, Code, and Novels, taken as one, with a short appendix of feudal law and the so called *Authenticæ Fredericianæ* added in the reigns of the emperors Frederick I and II, constitute the *Corpus Juris Civilis*.

Concerning the Institutes in particular, it was known that Tribonian's commission, in preparing their text-book for beginners, had made liberal use of a similar treatise written by one Gaius during the reign of the emperor Marcus Antoninus. They had simply taken the Institutes of Gaius and adapted them to the usages of the sixth century, by omitting certain portions regarded as obsolete, inserting fresh matter, and slightly altering the phraseology of the portions retained. But what had become of the original Gaius? No one could answer the question, and it was generally believed, until the beginning of the present century, that the Institutes of Gaius perished in the confusion of the Dark Ages. But in the year 1816, Niebuhr, who was then exploring the library at Verona, stumbled upon a manuscript that looked to him like a copy of the long lost work. Being unable himself to follow up the discovery, for want of time, he simply announced it. In 1817, Goeschen, then professor at Göttingen, was sent to Verona, on Niebuhr's recommendation, to undertake the critical editing of the manuscript. It was far more serious than had been supposed, and the final success was one of the greatest triumphs of modern scholarship and ingenuity. Not only was the manuscript a palimpsest, a manuscript of which the original text had been covered by a second, but sixty-two of the one hundred and twenty-five pages of the MS. were even a *double* palimpsest; the second writing had been in its turn covered by a third. For over a year Goeschen, assisted by Bethmann-Hollweg, worked assiduously; by the most careful application of certain chemicals, he succeeded in erasing the second and third writings — the epistles of St. Jerome — and deciphering nearly all the original text. His first edition appeared in 1820, the second, containing the emendations of Blume, in 1824; they created a revolution in the study of the Roman law. I doubt whether any other literary discovery ever wrought such wonders. Let the reader imagine, if he can, Greek literature without Homer, and then let him imagine a copy of the Iliad or the Odyssey suddenly unearthed in some convent of Wallachia. The study of the Roman law in Germany has been reconstructed from top to bottom, to such an extent that Vangerow dismisses the entire early literature on the subject of Roman pleadings in the following pithy sentence: All books written on this subject before the year 1820 are useless. But not only was the theory of pleadings understood *for the first time*, the entire body of the Roman law was overhauled. Passages in the *corpus juris* upon which whole libraries of angry controversial pamphlets had been written to no avail were now found to be quite plain; technical terms, once unintelligible, explained themselves in a very simple manner. The student had at last a small portable key with which to unlock three fourths of the mysteries that had haunted the *corpus juris* for a thousand years. I hazard little in asserting that at the present day the veriest tyro in the Roman law can glibly rattle off correct answers to many a grave question, and translate intelligibly more than one passage of the Digest that proved itself too difficult for the entire body of Italian, Dutch, French and German glossators and commentators from Irnerius down to Pufendorf and Glück.

The following extract may serve as a sample of the style of Gaius. It is taken from Lib. iv., § 16. *Si in rem agebatur, mobilia quidem et moventia, quae modo in jus adferri adducive possent, in jure vindicabantur ad hunc modum. Qui vindicabat festucam tenebat. Deinde ipsam rem adprehendebat, velut hominem* (i. e., a slave), *et ita dicebat:* HUNC EGO HOMINEM EX JURE QUIRITIUM MEUM ESSE AIO SECUNDUM SUAM CAUSAM SICUT DIXI. ECCE TIBI VINDICTAM IMPOSUI, *et simul homini festucam imponebat. Adversus eadem similiter dicebat et faciebat. Cum uterque vindicasset, Praetor dicebat:* MITTITE AMBO HOMINEM. *Illi mittebant. Qui prior vindicaverit, ita alterum interrogabat:* POSTULO ANNE DICAS QUA EX CAUSA VINDICAVERIS. *Ille respondebat:* JUS PEREGI SICUT VINDICTAM IMPOSUI. *Deinde qui prior vindicaverit dicebat:* QUANDO TU INJURIA VINDICAVISTI, D AERIS SACRAMENTO TE PROVOCO. *Adversarius quoque dicebat:* SIMILITER EGO TE, etc., etc. Nothing could be simpler than the wording of the above passage, but one must be more than a Latin scholar to understand it. Gaius is describing the old method of bringing a suit (*legis actio*) in the peculiar way called *sacramento*. The parties appear before the Praetor, with the object in dispute, if it is movable. Each claims it for his own. Thereupon the plaintiff challenges the defendant to a wager of fifty or five hundred asses, according to the value of the object, that he is the lawful owner. The money is deposited in some temple (hence the expression *in sacro*), and the judge settles merely the point who has lost the wager. The ownership is settled only indirectly, by implication.

The reading of Gaius was not completed by the end of the vacation, but continued for some time into the winter semester. My associates were at first P—— of the Westphalians and M—— of the Saxons, both candidates at the approaching state examination in Celle. They were of course far more advanced than myself, and also older by two or three years, so that I derived great benefit from their superior knowledge. We constituted a comfortable "clover-leaf," as the Germans call social trios. Our meetings were regular but perfectly informal. We met at one another's rooms in rotation for an hour or more every day. Each man had his own copy of Gaius, and the owner of the room was held to have in readiness the dictionaries and other works of reference. Our practice was to translate a paragraph at a time, in turn, trying to make the rendering as close as possible, in fact to make it what would be in print an interlinear version, line by line, word by word. The listeners had the right to interrupt the one translating and call upon him for explanations. Our progress was very slow. Although the style of Gaius is simplicity itself, we spent often ten or fifteen minutes over a single phrase to get its exact technical signification. Thus the phrase *hanc rem meam esse aio ex jure Quiritium,* means one thing, and *hanc rem in bonis meis esse* means something very different. It was the object of our reading, then, to bring out all such distinctions, to discuss them thoroughly, and, if necessary, trace them through the text-books. A German text-book on law always contains, besides the index of topics, an index of passages quoted from the *corpus juris,* just as an English law book contains the list of cases cited. By consulting these indexes of passages and comparing Gaius with Justinian, we were able to find whether the paragraph in question was cited by Puchta or Arndt or Vangerow in their works and, if so, what were the various interpretations put upon it and deductions made from it. This naturally took a good deal of time, but the results were very gratifying. I found that, by dint of repetition and collateral reading, not only the outlines of the law were fixing themselves in my mind, but I was acquiring a high degree of facility in construing law-Latin. This, it may not be superfluous to observe, is a language by itself, differing from the ordinary classic Latin as the phraseology of Blackstone differs from that of Byron. The *corpus juris* abounds in terms and phrases fully as technical as the *reliefs, primer seisins, estoppels* of English legal treatises, and unless one understands them precisely, the *corpus juris* is a sealed book. The best Latin scholar, not a jurist, could not read a title of the Digest without being "floored" in every paragraph by one or more of them. The Institutes of Gaius are not comprised in the *corpus juris,* it is true, but they serve all the better as a propaedeutic by reason of their exhibiting the Roman law in an earlier stage of development. Whoever has worked his way faithfully through Gaius, can read the Institutes of Justinian off-hand, and after he has read these, he can construe readily passages taken from the Digest at random.*

Besides reading the text of Gaius, we questioned one another every day on the substance of the preceding day's work, and tried to catch one another in a friendly way. This necessitated diligent review and preparation at home. The larger share of the benefit fell to me, of course, as the beginner. In one sense, my co-workers could teach me everything and I had nothing to give in return. But on the other hand, the duty of setting me aright obliged them to keep their own knowledge constantly in hand, as it were. They could not correct, they could not even interrogate me properly, without first putting their own ideas in perfect order. No one can realize —until he tries it—how much benefit he can derive from teaching, and how carefully he must overhaul his own

---

* If the reader is desirous of testing his ingenuity by a rather difficult passage, let me recommend the following from the Institutes of Justinian, § 2 I. III, 29. *Stipulatio enim Aquiliana novat omnes obligationes, et a Gallo Aquilio ita composita est :* " *Quicquid te mihi ex quacumque causa dare facere oportet, oportebit, praesens in diemve, quarumque rerum mihi tecum actio, quaeque abs te petitio, vel adversus te persecutio est, erit, quodve tu meum habeas, tenes, possides, possedisti, dolove malo fecisti quominus possideas,*' *quanti quaeque earum rerum res erit, tantam pecuniam dari stipulatus est Aulus Agerius* (one of the parties), *spopondit Numerius Negidius* (the other party). *Item ex diverso Numerius Negidius interrogavit Aulum Agerium :* " *Quicquid tibi hodierno die per Aquilianam stipulationem spopondi, id omne habesne acceptum ?*" *respondit Aulus Agerius : "Habeo acceptumque tuli.*" The entire transaction is simply a drawing up of all claims held by one party against the other, with a view to making a formal release.

information before he will succeed in imparting it to a beginner.*

As well as I can remember, we finished the Institutes of Gaius four or five weeks after the beginning of the winter semester. The six weeks from September 1. to October 15. passed like a pleasant dream, yet not without yielding permanent fruits. The work on which I was engaged, although difficult, was not discouraging, and was performed with pleasure, while the weather was simply faultless. The mornings and evenings were hazy, but the afternoons were resplendent. I devoted them religiously to recreation, either going over my rambles of the year before or playing an unlimited number of games of *Kegel*. The German game of nine-pins is different from our ten-pins. The pins are set up in diamond shape, and not in a triangle, and the count increases in a sort of geometrical ratio — instead of an arithmetical — with the number of pins thrown down. Each side begins with a minus number, say 300 or 400, and adds every count as a plus quantity. The game is over when the plus above zero on one side equals the minus below zero on the other. The alleys are much inferior to our own, but the game can be made to develop any amount of fun. The alleys are generally in the open air, in the garden of the restaurant, merely protected from the weather by a shed overhead. The game therefore affords a healthy exercise, free from the musty, whisky-laden atmosphere and other

---

* It was part of Dr. Maxen's plan to make his advanced students "coach" their weaker brethren.

disagreeable associations of the American bar-room. I look upon *Kegel* as the climax of amusement in the minor German towns. But then one must have an agreeable set of companions, and must be perhaps still in the twenties and a student, to enjoy it in perfection.

CHAPTER IX.

Anniversary of the Battle of Leipsic.— Commer.

AS the middle of October came around, I looked back upon the preceding six months with a pardonable feeling of satisfaction. Although some time had been lost by the false start taken at Berlin, I had made the loss good by industry during the vacation, and was fully prepared for the heavy work of the approaching winter. Becoming more and more intimate with Dr. Maxen, I fell into the habit of looking up to him as general adviser and father confessor and giving him a full and impartial account of my studies. He gave me in return the comfortable assurance that I was rather in advance of the average student of like standing. "Do not be discouraged, he often said, you have done almost work enough for two semesters. At all events, you are fairly started. Remain here in Göttingen, lose no more time, and all will be well."

After finishing Gaius, my friends P—— and M—— left for Celle, to enter the state examination. I had yet the Institutes of Justinian to read. Dr. Maxen was successful, however, in arranging a second "clover-leaf" quite as good as the first. The two new members were E—— and S——, both Westphalians. E—— was my superior in age and academic standing, being then in his fourth semester. He was also a young man of decided legal acumen and of quick perceptions, but had not yet developed into a very steady worker. S—— was a *Fuchs* in his second semester, like myself, but having spent his time after the approved fashion in *Kneipen* and *Pauken*, knew very little law. So far as he was concerned, then, I occupied the dignified position of teacher. Indeed, thanks to the regular working habits acquired in the vacation, I put E—— himself on his mettle to retain the lead. Between us, we succeeded in keeping our *Fuchs* busy. It always affords high moral satisfaction to know that there is somebody worse off than yourself, toward whom you can assume the air of superior information. We finished the Institutes by the middle of November. I should state that the edition which we used was that prepared by Gneist, of Berlin. It is a very handy, practical book. Each page is divided into two parallel columns. The left hand column is reserved for Gaius, the right for Justinian. The two works are thus placed side by side, so that the reader has the greatest facility for comparing them, and also for reviewing his studies. I improved the opportunity, while reading Justinian, by reviewing Gaius entire, passage for passage.

Before proceeding to give an account of the winter lectures, I wish to say a few words about *Kneipen* in connection with the most imposing student affair of the kind that I attended. The word *Kneipe* has a double meaning. It denotes the place where drinking is done, the drinking-hall or room or house, or it denotes the drinking itself, the carouse. The verb *Kneipen* means to drink, being used promiscuously with *trinken; bekneipt*, for instance, is the same as *betrunken*.

In whatever other respects the German student may be irregular, he always *kneips* according to rule. It is not necessary to go into all the particulars of the German beer-code; to be frank, I do not know them all myself, for they are as complicated and numerous as the provisions of the *Notherbenrecht* (doctrine of disinheritance) of the *corpus juris*. The reader who wishes to post himself thoroughly can study the famous Heidelberg *Bier-comment* or *Sauf-comment*. The chief point is that when you sit down with other students to a *Kneipe*, you must drink with the others and not according to your own fancy. Even if you are an invited guest, you will commit a breach of etiquette by drinking by yourself. You must always "come" to the health of some one in particular. The *modus operandi* is this. A calls out to B: *Es kommt Ihnen (Dir) etwas, Ich komme Dir einen halben, einen ganzen vor*, that is: "Here's something to you, a half glass, a whole glass," as the case may be. This is called *Vorkommen*. B's duty is to respond, which he can do in a variety of phrases, such as: *Prosit, trink'ihn, Trinken Sie ihn, sauf'ihn, in die Welt*, etc. B must also drink exactly the same quantity. This he can do either immediately, saying *Ich komme mit*, literally, "I come along with you," or after an interval, when he says, *Ich komme nach*, "I come after you." When B comes *mit* or *nach* to A, he can at the same time come *vor* to any third man C, thereby making one potation do double service. If A wishes to drink to the health of B without putting him under the obligation of *mitkommen* or *nachkommen*, he says: *Auf Ihr (dein) Specielles*, i. e., "To your especial good health." This is the usual way of showing attention to an invited guest, particularly one rather advanced in life or in social standing.

Every *Kneipe* has a master, or presiding officer, whose duty it is to see that each man meets the requirements of the *Comment*, and from whose decision there is no appeal. He gives tone and character to the entertainment, selecting the songs to be sung, and appointing the editor of the so called *Beer-gazette*. This is a sort of comic paper, either in prose or verse, composed impromptu, and devoted to the persiflage of the members of the kneipe and the incidents of the week. The master can punish disorder or disobedience, by ordering the unruly member to drink a quantity of beer *pro poena*, as it is called.

One of the side performances of a *Kneipe* is a "beer duel." Two students, wishing to ascertain which one is the better man, i. e., the faster drinker of the two, choose an umpire. This umpire places the duelists side by side, sees that each one has his glass properly filled, and calls off: One, two, three. At the word three, each one must put his glass to his mouth and empty it as fast as he can. The one who can rap his glass first on the table is the victor. It is the umpire's duty to see that the duel has been fairly conducted, i. e., that no heel-tap is left in the glass. The victor has the right to call the other his beer-boy, *Bierjungen*. To challenge another to the duel is, in technical parlance, *ihm einen Bierjungen aufbrummen*. I advise my countrymen not to venture upon a beer-duel without considerable preliminary practice, for the greenhorn may be sure of getting the worst. The veteran student has a knack at swallowing beer that would horrify any respectable professor of anatomy and hygiene. In truth, he does not swallow at all; he throws his head slightly back, opens his mouth and, holding his breath, simply pours the beer down the esophagus as if it were a long funnel. The rapidity with which a glass of beer can be made to disappear by this process is something incredible.

The 18th of October, 1863, was the semi-centennial anniversary of the great battle of Leipsic. German patriotism rose to fever-heat, the students of course catching the contagion. It was resolved to hold a grand *Studenten-kneipe* on the evening of the eighteenth in the large hall of the *Deutsches Haus*, outside the Geismar Gate. To those who know Germany merely as she is now, a compactly united empire, under one supreme head and one legislative body chosen by direct election, the days of the old *Bund* will appear, I suspect, a mystery. In 1863 there was no Germany, so far as concerned form, concert of action, anything beyond hopes and sentiments; there were thirty German countries pulling as many different ways.

In 1864, for instance, some of the students at Göttingen assembled in the railway station and gave three groans for Bismarck, as he passed through on his way to Berlin; the university thought it advisable to transmit to the Prussian government an explanation and formal disavowal. Prior to 1866, certainly, the old saying, that wherever two Germans met there were sure to be three different opinions, still held good even to the details of common life. As to organizing any public entertainment without a squabble of one kind or another, it was quite impossible. The solemn commemoration of the battle of Leipsic gave rise at Göttingen to a quarrel between the *Corps-studenten* and the *Wilden* over the matter of precedence in the procession through the streets. Neither party would yield an inch. They came almost to blows in broad daylight in front of the Town Hall, and nothing but the personal interference of the Prorector and his "poodles" prevented bloodshed.

The result was that the *Corps-studenten* held the *Kneipe* by themselves. I had been invited two or three days before by my Westphalian friends; although regretting the disturbance, I did not judge that it compelled me to forego the *Kneipe*. Besides, there might not be another such opportunity of seeing all the *Corps-studenten* together.

Knowing the importance of keeping both mind and body fresh for the encounter, I passed the afternoon diligently at *Kegel*. The banquet began at half-past seven in the evening. The hall was decorated with the Hanoverian colors, and with the colors of the several corps. Each corps sat by itself, at its own table. The Westphalians had the presidency,* as well as I can remember. Being on speaking terms with nearly all, and knowing three or four quite intimately, I felt at ease at their table. A plain but good supper was served in two or three courses. The toasts were then in order. After the lapse of so many years, I do not pretend to remember any of the speeches; indeed, I made no attempt to charge my mind with them at the time. Partiality for German scholarship and German books does not imply admiration for German oratory. Now and then one hears a strong address in the Prussian House of Deputies or the Imperial Diet. Bismarck, Lasker, Gneist, Windhorst-Meppen, and the other leaders of debate say very good things, and say them to the point, with a refreshing absence of "buncombe." Still, we shall scarcely do the Germans injustice by declining to rate their public speaking as true oratory. It does not appeal to the soul, it does not sweep the soul off in a tide of passion tempered by reason, or reason quickened by passion.

Public speaking in Germany is rather didactic. I doubt whether the language will permit flights of oratory. The structure of the sentence, especially the dependent clauses, is such as to make the orator appear almost of necessity halting and diffuse. He can not place his

---

* This shifts from year to year in rotation.

emphatic words as he wishes, but must run the risk of blunting the point of an expression by a trail of procrastinating verbs and separable particles. Furthermore, the Germans are not very happy in after-dinner speaking. They are too ponderous, they do not possess the art of saying clever nothings that provoke mirth and facilitate digestion.

The speeches delivered at the banquet in question were not above the average. Several professors were present as invited guests and made short formal harangues. One or two of the students, it seemed to me, did better than their instructors. At least they had more fire, more "snap." The key-note was of course German patriotism and German unity. Germany was faithfully praised and no less faithfully exhorted. France, I am able to state, was not abused. Frenchmen were spoken of as "invaders," and Germany was congratulated on having rid herself of them and undertaken to work out her destiny for herself. But patriotism did not degenerate into *chauvnisme*. The general tone was healthy; there was plenty of thankfulness for what had been done, and exuberant confidence in the future, but there was no trace of aggressive rancor.*

The professors and other elderly guests beat a retreat before ten o'clock, leaving the students to display their peculiar youthful qualities without restraint. I shall not

---

* The reader may find fresh proof of the absence of malice from the German character in the circumstance that the *Marseillaise* was played repeatedly at public concerts in Berlin in 1872 and 1873, and nearly always encored.

attempt to describe the babel that ensued. The reader has only to imagine half a dozen students haranguing at once in varying degrees of "inspiration," healths drunk right and left, glasses jingling, masters of ceremonies bawling to order, waiters rushing to and fro. But has the reader ever heard of that august ceremony called "rubbing a salamander?" Let me give it. The president rises from his chair and, carefully clearing his throat and filling his lungs, lets the thundering words resound through the room: *Silentium, meine Herren, silentium!! Schmidt, du trinkst einen pro poena.— Pst! Ruhig, sonst trinkst du noch einen.* "Smith, you've got to drink one as a fine (for having interrupted me). Pst! be quiet, or else you'll get another." *Silentium! Fischer, zwei pro poena!* "Gentlemen, in consideration of the glorious occasion we celebrate, I herewith call upon you "—— *Förster, du kriegst zwei pro poena, will mir keiner den Kerl herausschmeissen,* "two for Foster, will nobody do me the kindness to put the fellow out "—— " call upon you, gentlemen, to participate in the joyous exercise of rubbing a salamander." *Ad exercitium salamandri, dro, drum. Aufstehen, aufstehen,* "get up! Hannemann, why don't you get up, I say?" (H——'s neighbors inform the president that H—— is *abgefallen,* too far gone to rise). "Well, then, help him up, stand him on his legs. Gentlemen! All glasses full?" *Ad exercitium salamandri,* "One, two, three! Drink out!" *Hannemann, du hast nicht ausgetrunken.* (Here H——, assisted by his friends, succeeds in getting some of the beer down his throat, but the larger share over his shirt). *Silentium,* " One, two, three." (Here every man pounds his glass furiously on the table). *Ad loca! Ad loca!* " Take your seats."

The salamander is bad enough, but something infinitely worse is the *Bierwalzer,* one of those thumping waltzes of which the Germans are so fond. The music rises and falls, a slight pause is made; suddenly every one commences to keep time with the music, first by stamping on the floor, next by whistling, lastly by jingling glasses; then comes the final outburst *unisono* in the thrilling words: *O jerum jerum jerum jerum, la la la,* etc. On reaching the fourth or fifth verse of this simple melody, one need not be surprised to notice that his head shows a remarkable proclivity to roll all over the room, while his heart is expansive enough to embrace the universe. My remembrances of the finale of the great Eighteenth-of-October *Commers** are that I became involved in a very elaborate and eloquent discussion with two Westphalians, likewise *studiosi juris,* upon the *dominium ex jure Quiritium* and the equitable functions of the Praetorian Edict, very fertile topics, upon which one can talk all night without coming to a conclusion. My friend P——, the veteran of a hundred *Kneipen,* who had me under his especial charge as his guest, came to the rescue, by suggesting, in a whisper, that perhaps " we " had better make our escape. So I took French leave of the

---

* *Commers* is the name given to a *Kneipe* of a more grandiose character than usual.

Commers, and reached my quarters in safety. The next morning I had a slight touch of *Jammer*, not serious, just enough to make me feel disposed to be out in the open air, and indisposed to work. As lectures had not yet commenced, I lost nothing. It may not be going too far out of my way to observe that *Jammer* has its degrees, its *gironi*, as the student of Dante might term them, three in number: *der gewöhnliche Hauskater, der Wildkater*, and *das graue Elend*. Woe to the man who has plunged recklessly into the abyss of the *graues Elend*. I remember seeing once a fellow-countryman, anything but a neophyte in such matters, after he had fallen into the hands of the Philistines. He had been beguiled into accepting an invitation to pass the evening over a bowl of Swedish punch, an infamous decoction brewed after Father Tom's recipe, except that arrack is substituted for whisky. You take a little sugar and some arrack, and then you put in some more sugar, and then some more arrack, and every drop of water you put in *after that* only spoils the punch. My poor friend, relying upon general experience, and ignorant of what he was dealing with, had been completely fooled by the sweetness of the beverage into drinking an inordinate number of glasses. The consequence was that by four o'clock in the afternoon he had just crawled out of bed, and was lying hopeless on the sofa, trying to recall his vanished animation with an occasional sip of very mild brandy and water. A more woebegone, spiritless countenance it would be hard to imagine.

The students have a superb collection of songs in their *Commersbuch*. The reader is doubtless familiar with *Was kommt denn von der Höh*, and one or two others in Longfellow's charming translation. It gives me pleasure, even now in these later years, to turn over the leaves of the *Commersbuch* and read as chance may direct. Many of these songs are quite old. *Volkslieder*, perhaps, that sprang up among the *scholastici vagantes* of the fifteenth and sixteenth centuries; others bear the names of the most famous poets of Germany, such as Goethe, Körner, Bürger, Uhland, Arndt. There is a wonderful poetic vein running through them, a mingling of wit, humor, pathos, rude physical life, beautiful imagery, absurd slang. The *Commersbuch* is as chaotic, as irrepressible, as full of good and evil in glaring juxtaposition, as the student-life itself. Generations of young men have labored upon it to make it what it is, the one student song-book in the world. Yet the singing, I regret to say, is scarcely equal to the music. Whether the voices are made gruff by excessive quantities of beer, whether there is a want of tenors among the students, at all events the singing, although hearty and correct in time, is not as melodious as it should be. It has always left me unsatisfied.

CHAPTER X.

The Pandects.

ONE might while away many an unoccupied hour not unpleasantly in speculating upon the general character of Justinian's codification. That the emperor himself, whom the modern critic is constantly tempted to set down as a "prig," fondly regarded his codification as something wonderful, is evident from the extravagant self-laudation in the *Digestorum confirmatio*. *Imperator Caesar Flavius Justinianus, Alamannicus, Gotthicus, Francicus, Germanicus, Anticus, Alanicus, Vandalicus, Africanus, pius, felix, inclytus, victor triumphator, semper colendus Augustus,* etc., etc. § 1 — *nunc vero omnium veterum juris conditorum colligentes sententias e multitudine librorum, qui erant circiter dua millia, numerum autem versuum habebant tricies centena millia, in moderatum et perspicuum collegimus compendium. Quinquaginta itaque nunc fecimus libros e superioribus colligentes utilia, et omnes ambiguitates resecantes, et nihil adhuc dissidens relinquentes. Quem librum Digesta sive Pandecten appellavimus, tum quod legum contineat disputationes, ac decisiones, tum exeo, quod omnia in unum collecta recipiat, hanc ipsi ponentes appellationem; non ultra centum quinquaginta versuum millia ipsi dantes, et in septem illum digerentes tractatus, idque non temere, verum numerorum naturam et concentum spectantes.*

The idea of simplifying the great body of the Roman law, by substituting one compact work for a whole library, was praiseworthy. But the execution was anything but faultless. There are many places, indeed, where the work of Tribonian and his fellow Commissioners seems to have amounted to little more than a diligent use of scissors and paste. The Commission drew up a scheme of work, laying out the law like a vegetable garden, here a place for cabbages, there a patch for turnips, potatoes, or the like, and then filling up the several compartments by the mechanical process of transplanting. The Digest makes a stout volume of 900 lexicon octavo pp., double columns, solid matter, divided into fifty books, each book subdivided again into titles. The subdivisions of a title are called *leges*, and each *lex* may have one or more paragraphs. The German mode of citation is thus: l. 2, § 32 D. de orig. jur. (I, 2). One might suppose that at least each title would be worked up into something like homogeneity, that is to say, that the Commission, after collecting their authorities, would really *digest* them, would extract the *principles* embodied in the works of Papinian, Gaius, Paulus, Ulpian, etc., retaining perhaps the phraseology to a large extent, but nevertheless recasting the whole. But this they did not do. They simply extracted *passages* from the great Roman jurists of the classic period, putting them together as beads are arranged on a string. Their work accordingly is nothing more than a mosaic of quotations. To such an excess did they carry this patching process, that in some instances they even made up a complete sentence or opinion with fragments of sentences from two or more authors. Thus, in the Title *de procuratoribus et defensoribus* (III, 3), lex 8 (taken from ULPIAN) ends : *Item si dignitas accesserit procuratori, vel reipublicae causa abfuturus sit,* lex 9 (GAIUS) *aut si valetudinem, aut si necessariam peregrinationem alleget,* lex 10 (ULPIAN once more) *vel hereditas superveniens eum occupet, vel ex alia justa causa. Hoc amplius et si habeat praesentem dominum, non debere compelli procuratorem,* lex 11 (PAULUS) *si tamen dominus cogi possit.*

To read the Digest, then, is hard work. The Latin is simple, but the reader must have the exactest understanding of technical terms, and such a grasp of the subject as to be able to master the most condensed expressions of thought and very abrupt transitions. A *lex* is usually either a passage selected from a theoretical treatise, or an opinion in a case. If it is the latter, nothing but the facts are given and the opinion. I offer specimens of both.

Lex 1 (PAULUS) D. *de usufr.* (VII, 1). *Ususfructus est jus alienis rebus utendi fruendi salva rerum substantia* is merely a theoretical definition. Lex 20, ULPIANUS, same title : *Si quis ita legaverit, 'fructus annuos fundi Corneliani Caio Maevio do, lego,' perinde accipi debet hic sermo, ac si ususfructus esset legatus,* is an instance of equitable construction. The intentions of the testator, manifested in the words *fructus annuos,* are to be carried out, although he has failed to use the technical expression *ususfructus*.

Until comparatively recent times, the study of the Pandects consisted in listening to or reading a sort of running commentary upon the principal passages of the fifty books, in the order in which they occur. But this method has gone out of use, in Germany at least. A professor who lectures on the Pandects arranges his own order of topics, or follows that of some popular text-book, generally that of Arndts. In either case, the order is strictly scientific and the subdivision very minute. The course is a systematic grouping and exposition of the principles scattered throughout the *corpus juris*, each statement being supported by references.

The winter's work was heavy. I had Pandects with Professor Mommsen every day, including Saturday, from nine to eleven, Criminal Law with Professor Zachariæ every day from twelve to one, Doctrine of Inheritance with Dr. Schlesinger five times a week, in the afternoon, History of Civil Procedure among the Romans with Dr. Maxen twice a week. In all, twenty-five hours of rapid writing a week. The lecturers, Dr. Maxen excepted, gave very little *tempus;* Mommsen, in particular, scarcely any.

I have an indistinct remembrance of reading years ago a well written magazine article on German university life, but the author's name has escaped me. Whoever he may be, he has made one serious misstatement which I feel called upon to correct. He says that, with a view to acquiring facility in translation from German into English, he made a practice of translating in the lecture-room, writing down his notes (from the lecturer's words) in English and not in German. To me this sounds like an impossibility. I have heard many lectures from many different men, but never a lecture that could be translated off-hand after this fashion. A hearer thoroughly familiar with both languages might select a sentence here and there and put it into crude English. But he would certainly not succeed in getting complete notes. The best proof that I can give is my own experience. Having always been a ready penman, and having acquired a high degree of proficiency in German through a residence of two years and constant attention to the language in general, and to legal phraseology in particular, I could take notes as fast as any of the German students. By exerting myself to the utmost, I succeeded in taking down everything said or dictated by Mommsen and Zachariæ. The others spoke too fast. My notes on the Pandects, on Criminal Law, and on Ecclesiastical Law were as full as those of any other student in the class, and were borrowed continually by my colleagues. Yet I can assure the reader that, in order to succeed, I had to put forth every effort in the way of concentrated attention and systematic abbreviation. As a specimen of note-taking, I give the following passages, one from Mommsen, the other from Herrmann; assuring the reader that both were written as fast as the pen could be made to move over the paper:

MOMMSEN. "*Unter* DOS *vrstht man ein Gut welches von d. Frau od für dieselb. d. Manne. gegeb. wird, damit ihm durch d. Genuss desselb. fur d. Dauer d. Ehe ein fortgehend. Beitrag zr. Bestreitg d. Kosten d. ehel. Lebens gewährt werde.*"

Written out in full: *Unter* DOS (dower, according to the Roman Law) *versteht man ein Gut, welches von der Frau oder für dieselbe dem Manne gegeben wird, damit ihm durch den Genuss desselben für die Dauer der Ehe ein fortgehender Beitrag zur Bestreitung der Kosten des ehelichen Lebens gewährt werde.*

"Upset" into English on the spot, the passage could not possibly be put into more tolerable shape than the following: By "dower" we understand a piece of property which by the wife or on her acc't is given to the husband, in order that to him through the use thereof for the duration of the marriage a permanent contribution toward meeting the expenses of matrimony may be secured.

HERRMANN — "*D. Kirche ist d. v. χtus gestiftete, mit d. zr. geschichtl. Fortführg. d. Erlosgswerks erforderl. Vollmacht. u. Gaben ausgerüstete u durch. Einsetzg d. immer während. Apostolats verfasste Anstlt.*"

Die Kirche ist die von Christus gestiftete, mit den zur geschichtlichen Fortführung des Erlösungswerkes erforderlichen Vollmachten und Gaben ausgerüstete und durch Einsetzung des immer währenden Apostolats verfasste Anstalt.

This would look still worse, "upset:" The Church is

the by Christ founded, with the for the historic carrying out of the plan of redemption needful powers and gifts furnished and by the institution of the perpetual apostolic succession constituted establishment.

Will any one believe that a succession of such sentences, kept up by the hour, can be translated *currente calamo?* Or that the attempt, if seriously made, will lead to anything but the direst confusion of both languages? I never thought of making the attempt, but was satisfied, and very justly satisfied, with holding the thread of the discourse in my mind, while my fingers formed the German letters mechanically. Furthermore, I venture to doubt whether a man can be found able to translate off-hand, even from a printed book, provided the style be at all above the simplest narrative prose. The structure of the German sentence forbids rapid translation. The translator has to change the order of words and ransack his vocabulary for equivalents. Although knowing men by the score, who could read a German book as rapidly and get as clear an idea of the meaning as if it were expressed in English, I have never yet seen one who could put the same book into even intelligible English without stopping to consider carefully each sentence.

I should therefore dissuade every countryman of mine from attempting to translate in the lecture hour, so long as he regards the lecture as a mode of imparting substantial truth, and not as a mere occasion for practice in language. Translation is a most excellent exercise, but it cannot be cultivated to advantage when reader and hearer have not a moment to spare for mere matters of form. Training is one thing, knowledge is another; the shortest cut to knowledge will generally be found to be the best. After one has resided long enough in a foreign country, he acquires the power of catching directly ideas expressed in the language of that country, without having to subject the words to any intermediate process of translation. When one has reached this stage, he cannot do better than to receive statements of fact and opinion just as they are given, to let them act upon him with undiminished force, instead of weakening their impression by seeking to give them an intermediate and necessarily imperfect shape.

The labor, it is perhaps superfluous to say, was wearing. One cannot attend twenty-five hours of lecture per week, taking full notes, and not feel his brain and fingers grow weary. In addition to the lectures, I had a good deal of collateral reading. Besides finishing the Institutes of Justinian, I also read with an older student a number of selected titles from the Digest, worked up my notes as fast as they accumulated, consulted such works as Vangerow and Goeschen on the Pandects, and Berner on Criminal Law, to say nothing of Rudorff's *Rechtsgeschichte* and Keller's *History of Civil Procedure by Formulae,* and reviewed the greater part of Puchta. My relations with Dr. Maxen became more and more intimate. The doctor had several ways of extracting information without seeming to question; his favorite method was to start some very heretical proposition and lure his victim on to combatting it vigorously. He was, therefore, accurately posted, not only as to what I was hearing and reading, but also the greater or less extent to which I had really mastered the subjects. At the end of the semester, he said to me in an encouraging manner: "You have certainly done well so far. I don't know how long you will be able to keep up this rate of work, but if you can only hold out until next Fall, and can be exempted from examination in German law, you might perhaps "go in" for your degree. But you must consult Ribbentropp. He is not the dean of the faculty at present, but he is the Nestor, and if he takes an interest in you, your chances are good. I cannot help you directly in the matter, but I can do something indirectly. There is a mass of work yet to be done. You must have Ecclesiastical Law and a *Pandecten Practicum*, and go through a regular *Repetitorium*. I hope to be able to organize one this summer. Several students have made application, but I am not willing to take everybody, and four is the limit. If three of the right kind offer themselves, shall I reserve the fourth place for you?" I thanked him warmly, and assured him that it would meet my wishes exactly to place myself for an entire term under his personal supervision.

CHAPTER XI.

The American Colony — Birthdays.

GÖTTINGEN has always been an attractive place to Americans. Scarcely a semester has elapsed in the past twenty or thirty years without the attendance of at least four or five. In the summer of 1861, just before my arrival, the number amounted to eighteen, just enough to organize a base-ball club and play one game on the Lower Marsh. The fame of that trial of athletic skill has not been dimmed by the course of time. Those who participated in it will know what I mean. During the winter of 1861-2, the number was nine or ten. The next summer it dropped to two. The following winter it rose to eight. In the summer it again dropped to four. In the winter of 1863-4 it was ten, in the following summer only four. The reader will observe that the falling off took place in summer. This was due, I am inclined to believe, to the superior attractiveness of Heidelberg as a place of summer resort. In my student days Heidelberg was the fashionable university, and a wonderfully cosmopolitan place for its size. When I visited it in the autumn of 1864, there were nearly forty American students, almost as many Englishmen, not a few Frenchmen, Greeks, Poles and Italians, to say nothing of the numerous English and American families residing there permanently. I counted, one evening, eighteen or twenty of my countrymen at one time in the same café. At present, the fashionable university is Leipsic.

The Americans in Göttingen styled themselves the "colony." Who invented the name, I am unable to state. It certainly outdates my recollections. The oldest American resident was eo ipso "the patriarch." It was his duty to be on the look-out for newcomers, give them assistance in the way of finding rooms and the like, and take charge of the colony record and flag. The record was a simple note-book, rather handsomely bound, in which the newcomers entered their names and residences at home. The flag was a small piece of canvas painted in the likeness of the stars and stripes, and framed. When a patriarch left Göttingen, it was his duty to transfer the flag and book to the next oldest resident.

Not having the record before me, I am unable to speak with any certainty concerning the earlier members of the colony. Only three or four names occur to me, namely those of Mr. Bancroft, our Minister at Berlin, Professor Goodwin of Harvard, Professors Joy and Chandler of Columbia College, and Professor Nason of the Rensselaer Polytechnic. The Göttingen colony, although never very numerous, had one decided superiority over Heidelberg and perhaps also over Bonn. It was more homogeneous, the individual members were well disposed one toward the other. In my student days, which covered the period of our great civil war, the party line between Southerner and Northerner was drawn very sharply in Heidelberg. The two sets did not quarrel, to any extent, but they kept aloof from each other. In Göttingen, there were never more than two Southerners together at a time, and they did not, I am happy to say, constitute an element of discord. Although holding their own political views, they did not put them forward in a way to offend others. The consequence was that our little colony lived in perfect harmony. We saw a good deal of one another, and were in the main what might be called a "jolly set." We certainly were very jolly during the winter of 1863-4. For my own part, I shall always look back to that winter with feelings of peculiar pleasure. We numbered ten, and did not count a single black sheep, a single idler. We represented nearly all the leading branches of study; there was one man in theology, another in philology, myself in law, two in medicine, the rest in chemistry. Each man worked away for himself, in very independent style, but our social reunions were numerous. To say nothing of casual meetings on working days, in one or another of the dozen *Kneipen* and cafés about town, we invariably turned out in force at the *Kaffee-concerte* held every Saturday afternoon in the music hall of the Museum. These *Kaffee-concerte*, otherwise styled family concerts, were open only to members of the Museum and their families, but as nearly all the students were members, the student attendance was the leading element. Philistia alone was excluded. The music was instrumental, and was given by the University orchestra. It was good, but — for Germany — not very good. Still, it was all that could be had in those days.* The order, I need scarcely say, was excellent. There were no seats in the English or American fashion. The body of the hall was filled with small tables, around which the audience sat on detached chairs. Although in theory any one was free to sit at any table, as a matter of fact the professors and their families occupied one part of the room, the Privatdocenten another, the students still another. Smoking and drinking went on uninterruptedly, conversation was suspended during the performance of a piece. One was at liberty to pass from table to table during the intervals, and exchange salutations with his friends and acquaintances. The "women-folk" occupied themselves with their knitting or crochet-work, and sipped coffee. The men generally preferred something stronger. It may be interesting to study the table of say Hofrath So and So. The learned Hofrath himself sits puffing philosophically from a twenty dollar (per mille) cigar and evolving all sorts of theories and definitions with the gray-blue smoke. Opposite sits the Frau Hofräthin, her attention divided between trying to knit a stocking without looking at the needles and keeping watch over the youngest child, a hopeful youth of four, who has a partly filled glass of beer all to himself, in honor of the occasion, and who seems bent either upon upsetting said glass or sliding off

---

* I have learned that since Göttingen has become a Prussian town, it rejoices in one or two excellent military bands. *Sic venit gloria mundi.*

his chair. *Pfui Fritz, wie du unartig bist, heute,* for shame, how naughty you are to-day, says the mother reproachfully, whereupon Master Fritz makes a desperate effort to sit upright and drink his beer "like a man," only holding the glass in both hands. The Hofrath's sons are off at some other table, kneiping with their student brethren. The three unmarried daughters, securely sandwiched between papa and mamma, scarcely lift their eyes from their work, but ply needle and thread as though running a race. Herr Dr. ——, who is *verlobt* with the eldest, sits at a respectful distance from his fiancée, not saying much, but stealing a sly squeeze of the hand now and then under the table, at the risk of getting his fingers pricked. You cannot hear what is said at the table, but, judging from the looks and smiles interchanged, you are led to suspect that there is a deal of gossip going on. In fact, the students have nicknamed these musical entertainments *Klatsch-concerte.**

Our "American" table was in one corner of the hall, by a side-door, and conveniently near the source of supplies. As the waiters all knew us by face and name, and had an abiding faith in our *Trinkgelder*, we did not suffer from thirst. Many a learned professor and doctor at the other end, irate from long waiting, must have anathematized the wretched "service." If they had but known how the Yankees were intercepting their supplies!

---

* It may not be amiss to state that German married women are fond of meeting in knots of three and four in the afternoon at each other's houses, for the purpose of enjoying a social cup of coffee. To these innocent gatherings their unfeeling liege lords have given the name of *Kaffeeklatsch.*

The reader need not infer, however, that our concert-sessions amounted to orgies. German students, or students in Germany, as the reader may prefer, lead in the main a free life, but in certain particulars they are scrupulous observers of rule. Among themselves, they throw aside restraint and drink to their heart's content, or discontent. On the other hand, in the presence of their superiors, they invariably keep within bounds. I doubt whether the wildest *Corpsbursch* would suffer himself to become befuddled with the eyes of the whole university as it were upon him. The thing has happened, I am aware. The most flagrant instance was in 1837, during the ceremonies attending the centennial anniversary of the founding of the university. The students broke into the banquet-hall before the appointed time, and literally ate and drank up everything, even the dishes prepared for his Majesty, the King of Hanover. But then those were troublous times. Only six years before, in the winter of 1830–1, the town had been the scene of a political insurrection. The students took the lead of the democratic movement, disarmed the town-watch, set up their own patrols and sentinels, and had possession of the town for several weeks. The insurrection was quelled only by the interference of an entire Hanoverian army-corps, under the command of General v. d. Busch. I cannot undertake, of course, to speak of the political history of Germany. I can only allude to it in a general way, where it happens to be connected with the universities. Whoever is familiar with the history of Germany in the years between the Restoration of 1815 and the Revolution of 1848-9, will know that the country was in a state of constant fermentation. The people, finding itself disappointed by the Metternichian policy in its hopes of political reform, betook itself to underhand agitation and conspiracy. The universities, or rather the university students, as representatives of liberal, progressive ideas, were naturally foremost in this agitation. They were not the actual planners of the revolutions of 1831, 1833, 1846, and 1848, for the head-centre of the movement was in Paris. But German students were among the most conspicuous agitators and agents. I need only allude to such incidents as the murder of Kotzebue and the Wartburg Festival, and to a circumstance which is not generally known, at least not stated in published works, namely, that the Polish-Galician revolt of 1846–7 was managed by Polish students of the university of Breslau. I make this statement on the verbal authority of one of those students himself. The great year '48–'49 came and went like a whirlwind. Foremost in the cause of democratic ideas were the student legions of Berlin and Vienna. There is many a German, from Senator Schurz down, now residing among us as a quiet American citizen, who could tell a thrilling story of his hairbreadth 'scapes from bayonet and dungeon. The history of those days has not yet been written, but when it is written, the world will know more exactly what share in it belonged to the German students. Meanwhile I must content myself with saying that the universities were not places for study alone, and that the students paid anything but exclusive devotion to books and lectures. Each university was a larger or smaller center of political agitation, and attracted to itself the disturbing, aggressive elements of society. The manners of the students in those days were boisterous, turbulent, defiant. The young men regarded themselves as the *coryphaei* of New Germany, and asserted their mission with all the recklessness of youth. The year '48–'49, I have said, came and went like a whirlwind. Apparently it wrought no change, it only confirmed the existing dynasties in the possession of their prerogatives. In reality, the country was revolutionized. Kings and princes, although theoretically absolute, found that the unquestioned divinity which once hedged about their kingship was gone, that there was such a thing as public opinion which could not be defied. The end had not yet come, but it had been prepared. Political agitation was still kept alive, but the scene for it was shifted. Instead of University *Burschenschaften*, conspirators, clubs, anonymous pamphlets, there was a press freed from censorship, and there were the several state diets. In the press and in the diet, then, the battle was to be fought. The universities ceased to be political centres and became once more, what they always should have been, mere seats of learning. When I came to Germany for the first time, in 1861, the change had been substantially effected, although traces might still be detected now and then of the old feeling. I have mentioned elsewhere the circumstance that Bismarck, then representing the Prussian squirarchy, was groaned by the students of Göttingen on his way to Berlin in 1864. Still these were mere trifles, they did not constitute a distinguishing element in student life.

In making this digression, I have had in view a practical object, namely to put the reader on his guard. Everything written about German university life before the year 1860 must be taken *cum grano salis*, and a very liberal dose, at that. The manners and character of the students have, beyond all question, undergone a marked change. The student of the present day is not the student of 1830 or 1840 or even 1850. Retaining all his disdain for Philistia, and still regarding himself as a child of light, he no longer looks upon himself as an armed apostle of the new gospel and subject only to the martial law of his own invention. He feels more and more that he is but one and not the most important link in the great political nexus. He is soberer, toned down, disposed to look upon his university membership as a means of social and intellectual enjoyment rather than a stronghold for offense and defense. He drinks less, duels less, studies more, and intrigues not at all. I was impressed with the metamorphosis on revisiting Germany in 1872-3. Although then occupying a position which obliged me to study the press and political movements very closely for months, I never had occasion to note any political demonstrations on the part of students. I met many of them who had served in the campaign against France and had returned home to finish their studies. They had their opinions, and expressed them freely enough when invited to do so. But they certainly did not obtrude them, and seemed to hold rather aloof from domestic politics. The only topic of general interest was the relations of Germany to the rest of Europe, and here national pride and the flush of success made them as one man.

The *Kaffeconcerte* — to return from this digression into politics and history — are as good an illustration as I can give of the great freedom of intercourse existing in Germany between professor and student. I say freedom of intercourse, rather than intimacy. There is no such thing in general as intimacy between students and professors, and there never will be. The reason is obvious; personal intimacy implies equality of age and standing and congeniality of taste and character, things which do not exist as between old and young, the mature and the immature. So far as my observation extends, the relation between student and professor is formal, ceremonious. In the majority of cases, the student does not come in personal contact with the teachers in his own department; he merely salutes them in the street and in other public places. As to the professors in other departments, he does not even know them by sight. It is difficult to make this relation intelligible to the ordinary American collegian, who, I venture to say, regards his professor as one either to fight or to run away from. Perhaps the best way of making the case clear is to show what the relation is *not*. In the first place, the student has not to look upon his lecturers as men whose daily business is to gauge his weakness and keep an exact mathematical record of the same. In the next place, he knows that his lecturers have nothing to do with his general deportment, and are not even his judges. Finally, he knows that they are men who exact nothing from him but a decent observance of etiquette, and men from whom he can expect nothing in the way of protection or favor. In consequence, the student experiences no temptation either to annoy his professor or to flunkey to him. He preserves a manly independence, while paying to age and talent the proper tribute of respect. At Göttingen, where there was in my day but one tolerable billiard table,— the one in the Museum,— I have taken part in many a game of "pool" with the *Privat-docenten*, professors of the university, and teachers in the gymnasium. No one seemed to think that there was anything out of the way in a full professor of mathematics and a *Fuchs* in the legal department trying to "kill" each other and laughing at each other's "scratches." In Leipsic, I have seen Zarncke, the leading professor of Germanistic philology and then (1872) rector of the university, drop in at the *Universitäts-Keller* of an evening and sit down to a glass of Pilsener with a naivety that would have horrified our college trustees and faculties. As to such a university as Marburg, there was one *Kneipe* in particular where one might see, every evening in the week, a perfect medley of students, *Privat-docenten*, professors, and officers. I do not wish to be misunderstood. Professors and *Privat-docenten* are anything but hard drinkers, or even regular frequenters of beer-saloons. They have too much to do, and lead a rather abstemious life. But this much at least I can say with safety, that they feel none of that false restraint which hangs over the American professor like a cloud and makes his life so isolated. No man in Germany hesitates as to the propriety of taking his supper and meeting his friends in a beer-saloon, for he knows that his coming and going will be looked upon as a matter of course.

There are many conditions of things where it is difficult to ascertain what is cause and what is effect. Do respectable people frequent public saloons in Germany because they are orderly, or are the saloons orderly because of the respectable people who frequent them? I cannot take it upon myself to decide this delicate question. I can only state the broad fact, that what in America would be considered undignified, a sort of loss of caste, is in Germany an every-day affair. Men of the most eminent scholarly attainments, leading the most irreproachable lives, as jealous of their reputation as men well can be, not only attend beer concerts and other places of public amusement, but take their wives and daughters with them; they enjoy an hour or two of music, in the open air if possible, meet their friends and neighbors, and return to their homes refreshed by innocent recreation. Are the Germans so much better than we, or do we fear the devil so much that we cannot confront him boldly and banish him to the realms of outer darkness?

In addition to the *Kaffeeconcerte*, the work of the winter of 1863-4 was enlivened by a number of private social gatherings among the Americans. Our colony numbered, I have said, ten. It was a curious phenomenon that no less than six of the ten had their birthdays to celebrate during the three months of December, January, and February. It would be ungracious in me to insinuate that the calendar had been tampered with. When a countryman surprised me at my books, staying long enough to help himself to a fresh cigar, and state, in an off-hand way, that he would be glad to have the pleasure of my company the next Saturday night, at such a place, in honor of his birthday—" merely a few friends "—of course the only thing to do was to put on a smiling mien and make the best of it. But it *was* remarkable that a birthday should come around regularly every fortnight, to say nothing of the convenience of its always happening on a Saturday.

Our birthday celebrations were an odd mixture of the German and the American. The eatables and drinkables were German, and we observed, in the main, the rules about *Vortrinken* and *Nachtrinken*, but the toasts and speech-making, and the general atmosphere of the entertainment, were intensely trans-Atlantic. The few Germans who were invited had a good opportunity of becoming acquainted with the merits of such stirring ditties as "John Brown," "Rolling Home," and "Smith is a Jolly Good Fellow, Which Nobody can Deny." H——, who was understood to be "cramming" for his degree in classic philology, was invariably called upon for the boat-song of the Argonautic Expedition.

Further description is unnecessary. The reader can easily imagine what a party of the kind must be. Our birthday celebrations were no better and no worse than such affairs usually are. There was some sense talked, and a good deal of nonsense; but there was no quarreling. We were friends, glad to meet one another and have a good time together. Our reunions broke up the dull monotony of work. As to the morality of wine-parties, especially among students, that is a question which the reader can settle for himself, bearing in mind the truism that Germany is not America. Out of the ten who composed our set, not one was intemperate at the time, or has since become so. Most of the ten are now married and occupying responsible positions in society. We all worked fairly at that time, and some worked very hard. Not one of us ever dreamed for an instant that he was committing an impropriety in knocking off work at the end of the week and kneiping with his associates. We learned to distinguish very clearly between a man who knows how to live, and a sot. It was not a difficult lesson. Every schoolboy in Germany learns it in *Prima*.

CHAPTER XII.

"*Spurting.*"

HAVING every reason to expect that the coming summer semester would probably decide my chances as a candidate for the degree of Doctor Juris, I thought it advisable to prepare for it by taking a rest in the spring vacation. There was no necessity for revisiting Wiesbaden, as my health throughout the winter had been unexceptionable. But feeling attached to the place, and confident that the bathing would at least do no harm, I took a second *Cur* of a fortnight. The spring of 1864 was quite backward, and the weather, even on the Rhine, uncomfortably chilly. The season had not yet commenced, and the number of guests was extremely small. As a matter of course, the place was *langweilig*, yet the change and the entire absence of excitement were probably the best thing for me under the circumstances. After suffering myself to be bored unmercifully for a fortnight, I ran over to Heidelberg and from there down the Rhine as far as Coblenz, returning to Göttingen by the valley of the Lahn and Cassel.

The last week of the vacation was passed in making preparations for the semestrial work. I decided to hear only two lectures, one on Ecclesiastical Law, by Herrmann, and one on *Erbrecht*, by Francke. This latter subject I had heard in the winter, but as Schlesinger had not succeeded in making the subject clear to me, and as Francke, if I went into the examination, would be one of the chief examiners, I deemed it expedient to take the course over again.

Subsequent events proved that I was right. Besides these lectures, I took a *Pandecten-practicum* with Thöl. This bears a strong resemblance to the Moot Courts in our Law Schools. Thöl met his hearers once every week for two hours. At each meeting, a practical case was given out for discussion. Our opinions upon it were submitted, in writing, the next week, and returned to us, with the professor's criticisms, the third week. This returning did not consist in merely handing the papers back, like compositions with marginal corrections. After each member of the class had placed his paper before him, the professor took up the question and discussed it in all its bearings, stating what his own views were, showing what views had been presented by the members of the class, which of those views were correct, which incorrect, but not mentioning names. Each student could see for himself, however, where he had made a mistake. These verbal discussions — they were not arguments in our legal acceptation of the term — were very informal. The students were at liberty to interrupt the professor whenever they felt the need of fuller explanations. If any time remained after this exhaustive discussion of the question set for the day, the professor utilized it by sub-

*15

mitting one or more short cases to be analyzed on the spot.

I give one of the set cases. It is a very easy one. A has a claim against B of $100; B against C of $120; C against D of $130; D against A of $140. Meeting by chance, they discover, in the course of conversation, that there is the sum of $100 mutually claimed and owed by all four. This they agree to cancel, leaving the balance of the claims to run. Some time after, C finds among the papers of his father, from whom the debt of $120 devolved by inheritance, evidence that this debt had already been paid to B. What remedy has C, and what is the legal character of the agreement entered into by the four to cancel the common claim of $100?

These practical exercises are of great advantage to the students. They are, I believe, better than our Moot Courts. The questions submitted are generally of a higher order, and more complicated in their nature,* and — the main point — the exercises are better adapted to teaching the class. The necessity of writing out one's opinions at length every week and submitting them to the deliberate inspection of the professor, has the tendency to make one careful. Now and then a Moot Court case is well argued, but generally the so called arguments are too wordy and rhetorical. Besides, there is a great difference between speaking once in three months or six

---

* The one given above is by no means a fair specimen, but the others contained in my Lecture Ms. are too long and presuppose too much knowledge of Roman law.

months, and writing out an opinion once every week for an entire semester.

The *Pandecten-practicum* covers only the substance of civil law. The more advanced students have practical exercises of a similar nature in Criminal Law, in Ecclesiastical Law, and in Procedure and Evidence.

Francke's lectures on the Law of Inheritance were extremely clear and satisfactory. As the lecturer spoke slowly, there was no difficulty in taking him down verbatim. The subject is complicated, so complicated, in fact, that I can not hope to give the reader even an outline. I can only call attention to one or two cardinal points. The Roman Law has a much more philosophical conception of succession by inheritance than the English Law. It regards the personality of the deceased as in a measure continued after death, that is to say, all the property, whether real or personal, all claims held by, all debts due by the deceased, everything in short that does not perish with him, devolves as a unit upon one or more persons who represent him, who continue his existence, as it were. The *heres* succeeds to the defunct, is entitled to all his property, is under obligation to pay all his debts, *heres defuncti locum sustinet*. Our Common Law, hampered from the outset by the feudal distinction between real and personal property, has never yet succeeded in elaborating a satisfactory theory of inheritance. The Roman Law, on the other hand, labored under a difficulty peculiar to itself. It was in the beginning extremely illiberal in doctrine and rigid in its forms.

The Praetorian edicts effected gradually a thorough equitable reform, by admitting the claims of kinsmen who were not entitled under the old law of the XII Tables, by smoothing over mistakes in drawing up wills, and by checking as much as possible, in favor of lineal descendants, the privilege of disinheritance. The development of the Roman law of inheritance is, in fine, the history of a protracted struggle between the narrow-mindedness of the old *hereditas* and the equity of the Praetorian *bonorum possessio*. The Praetor had no right to repeal or formally overthrow the old law, but what he was unable to accomplish directly, he did indirectly. Like the English Chancellor, the keeper of his Majesty's conscience, he could not say that such and such a claimant was not legally entitled, but he could in various ways prevent him from enforcing the claim.

A most interesting course of lectures was that delivered by Herrmann on Ecclesiastical Law. The lecturer's delivery was fluent, almost too fluent for those who wished to take complete notes, but his language was clear, and the substance of his remarks was, to me at least, intensely interesting. I can not but regret that no one of our law schools has seen fit to introduce such a topic in its curriculum. Surely, in view of the conflict between church and state now raging over Europe, it is of the highest importance that the lawyers and jurists of every land calling itself civilized should be acquainted with the principles involved in the issue. The primitive organization of the Christian Church, the growth of the hierarchy, the concentration of power first in the hands of the priests, then of the bishops, finally of the Pope, the Oriental Schism, the Reformation, the Declaration of Gallican Independence, Josephismus in Austria, the scope and functions of Concordates, the claims of the Church to the exclusive regulation of marriage and divorce, the provisions of the Council of Trent on this point, the Westphalian Treaty of Peace, are all subjects fraught with the deepest interest to every liberal thinker. Herrmann's lectures were to me a pleasure rather than a burden, while the notes then taken have since been of great service to me on more than one occasion. I am indebted to them for a very clear and comprehensive survey of the march of christian society during eighteen centuries.

Göttingen being an exclusively Protestant university, nearly all the professors and students were in my day Protestant. Herrmann treated the subject of Ecclesiastical Law, accordingly, from the Protestant point of view, but without becoming polemic. His exposition of the theory and doctrines of the Catholic Church, being based upon Catholic authorities, was eminently fair. Indeed, the object of the course was to acquaint the hearer with the facts of history and the actual shaping of principles and doctrines, rather than to defend or to controvert any one system. Herrmann now occupies the most important ecclesiastical position in Prussia, to wit, the presidency of the Upper Consistory in Berlin.

Before leaving this subject, I may add that, although

Prussia is nominally a Protestant country, a very large number, six or seven millions of its population, are Catholics. They are to be found chiefly in the Rhine provinces and in Polish Prussia. In organizing its system of education, the government has taken their wishes and needs into account, by constituting what are called paritetic universities, in addition to the Catholic gymnasiums. Bonn is one of these universities, Breslau another,* and Münster is an exclusively Catholic academy, falling very little short of a university. In such paritetic institutions, all departments where there is conflict of religious opinion are supplied with double sets of professors. The Catholic professor of Ecclesiastical Law at Bonn was Walter, between whom and Richter, the Protestant professor in Berlin, there was unceasing warfare. Both men being aggressive by nature, neither could let the other alone. It is entertaining to read their respective treatises and observe the numerous flat denials, corrections, and sneers that each hurls at the other. Schulte, probably an abler man than the other two, is less dogmatic and positive; his text-book of Catholic Ecclesiastical Law is the best of the kind produced in modern times.

The reader can perceive that two lectures a day, and an elaborate opinion in writing once a week, to say nothing of collateral reading, did not leave much unemployed time. But the most searching part of the semestrial work has yet to be mentioned. Dr. Maxen succeeded in

---

* Tübingen is also paritetic, although not a Prussian university.

forming his *Repetitorium*, or *Exegeticum*, as he called it.*
The three members beside myself were students in their
sixth semester, preparing for the State examination at
Celle in the fall. We met six times a week, at the doctor's rooms, from twelve to one o'clock. The exercise
was what medical students call a "quiz," and did ample
justice to the name. We students naturally thought that
we knew at least some law, but one or two quizzes were
sufficient to convince us that we knew nothing. The doctor's method was, in appearance, as immethodical as one
could imagine. We never knew before the hour what
topic he might take up, and consequently were unable to
prepare ourselves. This seemed to me unsatisfactory,
and I ventured to say as much to the doctor, in private.
At this he only laughed, and replied : "That is precisely
what I aim at doing, to make you dissatisfied. If I gave
you ten or twenty pages of Vangerow or Arndts to
recite upon, you would get the work by heart, I dare say,
and forget it again in a week. But if I catch you to-day
on some point that has never occurred to you, you will
feel vexed at yourself, and when you return to your
room you will look it up carefully, and then you will not
forget it. My business is not to discover what you know,
but what you do not know, and the best way of doing that
is to keep changing the subject unexpectedly. I wish to
catch you unprepared, for then I shall certainly detect

---

* It was in reality a course of private lessons. Each one's share of the
expense, as well as I can remember, amounted to thirty or thirty-five cents an
hour.

the defects in your reading. Besides, is it not the best preparation for the examination? What you need is not only the knowledge of facts and principles, but the ability to answer all sorts of questions that may be sprung upon you. Relieve your mind by considering that every hour spent with me is an informal examination, and not a recitation, and be assured that you are not the first set of young men that I have had in training."

Notwithstanding the doctor's assurances, and the firm confidence that I had in his ability and sincerity, I felt many misgivings for the first month or two. It seemed as though we were making no progress, as though our modest but hard-bought attainments were a sort of ten-pins, set up only to be knocked down again. Perhaps the reader has taken boxing lessons himself, or at least has seen one or more of them. In that case, he will be able to appreciate the simile, when I liken myself and my three fellow-victims to pupils in the manly art of self-defense being "punished" mercilessly by the master. Mr. Bristed, in his book on Cambridge, p. 193 sqq. (ed. of 1873), has given a very racy account of the way in which "coaching" is conducted in an English university. I regret extremely my inability to sketch a like tableau of our quiz in the Georgia Augusta. Dr. Maxen "slanged" us plentifully, in the technical sense of that term; that is, he did not smooth over our ignorance with lavender-water, but made us feel it keenly. Yet his method differed radically from that followed by Mr. Bristed's coach, Travis, and, furthermore, the subjects themselves, the *Supplices* of Æschylus and the body of the Roman Law, can scarcely be treated after the same fashion. Mr. Bristed's coaching is a mere recitation, that is, a literal translation, with running commentary, of a given passage in the *Supplices*, reproduced, I presume, from notes taken at the time. The reader, even if not a classical scholar, can at least follow the recitation line by line. With regard to our quiz, on the other hand, I must remark, in the first place, that the subject is so foreign to the reader that, in order to make a description barely intelligible, I should be forced to give about six pages of prefatory explanation to one of description, and, in the next place, that the quiz was an examination, not a recitation, the subject being changed abruptly every few minutes. My note-book is filled with names and dates, detached fragments of law, references to authorities, queries to be pursued at leisure, and the like, but it contains nothing that would give the reader a satisfactory idea of how the work was done.

At all events, there was the satisfaction of perceiving that my three co-workers were not much better off than myself. They knew more law, but they did not have their knowledge in a more available shape. Practically, we were on an equality. The real benefit of the quiz came after the hour. Having the afternoons and evenings to myself, I spent the time in reviewing, with the utmost care, what the doctor had run over hastily in the forenoon. Still smarting under the lash of criticism, to speak figuratively, and having some definite object of search, I ransacked Puchta, Arndts, Goeschen, Vangerow, and my notes, for everything that might throw additional light on the topics that were started by the doctor from day to day. I made no attempt to prepare for the doctor in advance. There was enough to do to follow up his hints as fast as they were given. After pursuing this method for two months, the conviction finally dawned upon me that the doctor was correct. The quiz was not only a powerful stimulant, but it gave some object to my private reading. Instead of droning over one book at a time, page after page and chapter after chapter in consecutive order, I was forced to go through each book every day, from cover to cover, in search of examples, definitions, exceptions, authorities, whatever, in short, might aid me in understanding more clearly half a dozen points raised but not exhausted in the quiz.

By the end of the semester I made a further discovery. Dr. Maxen's plan, seemingly immethodical, was in truth the highest kind of method. Running over my notebook, I could see that the doctor had covered the law of obligations, at least in its general principles, almost entire, and had taken in a large share of the law of real property and family relations, and not a little of the law of inheritance. While zigzagging to right and left in a manner that gave no indication from one day to the next of a deep-laid plan, the doctor had succeeded nevertheless in starting us on all the more important subjects. One object he had certainly realized: he had taught us how to study. When the last quizz was ended, and we broke up as a class, I felt that I had been shifted to an altogether new stand-point, that success in the examination would probably resolve itself into a matter of time and endurance.

I have stated, on a previous occasion, that the relation between student and professor is generally formal, savoring little of intimacy. There are brilliant exceptions, however, and it was my good fortune to profit directly by one of these exceptional cases. About the middle of July, Dr. Maxen said to me: "It is time that you should call on Ribbentropp and confer with him on the subject of your examination. He is not the Dean of the faculty, but he is the oldest and most influential member. You must make him interested in you. There is no need of a letter of introduction; you will find him very charming and affable."

The *Geheimjustizrath* v. Ribbentropp occupied a most enviable position. He had made his reputation as a jurist while still a young man, by his treatise on the law of *Correal* Obligations. Coming into the possession of a handsome property by inheritance, in addition to his salary as professor, he was able to live in what, for Göttingen, was decidedly style. He occupied a large house by himself, something very unusual in a German university town; the parlors and dining-room were on the second floor, his study and private apartments on the third. Over the ground-floor the housekeeper reigned supreme. Gossip had it that the housekeeper was the only person in the town who disturbed the mental quiet (*Gemüthsruhe*) of the *Geheimjustizrath*. Not that she was vinegar-aspected or harsh of manner; but, like all spinsters of a certain age, she had come to regard men in general, and old bachelors in particular, as helpless beings, whom it was never safe to trust too long or too far out of sight. The object of this anxious supervision often made a jest of it to his friends.

Summoning up courage, I called upon the *Geheimjustizrath* one evening, and running successfully the gauntlet of the housekeeper and under-servant, obtained admission to the sanctum sanctorum, the library. I found a gentleman not over sixty, as well as I could make out, of decidedly *distingué* bearing, rather short in stature, but with a superbly shaped head, a winning smile, and the most fascinating pair of eyes that I have ever encountered. Whether perfectly black, or only of a very dark brown, I am unable to state from memory; but the play of lambent light emitted from them, joined to the witchery of a humorous smile around the corners of the mouth, gave to the massive forehead and classic features a grace and an animation that were irresistible. I perceived, at the very first glance, that I was dealing with one of nature's noblemen. Speaking frankly, I fell quite in love with the elderly gentleman who received me with such an uncommon blending of French suavity and German simplicity. It was the gracious commencement of an acquaintance that — to me certainly — was to be fraught with benefit and pleasure.

I stated as briefly as possible the object óf my visit, mentioned the lectures I had already heard or was then hearing, the text-books I was using, the amount of private reading already accomplished, the private instruction received from Dr. Maxen. I said that I was perfectly aware of the incompleteness and hurried nature of my course of study as a jurist, but that it would be impossible to remain in Germany beyond the coming Christmas, and that I was anxious to take back with me to America tangible evidence of my industry in the shape of a degree. Would he have the kindness to give me his opinion frankly as to my chances of being admitted to examination, and advise me generally as a friend?

He listened patiently, with the same bright, flashing look of the eye, and the same good-natured smile. "Stop a moment," he said, "don't you smoke?" I hesitated. I *was* a smoker, but then it did not seem to be exactly "the thing" to be puffing at such a solemn audience in the sanctum of a *Geheimjustizrath*. "Ah!" he continued, "you hesitate. I *know* you smoke, but you don't like to say so. Wait a moment." So the great jurist frisked into the adjoining room with the alacrity of a boy let loose from school, and returned, presenting a box of unimpeachable Havanas. "There," he exclaimed, "now we can talk up this matter of yours at our leisure."

Under ordinary circumstances, the offering of a cigar means very little. But when you call upon a great man for the first time, without any other recommendation than yourself and your own story, and he insists upon your smoking one of his best cigars, you may safely take for granted that he is kindly disposed toward you.

My visit was protracted until a late hour. The *Geheimjustizrath* had a great many questions to ask me, but they were about everything else than jurisprudence. He wished to know what I had seen of Switzerland and Germany; what I thought of the war in my own country (then approaching the crisis); how I liked Germany as compared with America. In fine, I passed a most delightful evening in easy conversation. I was treated, not as a student, scarcely even as a very young man, but as a welcome guest, or as one who had presented strong letters of recommendation. I did not elicit any definite expression of opinion as to my chances of a degree. In truth, that was not what I expected. I knew enough of the ways of the world to refrain from urging the matter to an immediate decision, and to be satisfied, and more than satisfied, with having created a favorable impression and excited the interest of the most influential member of the Examining Faculty. On my taking leave, the *Geheimjustizrath* said: " Herr Hart, you must come and see me often, once a week. Come to tea, and then we can have the entire evening to ourselves. Just consider that as part of your legal education. I must become well acquainted with you."*

---

* It may surprise the reader to learn that I waited so long before making the acquaintance of the *Geheimjustizrath*, and that I heard none of his lectures. The latter circumstance is easily accounted for. Ribbentropp read the Institutes and *Rechtsgeschichte* in the winter, and Pandects in the summer. My first

On relating my experience to Dr. Maxen, the next day, he said, in his blunt, off-hand fashion: "Well, I think you will do. Keep on as you have begun."

I obeyed the *Geheimjustizrath's* friendly injunction to the letter. Scarcely a week passed without my dropping in to tea in an informal way. I always found the same hearty, unaffected welcome, and the same animated flow of conversation. The host was not merely a profound jurist, but thoroughly versed in the classics, and in the literature of his own country, and an amateur in art. His collection of engravings was not large, but it was very choice. I cannot better illustrate his genial character and his thorough, unselfish appreciation of the best efforts of human genius in every line, than by narrating the following incident. One evening the conversation happened to turn upon Goethe. I believe that I introduced the subject by alluding to the great number of poets who had begun their career as students of the law. "*Ja, ja,*" said the *Geheimjustizrath,* "*Goethe, das war ein ganzer Kerl!* You know, of course," he continued, with a most mischievous twinkle in his eye, "you know, of course, his stupendous lines in *Faust* on the study of

---

summer as a student of law was passed at Berlin, where I heard the Institutes from Gneist. On returning to Göttingen for the winter, I was ready to take up the Pandects, which were read in winter by Mommsen, not by Ribbentropp. As for the acquaintance, it was none the worse, but probably all the better, for the delay. Professors are not apt to interest themselves in *Füchse*. It is too much of a bore to have to deal with a mere beginner, one who is not yet out of the rudiments The circumstance that a student may pass nearly two semesters before making the acquaintance, or even recognizing by sight, the most prominent professor of his own faculty, throws a strong side-light on the character of German university life.

law." I had read the Faust, as already stated, very carefully in my second semester. But what with Pandects and *Erbrecht*, *Practica* and *Exegetica* the muses had been strictly banished from my thoughts for many a month. I had become a stranger to everything that could not be demonstrated logically from the *corpus juris*, and was forced to plead forgetfulness as to the passage in question. "What," exclaimed my host, "you don't mean to say that you, a *studiosus juris*, have forgotten the very best thing ever said by mortal man on the science of law? Really, I must give it to you on the spot. Take it to heart." Thereupon, assuming somewhat the pose of an actor on the stage, but not rising from his seat, he declaimed, from memory, in a rich, sonorous voice, and with the most expressive emphasis, the magnificent lines:

> *Es erben sich Gesetz' und Rechte*
> *Wie eine ew'ge Krankheit fort,*
> *Sie schleppen von Geschlecht sich zum Geschlechte,*
> *Und rücken sacht von Ort zu Ort.*
> *Vernunft wird Unsinn, Wohlthat Plage,*
> *Weh Dir, dass Du ein Enkel bist!*
> *Vom Rechte, das bei uns geboren ist,*
> *Von Dem—ist leider nie die Frage!* *

---

* I am unable either to make a metrical rendering of the passage, or to quote one. Bayard Taylor's translation of the Faust, so admirable in the main, breaks down signally in this very passage. Put into tame prose, the lines run:

> Our laws and legal systems do transmit themselves
> Like an inherited disease;
> They drag themselves along from race to race,
> And softly crawl from land to land.
> What once was sense is turned to nonsense, the boon becomes a torment.
> Alas for thee, that thou'rt a grandchild!
> The right that's *born* with us,
> Of *that* — good lack — we never hear the mention.

The reader must bear in mind that the speaker is Mephistopheles, who, wrapped in Faust's mantle and seated in his chair, proceeds to give the young student advice as to his studies, and the respective merits of the different faculties.

"Now, just see how the great poet has hit the thing off. What venom there is in every line, in every word! And how the climax is reached in the line: *Weh Dir, dass Du ein Enkel bist!* Ha, ha! Not only has a man to bear the consequences of all the foolish legislation and stupid decisions of his own day and generation, but he is crushed with the accumulated burden of his father's and his grandfather's asininity. Isn't it sublime? *Ja, ja, der Goethe, das war ein verzweifelt schlauer Kerl, er wusste, was er sagen wollte.*

Looking back upon this phase of my Göttingen life through the vista of a decennium, I am impressed more strongly than ever with its uniqueness and its appositeness. It was the one bright side of my then daily round of dull work. The sociable set of Americans of the previous winter had broken up. Many had removed to other universities; only a few were left, and a spell seemed to have come over both them and myself. We met occasionally, but the old spirit of friendly intercourse was suppressed for the while by more urgent needs. The hebdomadal visits at the *Geheimjustizrath's* were almost my sole diversion for months. The relationship, if I may venture to call so simple a thing by so ponderous a name, was something for which an Americam college can furnish no analogy. The nearest approach to it is to be found in our schools of science. I have no personal knowledge of the Sheffield Scientific, but from what has been told to me by graduates, I infer that a certain degree of freedom exists there between the instructors and the pupils. Herein probably lies the secret of success, of the rapid growth of scientific schools as distinguished from colleges. The teachers, at least very many of them, have been trained under the German system, and have caught its tone. They work more with the students, and seek to guide and stimulate them, rather than to play the pedagogue. Yet there is this difference, I believe, between the Sheffield Scientific, taken even at its most favorable estimate, and my Göttingen experience. The intercourse between professor and student at the Sheffield Scientific is, although free, not what can be strictly called social, but is confined to what the Cantabs and Oxonians call "shop." This was not the case in my tea-drinkings at the *Geheimjustizrath's*. The conversation rarely turned upon legal matters, and then only incidentally. On one occasion, it is true, I was subjected to an impromptu and rather humorously conducted examination. But the great bulk of our conversation was made up of general matters, art, literature, science, and especially national peculiarities. My host never grew weary of listening to all that I could tell him about my own country. He was possessed of an insatiable curiosity to know how Americans lived and fared; what kind of houses they had; what views they took of life; how they passed their leisure hours. Like most educated Germans' who have never traveled in America, he was accurately posted on certain minor details of American life, but failed to seize its essential spirit, to comprehend the broad sweep of its movement. The recklessness and turbulence, the aggressiveness of the American character, evidently impressed him more than its acuteness and its capacity of quiet endurance. I cannot flatter myself with the belief that I made a convert. From one position the *Geheimjustizrath* was not to be dislodged. He wound up all our discussions with the triumphant assertion: "Yes, that is all very well. You Americans do great things, but then you have no *Bildung*. You have *gebildete Leute* in the larger cities, especially men who have been in Europe and profited by what they have seen and heard here. But in the country at large you have no *Bildung* of your own." The reader may judge for himself whether the assertion was well founded.*

---

* After revising the above for the press, I read, in the supplement to the *Universitäts Kalender* for the summer semester of 1874, the sad announcement: *v.* RIBBENTROPP *ist am* 14 *April gestorben.* The event was not unexpected, the deceased having passed the scriptural term of three score and ten. Yet it must have been sudden, as the body of the *Kalender* announced his lectures for the then approaching semester. Von Ribbentropp's cherished wish was gratified: he died in the harness. His associates, who knew him so long and loved him so well, though scarcely better than I did, must write his eulogy. But they will not grudge me the minor consolation of laying upon his tomb a chaplet of wild flowers culled on American soil:

> "Happy their end
> Who vanish down life's evening stream
> Placid as swans that drift in dream
> Round the next river-bend!
> Happy long life, with honor at the close!"

Three of my examiners have passed away: Kraut, Francke and Ribbentropp.

CHAPTER XIII.

The Final Agony of Preparation.

BETWEEN the middle and the end of the summer semester, I made my formal application to the dean of the legal faculty to be admitted to examination for the degree of *Doctor juris*. The paper, or document, consisted of a concisely worded but full statement of the place and time of birth, and the schools and other institutions that I had attended in America, and a more detailed account of my studies in Germany. I gave the titles of all the lectures I had heard, all the text-books on law that I had read or was then reading, all the practical exercises that I had attended. Nothing was omitted that could help in putting my studies in the proper light. This *curriculum vitae*, as it is styled, concluded with a brief petition. Accompanying it was my *Anmeldungsbuch*, duly signed and certified by the professors with whom I had heard.

The semester drew to an end, but the question whether I should be permitted to enter myself for the doctoral examination in the fall was not yet settled. The state of affairs was briefly this. At Göttingen — and I presume the same arrangement exists in the other universities — the conferment of degrees is in the hands of a limited number of the regular faculty in each department.

This select body, called the *Honoren-facultät*, comprised, in the law faculty, five men: Kraut (then dean), Ribbentropp, Francke, Zachariae, and Briegleb. Ordinarily, the application for an examination is granted as of course. My petition, however, was a special one, involving special concessions. In the first place, I had not studied law the ordinary number (six) of semesters. In the next place, I desired to be examined only in Roman, Canonical, and Criminal Law, with the exclusion of Practice and German Law. The faculty of honors in law at Göttingen was governed at that time by strict principles, and was not disposed to make any concessions that looked like lowering the standard of scholarship. Ribbentropp, I knew, was in favor of granting my request, and so was the dean, Kraut. With regard to Zachariae, I was not at all certain. The remaining two, Briegleb and Francke, were set against me. The latter, indeed, told me as much, saying very frankly that he did not believe that I had studied long enough and knew enough. No final vote was taken during the semester, I was "kept on the hooks," as the saying goes, until I felt tempted to give over the effort altogether and return home without further delay. I made a last visit upon the dean just at the close of the semester, but did not succeed in eliciting a decisive answer. This was Friday or Saturday. Monday morning, as I was idling over my books and papers in a rather listless, because hopeless, frame of mind, I heard a heavy tramp down the passage-way leading to my room. The steps came nearer and nearer, there was a sharp, authoritative knock at my door. I answered, *Herein*, and one of the university beadles entered. Touching his cap with a half-military salute, he said: "*Empfehlung von Herrn Hofrath Kraut, und er schickt Ihnen dieses*, Hofrath Kraut sends you his compliments, and *this*," handing me a slip of paper. On it was written in curt, cabbalistic characters:

> Cap. *Non est vobis* (11) *X de sponsal.* (4, 1).
> *l. Dedi* 16 *D. de condict. causa dat.* (12, 4).

Nothing more. Not a word of explanation; not even a signature. But it was enough. I knew that it was the summons, the token that my request for examination was granted. The paper contained the references to two passages, one from the *corpus juris civilis*, the other from the *corpus juris canonici*, upon which passages I was to prepare and hand in elaborate dissertations. Should these dissertations prove satisfactory, I must be admitted to the oral examination; if unsatisfactory, I was barred from applying again for a semester or two.

The reader will easily appreciate the reverent fondness with which I gazed upon this scrap of paper, unintelligible save to the initiated. It was the glad announcement that I should have at least a trial, and not be turned away unheard. Wishing to break the good news to myself as gently as possible, I spent the rest of the forenoon over the billiard-table, and as it never rains but it pours, I had an uncommon run of good luck, that quite upset Prof. L—— and Dr. S——. The afternoon I passed, in part, with Dr. Maxen, in conference as to the best way of taking up the dissertations, and the authorities to be consulted. What puzzled me at the time was to account for the sudden change since Friday. I learned afterward that the faculty met on Saturday to take a formal vote. The voting stood two against two, Zachariae being absent in the country. At Ribbentropp's request, Kraut wrote to him and left the decision in his hands. He immediately telegraphed his reply in my favor.

The time set for handing in the dissertations was October 15th. But on this point the greatest liberality is shown to candidates. Practically, they can take all the time they wish, and even after the day for examination has been fixed, it can be postponed for good reasons shown. The faculty will not interfere unless they are induced to suspect that the candidate is trifling. My own case is in proof. I was not examined until the 20th of November.

In order to simplify matters, I decided to dispose of the dissertations first, before subjecting myself to the "cramming" process for the oral. I spent an hour or two a day in making ready for the "cram," after a peculiar fashion. The reader who has had the patience to follow the account of my lectures and collateral study will admit that the ground covered was extensive. In notes alone there were nearly 1,800 closely written manuscript pages, excluding Schlesinger's lectures on *Erbrecht*. So far as the Pandects were concerned, I saw that any attempt at memorizing them in mass would be useless. The field was too large, and there were too many details. I should have to trust to a clear understanding of definitions and general principles, and — to luck. But the other subjects, namely, Criminal Law, *Erbrecht*, and Ecclesiastical Law, I could and should have, so far at least as concerned the lectures that I had heard upon them, at my tongue's end. Accordingly I reduced them (250 pages each) to the smallest and most manageable shape, by re-writing. Not omitting a single point, but using all sorts of abbreviations, catch-words, and other mnemonic helps, I cut them down to a third or a fourth of their original bulk. To make sure of the historical growth of the Roman Law, I also abbreviated the more important and difficult sections in Puchta, such as Family Rights, *Erbrecht*, Rights of Persons, Procedure. Working regularly for an hour or two a day, I succeeded, in four or five weeks, in completing this preparation for "cram." It was not difficult, and it served as an excellent preliminary review.

As to the dissertations, I began with the passage from the *corpus juris civilis*, as being the more important of the two. The text runs thus:

CELSUS (the name of the jurist from whose writings the extract has been excerpted). *Dedi tibi pecuniam, ut mihi Stichum* (the conventional name for a slave) *dares; utrum id contractus genus pro portione emtionis et venditionis est, an nulla hic alia obligatio est, quam ob rem dati re non secuta? In quod proclivior sum; et ideo, si mortuus est Stichus, repetere possum, quod ideo tibi dedi, ut mihi Stichum dares.*

The examiners had assigned to me — whether in a spirit of kindness or unkindness, I could not divine — one of the most bristling *vexatae quaestiones* of the Roman Law. I fear that I cannot make the case itself intelligible to the reader, even should he be a proficient in the English Common Law, much less furnish him with all the materials for forming a proper judgment. Roughly translated, for our language is scarcely adequate to rendering the concise and technical forms of law Latin, the passage might read after this fashion: "I have given you money to the end that you should give me in return your slave Stichus; question, is this in a part a contract of sale, or is it nothing but an obligation *ob rem dati're non secuta?* To which latter opinion I am inclined, so far that if Stichus has died (or is dead), I can recover the money, inasmuch as I gave it to you that you should give me Stichus in return."

The sense of the passage turns on the word "give," the Latin *dare*. In the Roman Law, the three words, *dare, facere, praestari*, have technical meanings. *Dare* denotes the transfer of full property, the *dominium ex jure Quiritium*, as distinguished from mere putting in possession. If the one who transfers is not himself full and lawful owner, or if the forms prescribed by the old Roman Law are not strictly observed, the transfer cannot be called, in the Roman sense of the term, a "giving." It is only a *traditio*. Now the contract of sale, according to Roman notions, never aims at a "giving." The vendor does not promise to make the vendee the owner;

the vendee does not bargain for the ownership. The cardinal feature of the Roman *contractus emtionis venditionis* is simply this, that the vendor agrees to put the vendee in possession and keep him in possession against all comers, *ut rem sibi habere liceat*. So long as the vendee is undisturbed in his possession, he has no right of action against the vendor on the ground of defective title. This Roman contract of sale, then, is at once broader and yet more limited in its nature than that of our Common Law, and is governed by its own peculiar rules. Consequently, the jurist Celsus, after looking at the case submitted to him for an opinion, says to himself: "Can this be a sale, when I agree to 'give' some one money, and he agrees to 'give' me in turn his slave? No. It belongs to an altogether different and much more strictly construed class of contracts, and the rules applicable to an ordinary sale are not binding here."

The distinction is of importance. In the Roman *contractus emtionis*, the *periculum*, *i. e.*, the risk of loss or deterioration of the thing sold, passes from the vendor to the vendee from the moment that the contract becomes perfect. In a contract of sale made without conditions, this moment coincides with the mutual declaration of agreement on the part of vendor and vendee. A and B agree to buy and sell respectively a certain object. From that moment the *periculum* rests with the vendee. If the object is lost without the fault of the vendor, or if it deteriorates in value, the vendee must bear the damage.

This rule of the Roman contract of sale evidently does not apply to our case. Celsus says expressly, that the one who has "given" the money to the end that the receiver shall "give" in turn his slave, has a right to reclaim the money in case of the slave's death. The contract is not a sale, but what the Roman jurists called a *contractus innominatus*. A contract of this nature does not become perfect, *i. e.*, does not furnish a ground of action, with the mere declaration of mutual consent, but only with the fulfillment on one side. In other words, if B offers A one hundred dollars for a horse, and A accepts, from that moment the bargain is perfect. But if A and B merely agree to exchange horses (another form of *contractus innominatus*), the bargain remains imperfect, and becomes perfect only when A or B has taken the other's horse, so that the one who has parted with the possession has a right of action to compel the recipient to fulfill, in turn, his share of the agreement.

Yet, even assuming that the contract in our case is a *contractus innominatus*, as distinguished from a regular sale, the question still remains: Why does Celsus give such a decision? Is not the transaction, even as such a nameless contract, perfect, in the legal sense of the term? One party has "given," *i. e.*, has fulfilled his part of the agreement, consequently there is no further withdrawal. Both parties must abide by the result. If the slave dies, the loss (*periculum*) falls upon the would-be purchaser, not the late owner, provided there has been no neglect or foul play. The difficulty of explaining the decision rendered by Celsus is augmented by the circumstance that the *corpus juris* contains two other decisions, which are apparently in direct opposition to Celsus, namely: l. 5 § 1 D. de praescr. verbis (19, 5).

PAULUS (another jurist). "*Si scyphos tibi dedi, ut Stichum mihi dares, periculo mihi Stichus erit, ac tu duntaxat culpam praestari debes,* if I have 'given' you some drinking goblets to the end that you shall 'give' me in exchange your slave Stichus, then Stichus will be at my risk, and you will be liable only for laches." The other passage is: l. 10 C. de cond. ob caus. dat. (4, 6).

DIOCL. ET MAXIM. (the Roman emperors). "*Pecuniam a te datam, licet causa pro qua data est, non culpa accipientis, sed fortuito casu non est secuta, minime repeti posse certum est.* Where money has been 'given' for an object (*causa*) which — not through the fault of the receiver of the money, but by pure chance — has not been realized, it is certain that the money cannot be reclaimed."

I have endeavored to state as clearly as possible this vexed question, over which the ablest intellects have quarreled, from the glossator Azo in the twelfth century to authorities of the present day, such as Wächter and Vangerow. There was no lack of materials, then, from which to construct an essay. The only difficulty was to arrive at something like a clear opinion amid the tangled maze of argument and counter-argument. I found a condensed list of works of reference in Vangerow's textbook on the Pandects. This was enough for the start. My first "raid" upon the University library brought in about eight or ten works. By glancing over these, I found still further references. In this way I continued to add to my dissertation-library, until it amounted to forty or fifty volumes, big and little. What with my own private library, not very small, my quarters were overrun with books, superb glossated Leyden editions of the *corpus juris,* musty old tomes of the Dutch and French school, elaborate German treatises, volumes of law reviews, and monographs. It seemed at one time as if I were to be crushed under the mass of jurisprudence. I had much ado to find elbow-room. But this was a trifle in comparison with the bore of going through hundreds of pages, only to be no wiser than before. The more I read, the less apparently I knew. After three or four weeks of such disagreeable drudgery, I reached one conclusion, satisfactory to me at least. No two writers on the subject held the same opinion. Consequently, where doctors disagreed so flagrantly, a would-be doctor must have the right to think and write pretty much what he pleased. If the knot could not be untied, at all events it could be cut. Rejecting other works of reference as irrelevant and confused, I settled upon two or three, that had the merit of being clear and to the point, namely, two dissertations by Wächter (one in the *Civil-Archiv,* vol. xxxiv, the other a separate monograph, with the title, *doctr. de cond. causa data c. n. s.*), Erxleben's elaborate work on the *condictiones,* and Vangerow's Pandects, vol. iii, p. 228-242. I then endeavored to construct a plausible theory, by patching together Erxleben and Wächter (who is followed by Vangerow). I assumed that there was a contradiction, an antinomy, between Celsus and Paulus. The former, who lived in the times of Domitian, Nerva, and Hadrian, represented the older stage of the law, before the theory of the "nameless contracts" had been fully developed; whereas Paulus, who lived in the times of Septimius Severus and Alexander (and with Paulus, the emperors Diocletian and Maximus), looked upon such "nameless contracts" as analogous to the regular ones, namely, sale, hiring, loan, and the like. From the point of view of Celsus, the "nameless" contracts were scarcely contracts at all. There remained one point still unsettled. Assuming that Celsus and Paulus represented, then, successive stages in the development of the law, how did it happen that Justinian's Commission, who were appointed to prepare a digest of the law actually in force in the sixth century, *i. e.*, much later still, could commit the blunder of incorporating in their work two such conflicting views. In Justinian's time the old forms of *mancipatio* and *in jure cessio* had disappeared; there was no longer any distinction between *res mancipi* and *res nec mancipi*; the distinction between a contract of sale and a contract of exchange (with or without transfer of full ownership, *dominium*) was reduced to a minimum. On this point I followed the interpretation of Beloïus, Wächter, and Vangerow, who take the phrase *si mortuus est Stichus* to mean, if Stichus is dead at the time the money is received. Had the phrase been intended, says Vangerow, to state that Stichus died after the money was paid, it should have been worded *si morietur*. According to this interpretation, the passage comes under the general provision of the Roman Law, that an agreement based upon a performance which is impossible at the time, never becomes perfect. The only difference between a contract of sale and a *contractus innominatus* is, that the impossibility in the former case must exist at the time of the verbal agreement; in the latter case, at the time when one party begins to perform his share.

Having thus taken my position, the labor of mere composition became comparatively easy. I wrote off the dissertation in a few days, combatting hostile opinions as vigorously as possible, and fortifying my own statements with liberal quotations and references. The dissertation itself is, of course, on file in the archives at Göttingen, where, I trust, it will remain to accumulate the dust of ages in undisturbed repose. I have in my possession only the original notes of study and the rough draft. Judging from them, I should say that the dissertation filled twenty-five to thirty pages of legal cap. It would have been an easy thing to double, or perhaps treble, its length. But it seemed to me that the examiners would prefer a succinct, straightforward statement of opinion, something homogeneous in structure, and not loaded down with superfluous matter. The prime object of the dissertation, I took it, was to give evidence that the writer had been over the entire ground and understood the question in all its bearings. This view was the correct one.

Doubtless the reader has been bored more or less by the discussion of this notorious lex 16 D. "*dedi tibi pecuniam.*" I suspect that the above analysis will not be more than half intelligible, even to one familiar with the mysteries of the Common Law. Were it my object to produce a pleasing personal narrative merely, I should omit this part altogether. But as my object is rather to show precisely how students in a German university work, and what is expected of them, I do not feel at liberty to pass over in silence any essential part of my university course. It is well for the reader to know that the faculty, in admitting a candidate to examination, will not hesitate to set him very puzzling theses. And it will also be well to call the reader's attention, in this practical way, to one important circumstance in connection with the Roman Law. I mean the danger, not to say the senselessness, of making random quotations from the *corpus juris*. It is a work like many others, like the Bible itself, a work long and broad and deep, the product of many minds and many generations of minds, bristling with difficulties of interpretation, yet — to one who approaches it with due preparation — a work from which rare truth can be extracted; but only by one who has had due preparation. To the amateur civilian, the dilettante in Roman Law, the *corpus juris* is a book from which he can prove anything, and consequently nothing. There are many passages which are penned in the simplest Latin, and are intelligible to every reader; but they are interspersed with others that demand the widest collateral research. One who has not studied the Roman Law as a system can never be sure what sort of a passage he may have before him. No less a person than Blackstone himself is a signal instance of such blundering. The learned English judge is fond of ventilating here and there his would-be knowledge of the Roman Law. Coming to the study of the *Commentaries* fresh from my training in Göttingen, I was struck, nay more, thunderstruck, with Blackstone's ignorance. It is scarcely going too far to say that Blackstone, in a majority of the cases where he ventures upon some statement of Roman Law, is not only wrong, but grossly wrong; so far out of the way, indeed, that one wonders how he could possibly have fallen into such a predicament. On the other hand, Chancellor Kent, who studied the Roman Law carefully and systematically, is a safe guide to follow. Knowing that law as an expert, not as an amateur, he has succeeded in applying its principles to the elucidation of our English system with a sureness of insight and a breadth of vision that may possibly be rivaled by some future disciple, but will never be surpassed.

The full text of the citation from the *corpus juris canonici* runs as follows:

"*Non est a vobis (sicut arbitramur) incognitum qualiter Rex Anglorum pro discordia, quae inter ipsum et filios suos est suborta, uxores eorum detineat. Nos itaque attendentes justum et honestum esse ut viri suas petant uxores, mandamus, quatenus eundem Regem ad eas restituendas solicietè moneatis: et si juxta commonitionem vestram filiis suis uxores suas intra certum terminum non restituerit, ex tunc in quacumque provinciarum detinentur vel transferuntur donec ibi fuerint, nulla divina officia (praeter Baptismum parvulorum et poenitentias morientium) celebretis nec permittatis aliquatenus celebrari."*

Alex. III., papa, archiepiscopis, episcopis et aliis praelatis per Angliam constitutis.

After reading the passage carefully, to make sure of getting the exact meaning, I could not restrain an ejaculation of amazement. The papal message was clear enough, but, in the name of Alexander and all the other Popes, what was I to do with it? It furnished no materials for an argument, it did not conflict with any known principle of the mediæval church. How, then, was it to be expanded into the dimensions of a respectable essay? Or was the passage, apparently so simple, in reality a snare, a trap laid for me by the examiners? I studied it again and again, but could discover nothing that forced me to alter my first impression.

In this quandary, I submitted the passage to Dr. Maxen. He laughed over it after his usual fashion, and said: "That's easy enough. There is no trap in the passage The examiners have only given you an opportunity to display your historical knowledge. Consult Gonsalez Tellez and the text-books on the Interdict, and don't spare *padding*." Relieved by this assurance, I began work in earnest. The great Spanish commentator,

Gonsalez Tellez, to whom students of the *corpus juris canonici* can never be sufficiently grateful for his life-long labors, had treated the passage, I discovered, at length, in his fourth volume. From him I gathered the facts of the case. Henry II., that most amiable of English rulers, always in hot water either with the clergy or the nobility or his own family, had quarreled with his three sons, Henry, Richard and Godfrey. Thereupon the sons had set up the standard of revolt in the then English province of Aquitaine. To punish them and compel them to lay down their arms, the King seized and held their wives as hostages. The husbands appealed to the papal chair and succeeded in obtaining the decree in question, wherein the Pope, by virtue of his authority as God's vicegerent upon earth, enjoins the King to desist from his crime of attempting to put asunder what God has plainly joined. The archbishops (of York and Canterbury), the bishops, and the other clergy of England, are to induce the King, if possible, to restore the wives. But if their admonitions are of no avail, they are to pronounce over every province in which the wives are detained, or to which they may be removed, the great Interdict.

The first point in my dissertation was to discuss in full the Roman Catholic theory of punishment. The means of discipline are divided into two general classes: the *poenitentiae* (more correctly, *exercitia poenitentiae*, penance), and the *poenae*. The former, *poenitentiae*, are imposed upon the sinner who is already awakened to a consciousness of his guilt and seeks voluntarily to be reconciled with the church. The *poenae*, on the other hand, apply to the still impenitent. They are subdivided into *censurae* and *poenae* proper. The *censurae* serve as deterrents, to recall the sinner from his evil course, to compel him, as it were, to reconciliation. Hence they are also called *poenae medicinales*. The *poenae* proper are true punishments, inflicted to avenge the violation of holy law, and are called *poenae vindicativae*. They consist in imprisonment, flagellation, fines, degradation from the priestly office, and the like.

The *censurae* or *poenae medicinales* are of two kinds: the excommunication and the interdict. The excommunication may be either *minor* or *major*. The minor excommunication excludes the sinner from participating in the sacraments of the church. The major cuts him off from all church exercises; he cannot be buried in consecrated ground or with the ordinary ceremonies; his name cannot be mentioned in the prayers of the church, he cannot appear in court, either in his own behalf or in behalf of others, and he may be declared an outlaw. He can hold no intercourse with the faithful; in the words of the mediæval verse,

Os, orare, vale, communio, mensa negatur.

The interdict is a general suspension of church exercises, and not merely an exclusion of one or more persons from participating in them. It may be *local*, or *personal*, or *deambulatory*, as in the present case. The interdict, again, may be general or special, according as a whole district or only a single church is affected by it.

The excommunication strikes at the offender alone; the interdict, on the other hand, involves both the guilty and the innocent in the same punishment. The history of the excommunication dates from the earliest times of the Christian church, its institution being based upon the utterance contained in Matt. xvi. 17, in connection with 1 Cor. v. 5, and other passages. In excluding the sinner from communion with the faithful, the church (Catholic and Protestant as well) simply exercises a right common to all societies, namely, that of rejecting an unworthy member. With the interdict, the case is different. So long as the church was missionary and militant, engaged in the work of converting pagan Europe, the interdict was a weapon likely to do more harm than good. Although a few obscure instances are mentioned in the earlier centuries of the Christian era, the interdict, as a system of terrorism, was not fairly developed until the Middle Ages, that is to say, until the church had become the *ecclesia triumphans* and aspired to rule not only things spiritual but things temporal. An excommunicated sovereign could easily find ways and means of evading the penalties of the sentence and compelling the obedience of his subjects. But where the interdict was pronounced over his land, suspending all, or almost all, the public and private exercises of divine worship, the pressure brought to bear upon high and low was too great to be resisted. Every one felt a keen and direct interest in bringing about a reconciliation between the offending ruler and the offended church. The interdict thus became the chosen weapon of the mediæval Popes, the thunderbolt by which an Innocent or a Gregory struck down rebellious princes. Hurter, in his *Life of Innocent III.*, has a long and eloquent passage descriptive of the operation of the interdict suspended by that Pope over France because of the refusal of Philip to separate from his mistress, the celebrated Agnes of Meran. I give a few extracts, in paraphrase rather than in literal translation.

"Life, in all its higher phases, appeared dissevered from the church. The radiance of consecration was dimmed, earthly existence without communication with the heavenly. True, the new-born child was still received into the covenant of God, but only furtively, as it were; the day that else called forth joy and exultation from the parents' breast, now passed in mournful silence. The bond of matrimony was entered into, not before the altar, but over the grave, as by those worthy of death. The guilt-laden conscience was not lightened by confession and absolution, the weary were not cheered by the preaching of the word, the hungry not fed with the body of the Lord. Only from the steps of the church, and only on Sunday, was the priest allowed to exhort the people to repentance. Only in secret, with the faint hope of God's mercy, did the dying man receive the viaticum. But the last unction, consecrated ground, even funeral rites were denied him. Friend could not bury friend, children could not cover their parents with so much as a handful of earth, the corpse of the nobleman found no more favor than the corpse of the beggar."

After thus discussing the nature of church censure and its efficacy in the Middle Ages, I proceeded to show that according to the Roman Law (notwithstanding its *patria potestas*), the English, and the Canon Law, the son had a right to the undisturbed possession of his wife, even as against his own father. The act of Henry II., in seizing a wife as hostage for the misdeeds of the husband, conceding that the revolt was a misdeed, clearly contravened every known system of law and justice.* It was simply an act of arbitrary power, against which, coming as it did from the supreme ruler of England, the aggrieved husbands had no redress. They appealed to the Pope, as the judge of kings, to interfere in behalf of human right and divine law. Assuming that there was no complicity on the part of the wives, I took the broad ground that, in accordance with the spirit of the times, the stretch of papal power was in this instance, if ever, fully justified. There was scarcely any other way of reaching a sovereign like Henry II.

One point, which interested me more than all the others, I had to leave undecided. It was this, whether the threatened interdict was actually carried out, or remained a mere *brutum fulmen*. The Göttingen library is very rich in works of history; I ransacked the English department diligently, but did not succeed in finding an allusion either to the Papal threat or to any influence that it might have had upon the peaceable adjustment of

---

* Especially the English law, which, in some instances, even exonerates the wife as an accomplice, on the presumption that she has acted under marital compulsion.

the domestic quarrels of Henry II. In such researches, success is largely dependent upon the amount of time at one's disposal. After hunting over fifty or a hundred ponderous old folios in English, French and German, grim with dust and cobwebs, and boring the amiable assistant librarian, I dropped the attempt. Should any of my readers feel disposed to take it up, I wish him all success.

The dissertations thus disposed of, I suffered them to lie idle a while with a view to making verbal emendations from time to time, before submitting them to the dean, and turned my energies to the distasteful but indispensable labor of "cramming." The recollection of the days and weeks spent in this monotonous process makes me feel, even at the present day, unspeakably discomforted. What should have been spread over four or five months, and taken in homœopathic doses, had to be devoured in a few weeks. If there be one thing more than another to which I am opposed, on general principles, it is "cramming" for an examination. Not only is the brain worn out by the effort to master mere words and forms, but the chances are that when the object is attained, the examination over, one's dearly bought knowledge will slip away nearly as fast as it came. The task before me was not to learn any thing new, to develop new principles, to follow out some line of independent investigation, but to drum into my head definitions, names, dates, subdivisions of topics, exceptions, so as to be able to recite them glibly. This, of course, was not to be all the examination. But it would be undoubtedly a prominent part. Had I been able to prolong my stay until spring, I should have made things easier, by combining memorizing with collateral reading. As it was, I had to make the best of my limited time. The examiners, I knew, expected me to be thoroughly informed on certain subjects. Inasmuch as my examination would not cover the entire range of the law, but only so much as came under Roman and ecclesiastical jurisprudence, it behooved me to work up that portion all the more thoroughly, and thus prove to the examiners that they had not acted indiscreetly in giving me a trial. Being favored, I was under especial obligations. So I sacrificed my general principles to the needs of the situation, and "crammed" to the best of my ability.

As has been already mentioned, I had reduced my notes and portions of certain text-books to a compact and manageable shape. Allowing ten hours a day for four weeks, I drew up an elaborate schedule of study. So many hours or portions of hours every day were assigned to this topic, so many to that. I learned everything by heart, by sheer dint of repetition. Not being endowed by nature with a good memory, I had to proceed slowly and very systematically, catechizing myself at every step. The three main subjects were *Erbrecht*, Criminal Law, and Ecclesiastical Law. To the first I gave two hours and a half every day, to the two others two hours each. The remaining three hours and a half were split up in miscellaneous cram. The process was anything but an intellectual one. It consisted in going over the memoranda again and again until I had made sure of every point.

At the end of three or four weeks, I was surprised to see how much progress I had made, and how the memory had trained itself to retain names and dates and divisions. No one can realize the extent to which the memory can be trained, until he has tried for himself the experiment of memorizing an extensive and complicated subject. At first, the attempt seems hopeless. Names and rules slip in by the eyes and out again by the ears. What was learned one day, is forgotten the next. But the reader, if he does not know it already through his own experience, may take my word for it, that there will come a time when the knowledge *sticks*. Minor points may need occasional revision, but the solid frame-work of the subject will acquire a firm foothold in the memory. The subject itself has passed into the student's mind, it forms part and parcel of his very being, and cannot be dislodged, not even at will. What has been "crammed" into the memory, haunts the crammer like Banquo's ghost, thrusting up its hateful head on the most unseasonable occasions. At this stage of the work, it is a problem to decide whether the student has mastered the subject, or the subject the student.

By the middle of October, but for one unfortunate circumstance, I might have announced myself ready for the examination. The labor was substantially over. I had learned by heart all that had come to me in the shape of lectures on *Erbrecht*, Criminal Law,

Ecclesiastical Law, the History of Roman Jurisprudence, and was prepared to venture on the general principles of the Pandects. Francke's lectures, in particular, on *Erbrecht*, I had mastered so thoroughly as to be able to recite them from beginning to end, backwards or forwards, or to start in the middle and go both ways at once. It gave me a certain amount of pleasure to imagine that I was thus getting the better of one who had expressly declared his disbelief in my attainments. There was no ground for anticipating unfair treatment in the examination from any one, but there was ground for believing that from Francke I should get justice untempered with mercy. Accordingly, the uppermost thought in my mind for months was this: With the other examiners I may make a slip here and there, but with him I must and will answer every question. In this there was no feeling of personal animosity. On the contrary, I had the greatest respect for Francke as a man, and regarded his lectures as wonderfully clear and to the point. The oftener I reviewed them, the greater became my admiration for the intellect that had planned them. Were I a jurist in Germany, I should cherish my notes of those lectures as a *vade mecum* for the most subtle and knotty branch of all jurisprudence. Besides, a sense of justice forced me to admit that, taken at his point of view, he might be right. I was not, in strictness, entitled to an examination; he might have reason to suppose that one who had studied less than the usual time must be unprepared. I felt no resentment, therefore, but I was piqued and put on my mettle. In an American college there is friction enough, as every one knows, between professor and student, but it arises from personal dislike, and assumes a very petty shape. As our examinations are usually conducted in writing, each member of the class having the same questions, it would not be easy for the examiner, even if so disposed, to treat any one student unfairly. To do so, he would have to close his eyes willfully and heinously to the written paper before him. But in an oral examination, which lasts several hours, and in which the examiner has a free choice of questions, this element of personal antagonism may become a serious matter. The candidate who has reason to suspect that one or more examiners are opposed to him, must prepare himself with the utmost care. In law there is a certain latitude of opinion, but not nearly so much as in medicine, for instance, or philosophy, or history. It happens not unfrequently that the candidate in one of these branches, holding views differing from those of the examiner, will work up some controverted topic most elaborately, and turn the examination into a sort of word-duel between himself and the examiner. Nor does the examiner always come out from such an encounter the victor. An old-fogy professor — such men exist even in Germany — may be ridden completely out of the field by some half-developed Wolff, or Heyne. My ambition did not aspire to such a feat. All that I could aim at was to know thoroughly what every student should know, and answer legitimate questions promptly.

CHAPTER XIV.

Examination.

THE unfortunate circumstance that prevented my entering the examination by the middle of October was one that has frustrated many a well laid scheme of " mice and men." I broke down in health. For six months I had worked under what engineers would call a pressure of fifty pounds to the square inch. All through the enervating weather of spring and the depressing heat of the dog-days, I had slaved over books and notes, eight and ten and twelve hours a day, without a rest, without even a break in the dull monotony, and now nature resented the outrage. What injured me was not so much the amount of work performed, but the feverish haste with which it was driven, and the want of variety. I have studied quite as assiduously on more than one occasion since, without feeling the worse for it. But then I was not cramming for examination!

The week before the opening of the winter semester, I began to be conscious of a total want of energy, and an inability to keep my mind fixed on one subject for longer than half an hour. I could neither sleep by night nor rest by day, and was nervous to the last degree. It became evident to me that this was no fit state of mind or body in which to encounter a severe examination. The nervousness assumed such a violent shape that I suspected an attack of chills and fever, or possibly something worse. The physician, however, assured me that it was only a temporary prostration, and could be cured by rest and change of air, but by nothing else. To attempt to go on with my work would be downright madness.

Fortunately no day had yet been set for the examination, neither were there many candidates at that time. Both Ribbentropp and Kraut, whom I consulted more as friends than as professors, advised me by all means to drop everything and take a vacation. "It will make very little, if any, difference to us," they said, "whether you are examined in October or in November. In fact, the delay will rather suit us, because it will give us more time for working off prior applications. Hand in your dissertations, which we can then read at our leisure, take a holiday of a fortnight or more, and when you are back, inform us of your return. The rest can be easily arranged."

Accordingly I put the finishing touches to the dissertations, returned two or three basketfuls of books to the library, and turned my back upon Göttingen and the *corpus juris*. Having numerous friends at Heidelberg, I made that my first object-point. It mattered nothing to me where I went, so long as I could enjoy myself. No sooner had I taken my seat in the night express, than a heavy load seemed to roll off my mind.

Even the eight or nine hours of jolting and two changes of cars were welcome. Anything was better than books. The Heidelberg friends received me warmly. As it was only the beginning of the semester, they were not pressed for time. One or two *Kneipen* were arranged in honor of the guest, who had nothing to do but wander about from room to room, talking over old times, or to ramble over the castle and up to the Kaiserstuhl. One excursion, in particular, I shall never forget. On a glorious October day four of us set out in an open coach for the famous gardens of Schwetzingen. The road, after leaving the outskirts of Heidelberg, follows a straight line for five miles. It serves, I believe, as the base-line for the trigonometrical survey of this part of the Grand Duchy. Under ordinary circumstances, a straight line cannot be regarded as picturesque. But when it traverses rich fields filled with fruit-trees that bend under their load of golden fruit, so that the air is heavy with the fragrance, and you yourself, a prisoner snatching a brief respite from drudgery and confinement, are rolling along it in company with three jovial friends, you will be apt to take the good things of nature as they come, and not find fault with trifles.

The arch-ducal gardens of Schwetzingen, begun about the middle of the eighteenth century by the Prince Electoral Charles Louis, are on a large scale. They cover 186 *Morgen* of land. (A *Morgen* is about an acre.) The inner, or older, portion is laid out in the French style, in broad alleys, crossing each other at right angles, and lined with limes and orange trees in large wooden holders. At the crossings of the alleys are statues and statuettes, figures of nymphs, naiads, dragons, and other quaint garden devices of the order Louis Quatorze. To my taste there is nothing so disagreeable of its kind as a French garden on a small scale. It suggests the attempt to squeeze nature into a straight-jacket tricked out with finery. But on a generous scale, where the alleys are thirty and forty feet broad and hundreds of feet in length, the limes well grown and meeting at the tops, the vista closing in every direction with bubbling fountains, the French garden, more correctly called a park, is a consummate work of art. It shows off nature to advantage. The more so if, as is the case at Schwetzingen, the French part is surrounded and relieved by the charming irregularity of the so called English garden. The contrast of the two styles was to me something inexpressibly fascinating. In the English part, which is of much later date, the trees are chiefly horsechestnuts. On the particular day of which I write, the ground was covered with chestnuts and burrs. As we rambled through the winding alleys, we gathered chestnuts by the hatful and pelted one another in mimic warfare. What with this amusement, playing leap-frog, and getting up foot-races and jumping-matches, we behaved more like American Freshmen than dignified Heidelberg and Göttingen *Burschen.* There is not a little to see at Schwetzingen. The castle is usually open to visitors; then there is the Mosque, the Temple of Minerva, the Temple of Mercury, the colossal statues, the "Rhine" and the "Danube." But these did not interest me much. I cared only for the open air, the fresh turf, the fountains and miniature lakes, the grand old forest trees. I forgot Pandects and dissertations utterly, and did not even mourn the loss.

After a week thus spent in and around Heidelberg, I induced one of my friends to join me in a flying trip to Strassburg. We spent two or three days in exploring the wonderful cathedral, which is to me the most interesting in Europe. Standing almost under the great Rose-window, and letting the eye sweep down the aisle, one can trace, step by step, the development of the ogival, so called Gothic, style of architecture. The crypt, choir and part of the transept are still Basilican; the rest of the transept is early Gothic, the nave is Gothic in its prime, the part around the Rose is Gothic on the decline. The tomb of Marshal Saxe, in the Church of St. Thomas, is a charming allegorical group, in marble, life-size, commemorating the exploits of the great general of Louis XV. The marshal is descending to the tomb, conducted by France, a young woman in tears. Stalwart nude figures, crouching in fetters, symbolize the conquered nations.

Besides the objects of art in Strassburg, I became much interested in studying the mixed character of the population. I never could make out quite to my own satisfaction whether the person with whom I chanced to be speaking was French or German. Everybody seemed to use both languages with equal fluency and equal inelegance. By the third day, I began to speak polyglot myself, commencing a sentence in French and ending in German. The tone of the place was French. The hotels, cafés, public gardens were conducted after the French fashion. But it seemed to me, even then, that while the surface polish came from France, the substance was German. Now that Alsace is "restored," as the Germans say, the tendency among English and Americans is to look upon the annexation as a deed of violence that cries aloud to heaven, and to join the French in bewailing the hard lot of the "reconstructed" Alsatians. For my part, I certainly do not blame the French for taking the loss of a valuable province to heart. But whether they will ever recover it, whether, indeed, they ought to recover it, is another matter. Historic rights and wrongs aside, one thing is very certain. There is an underlying element in Strassburg and throughout Alsace that is essentially German, and can be incorporated in time into the German body politic. Given twenty years of undisturbed possession, with German schools, a German university, a German military service, the Hohenzollern dynasty may abide the French onslaught with the utmost composure. I hazard the prediction that, should war be renewed, the Alsatians will be found among the hardest fighters on the German side.*

---

* Goethe's account of his student-life in Strassburg and his flirtation at Sesenheim (given in *Wahrheit und Dichtung*), throws a strong light upon the thoroughly German character of the Alsatians and their mode of life at the middle of the eighteenth century. It is only after the Revolution had done its work of demolition and reconstruction that we observe the French putting forward any claims to having *Gallicised* their Rhine provinces.

The fortnight of vacation passed in this way only too rapidly. I bade my Heidelberg friends a last farewell and returned to Göttingen by the end of the month, determined to "go in" this time, and put an end to the uncertainty. At all events I was physically ready for the examination. Health and spirits were never better. My dissertations had been read and approved. The day of examination was fixed for the third Saturday in November, at four in the afternoon. The delay seemed almost too long, so great was my anxiety to reach a decision. However, there was nothing to do but to wait and work. Invigorated in mind and body, I took up once more the books and "cram" that had lain neglected on their shelves. There came over me one of those spells which the poets call inspiration. I worked as I had never done before. Everything was easy to me. Definitions, dates, names, intricate subdivisions were like child's play. So far from having forgotten anything, it seemed actually as if memory and judgment had continued to operate, unconsciously, all the while that I had been idling in Heidelberg and Strassburg. In the first two weeks of November, I reviewed the entire summer's work and made it thoroughly my own. The ten hours' reading a day was a pastime rather than a toil.

It was the Monday before the all-important Saturday. Wishing to go into the examination fresh, yet unwilling to fritter away the time, I devised the following plan for letting myself down gradually to do-nothingism. On that day I limited myself to eight hours, on Tuesday to six, on Wednesday to four, on Thursday to two. Friday was spent in sorting papers, answering letters, and disposing of odds and ends of business. A long walk in the afternoon and an inordinately long night's rest completed my preparation.

The morning of Saturday was dull and threatened rain. I lounged about the Museum, reading the papers and playing a few games of billiards. The excitement of the game was just enough to banish from my mind for the while all unpleasant ideas of examination. After dinner the clouds lifted for an hour or two and the sun came out warm. The opportunity for a turn around the wall was too good to be neglected.

I had been careful to keep the time of the approaching examination a secret. Nobody, as I supposed, but myself, the faculty, and the beadle knew of the precise day and hour. I had no desire to be congratulated too soon, only to be commiserated too late. Before three o'clock I was back in my room, dressing for the encounter. Perhaps the reader will smile at the idea of a student dressing for examination. But then Germany and America differ on this point, as they do on so many others. A university examination for degrees is a matter of ceremony. The professors come in full dress, and expect the candidate to do the same. Swallow-tail coat, silk hat, white cravat and white kid gloves are *de rigueur*. A sponge-bath,— which is *not* a part of any German official programme,— fortified me for wearing the swallow-tail with an equanimity that was as gratifying as it was surprising. Buttoning my overcoat up to the chin, so as to conceal my white cravat from prying glances, I slipped out of the house as quietly as possible and strolled down the Wende street toward the residence of the dean, Hofrath Kraut, looking in at the shop windows for new books. By this time the sun had disappeared, the brief winter twilight of North Germany had also disappeared, and the street was almost as dark as night. It was not very difficult, then, to avoid friends and acquaintances.

While waiting in the ante-room of the Hofrath's apartments, my equanimity was upset by one of the minor trials of life. White kid gloves are made in Germany to tear. One of mine, the left-hand, tore across the palm from side to side, when I attempted to pull it on. Necessity, it is well known, is the mother of invention. I used my left hand for holding my hat! The only drawback to the expedient was that it compelled me to retain the same position of the hand for three hours, no small item in an examination.

At four o'clock, punctually, the door of the Hofrath's study opened, and the beadle ushered me into the august presence of the examiners. Like myself, they were in grand toilet, seated in a sort of semi-circle facing the door, and looking quite unconcerned. An unoccupied chair stood in the center of the circle. Off in one corner was a small table; on it were two or three bottles of wine and a basket of cake. The festive aspect of the room suggested a reception rather than an examination. After I had bowed to the company in general and shaken hands with them individually, the dean motioned to me be seated.

The examination was opened without preamble or ceremony, by the head of the faculty, the dean. Hofrath Kraut's specialty was German Law, but as that did not form a part of my examination, he took up Ecclesiastical Law. He detained me not quite half an hour, putting his questions deliberately but not slowly. They were not difficult in themselves, although requiring precision in the answering. Not one bore any reference to church discipline. The reader may take for granted that, should he venture into an oral examination before a German faculty, he will not be questioned directly upon the subject contained in his dissertation, but rather upon something having a distant relation to it. A friend of mine, who took his degree at Leipsic, wrote his dissertation upon Homeric Greek. Thinking that he would probably be called upon to translate difficult passages in the examination, he crammed the entire Iliad and Odyssey. It was a case of love's labor lost; he was asked to translate from the dramatists. My examination in Ecclesiastical Law covered the entire field of matrimony and matrimonial rights and obligations, the mode of contracting marriage according to the early Roman Law, according to the law of the Empire, according to the practice of the early Church, according to the council of Trent, according to the Code Napoleon. I was called upon to state the Catholic theory of marriage as a sacrament, and the obstacles to marriage between certain parties, the *impedimentum aetatis, erroris, vis ac metus, cognationis,* and the like, the papal dispensations, divorce *a vinculo, a mensa et thoro.* The next topic was the nature of the priesthood in the Catholic church and in the Protestant, the right of patronage (advowsons), and the composition of the *corpus juris canonici clausum.* The chief difficulty that I labored under arose from the circumstance that Hofrath Kraut was slightly deaf. This obliged me to raise my voice more than was pleasant. The questions, I have said, were not hard, that is to say, they did not demand original thinking. But they were precisely worded and called for exact knowledge. A candidate who had not studied faithfully Herrmann's lectures or their equivalent, could not have answered more than one in three, possibly four. I missed a name or date now and then, but in the main was satisfied. When the Hofrath had finished, I felt that if the rest were no worse, I should pass with a margin.

The next examiner was Ribbentropp. His questions were much sharper than I had anticipated from one who had proved himself such a good friend. Perhaps the *Geheimjustizrath* had confidence in his protege's claims and wished to demonstrate to some of his colleagues that his partiality was not without foundation. Of course I did not get a single question on the *contractus innominatus* or the *condictiones.* But I was questioned most unmercifully on the general theory of contracts, upon suspensive and abrogating conditions, upon times and terms, and especially upon the contract of sale. Had I been writing a monograph on the subject, I could not have been called upon for more exact and detailed statements. Suddenly the topic was changed, and we were in the midst of the rights of real property. I had to give all that I knew or was supposed to know of the ways of acquiring and losing real property, from the laws of the XII Tables down to the codification of Justinian. This led to the servitudes (easements) of the Roman Law, their classification, their nature in general and in particular, and their operation. The questions came so fast that I had barely time to answer them. Perceiving that it was the examiner's intention to cover as much ground as possible, I deemed it expedient to assist him. Accordingly I wasted no time by asking for the repetition of a question; if unable to hit upon the answer at once, I said simply: do not know, cannot say. It became evident that this mode of procedure was well received. Nothing can be more exasperating to an examiner than the suspicion that the examinee is "beating about the bush," or "fighting against time." In an oral examination, if you do not know a thing at once, the chances are ten to one that you will not know it at all, and the more you talk, the deeper you sink in the mire. Having, in my turn, examined scores of young men, I can say frankly that to the examiner a prompt, honest "Don't know," is worth a dozen "Can't understand the question." The trouble is not with the question, but with the answer.

It was quarter past five. The Pandects had "blown" me a trifle. The dean, probably suspecting as much, said, with a good-natured smile: "We will now make a little pause." Going to the table, he filled the glasses with wine. The professors helped themselves liberally, and enjoyed the refreshments with a gusto that seemed to me rather cold-blooded. In such cases, it makes all the difference whether one examines, or is examined. Feeling that under the circumstances a drop might be a bottle too much, I declined the proffered wine, and contented myself with cake and water. At all events, the relaxation was very acceptable.

The pause did not last longer than five minutes. The third examiner was Zachariae, in Criminal Law. His questions, like those of Kraut, were not difficult, and were put even more deliberately. They were mainly upon the general theory of the right of punishment, the criticism of the Roman system, the views of Beccaria, Rossi, Bentham, Abegg, Feuerbach, and Mittermaier, the doctrine of punishment as a divine ordinance, the *lex talionis*, the theory of expiation, prevention, determent, reformation, self-preservation on the part of society. The nature and kinds of punishment, the death penalty, imprisonment, fines, the several penitentiary systems in force in Europe and the United States, the definition of criminal intent and criminal negligence completed the examination. At one question I suppressed with difficulty a smile. "Can you give me the precise meaning of *crimen*, as it is used in the *corpus juris?*" Ans. "The word denotes the *Strafsache* (the indictment and trial, procedure), rather than the criminal act itself. This latter is designated by the Roman jurists by the terms *delictum, maleficium, scelus,* and the like." In themselves considered, there was nothing about either question or answer to provoke risibility. The joke lay in the circumstance that I knew long before the examination that this particular question would be given. It had occurred in Dr. Maxen's Repetitorium, and the doctor warned us at the time, saying: "If any of you are examined by Zachariae, be sure that you know what *crimen* is. It is one of his hobbies."

So far, so well. But the two remaining examiners were the ones most to be dreaded. Francke opened the interesting field of *Erbrecht*. It was evident from his manner, and from the first few questions, that he meant to be thorough. Forewarned, however, is forearmed. During the forty-five or fifty minutes that he kept me on the "anxious-bench," I was sustained by one, and only one, reflection. It was this: Treat me fairly; give me such questions as ought to be given; examine me only on things that you yourself have explained, and I ask no favor. You shall have an answer to every question. And such was the case. The examination was very long and exhaustive. Each question came as quick and searching as though the examiner himself were in doubt and sought for information. The following specimen may suffice.

Q. What were the formal requirements of a private*

---

* *Private*, as distinguished from a will entered as a public act in the record of a court.

will, according to the law of the times of Justinian, as concerned the witnesses?

A. They must be seven in number.

Q. Who are incapable of acting as witnesses?

A. Women, the deaf, dumb, *furiosi, impuberes, prodigi* (legally declared spendthrifts), the blind, the *filius familias* of the testator, the one instituted as *heres*, and whoever is united with him in *patria potestas*.

Q. No matter about the others. What do you mean by the *rogatio testis?*

A. The witness must be asked to serve as such, that is, he must know that the act performed before him is the making of a will and not some other transaction.

Q. Continue your enumeration of the requirements.

A. The witnesses must be in the presence of the testator, must be situated so as to be able to see and hear all that is going on.

Q. What is the *unitas actus et temporis?*

A. It means that the act shall not be interrupted.

Q. When does it end? Any time specified?

A. Not until the testament is completed according to the full intent of the testator.

Q. What do you mean by a *suus heres?*

A. Whoever, as son or grandson (through the son), was in the *potestas* of the will-maker, the deceased, and became at his death *sui juris*.

Q. What were the claims of a *suus heres?*

A. He must be either instituted heir or expressly disinherited.

Q. To what particular share of the estate was he entitled?

A. To none. The testator could leave him as much or as little as he saw fit, only it must be something.

Q. Could any conditions be imposed upon a *suus heres?*

A. No, unless coupled with the alternative of express disinheritance.

Q. Who can make a will?

A. In general, any one.

Q. Who cannot make a will?

A. Whoever can have no property of his own.

Q. Whom do you mean by that?

A. A son, for instance, in the *potestas* of his father.

Q. Is every one *sui juris* entitled to make a will?

A. No. *Impuberes, prodigi,* deaf-mutes (born such).

Q. Can a person simply deaf or simply mute make a will?

A. Yes, according to Justinian, but only in writing.

Q. And deaf-mutes not born such?

A. The testament must be altogether in the testator's own handwriting.

Fifty minutes of such questioning are enough to shake any candidate who is not rooted and grounded in the faith. The close of Francke's examination was rather peculiar.

Q. What are the liabilities of one who has entered into the possession of an inheritance (*hereditas*) in good faith (*bona fide*), supposing that he was the lawful heir (*heres*), and is afterward sued by the real heir?

A. He is liable only for so much of the inheritance as actually remains in his possession, *in id quod locupletior factus est.*

Q. He is not liable, then, for what he has spent or wasted?

A. No; not if he has acted in good faith that he was the heir.

Q. Your answer is correct. Let me give you a practical case. A is in possession of an estate, supposing himself to be the sole heir. After several years, B comes forward and proves that he, B, is joint heir. In the meanwhile, A, leading a rather spendthrift life, has wasted half the estate. Can B say to A: You have spent your half of the estate; hand over to me now what is left, for that is my half?

I hesitated. The problem was wholly novel to me. I had certainly never met any thing resembling it, either in my books or lectures. Observing my hesitation, Francke said, rather sharply: "You understand me?" I replied: "Yes, I understand. B cannot claim this of A. If the two are joint heirs, they are joint heirs at all times. If part has been wasted in good faith, both bear the loss in equal shares. What is left must be divided between the two."

Breaking in so abruptly as to leave me scarcely time for finishing the sentence, he said, fixing his eyes full upon me: "Did you ever *read* any passage bearing upon this point?" I replied: "No; I answered on general principles." "Humph, humph," he said, "there *is* a pas-

*20

sage in the *corpus juris*, from Ulpian. You are right. That will do, sir."*

The fifth and last examiner, Briegleb, had things pretty much his own way. I had gone into the examination knowing that Procedure was the weak side of my preparation, and had supposed that I should be spared any questions touching upon the special developments of the Roman law in Germany. Had the examiner confined himself to the *Formular-process* (procedure by formulae) of the ante-Justinian law, he would have elicited more satisfactory answers. Instead of doing this, he dwelt, apparently with great delight, upon the theory of appeals according to the practice of the mediæval courts of the church, a matter about as familiar to me as were the laws of Manu. Fortunately Francke had consumed so much time with *Erbrecht*, that Briegleb had only twenty minutes left in which to punish me. I sat it out with as much grace as the circumstances would permit. After the excitement of Francke's examination was over, a decided reaction set in. I felt completely worn out, and answered almost listlessly, Don't know, to two questions in three.

About five or ten minutes past seven, Briegleb closed his examination. I withdrew to the ante-room, to await the decision. Over three hours, I muttered; they have not shown me much mercy. The suspense was almost intolerable. The ante-room was as much too cold as

---

* The words *heres*, *hereditas*, and *bona fide possessor* are technical terms of the Roman Law, for which we have no equivalents in English. The passage meant is, I believe, l. 25, § 15 D. de hered. pet. (v. 3.)

the other room had been too warm. What with anxiety, the consciousness of having done so poorly at the close, and the general reaction, I was overpowered by a nervous chill. The time of waiting was only five minutes, yet it dragged as though it had been as many hours. The beadle opened the door, and I was ushered once more into the presence of the judges, to listen to the sentence. They were all standing. The dean stepped forward and said, in a measured accent, as if to make sure of each word: "Candidate, in consideration of the dissertations submitted in writing, and of the oral examination just concluded, we, the faculty of degrees of the *Georgia Augusta*, have resolved to confer upon you the second degree, raised, *vera cum laude*. Permit me to congratulate you." With that, he extended his hand.

I took it mechanically. Had he told me that I had drawn the great prize in the Prussian lottery, my astonishment could not have been greater. The second degree raised? Was there not some mistake about it? The utmost that I had hoped for was to pass. But to take two degrees above pass, sounded incredible. That the reader may understand the point, I should state that the legal faculty of Göttingen distinguished three grades. The lowest was entitled simply *examine superato*. The one above it was entitled *examine cum laude superato*. The next in order was the *vera cum laude*. There was still another, nominally the first, called *insigniter*, or *post insignia exhibita specim na*. It was given, however, very seldom, and only to such candidates as displayed extraordinary knowledge, both in their examinations and in their dissertations. The last instance of its conferment had occurred eight or ten years before. Even had my work been twice as good as it was, it would not have entitled me to an *insigniter*, for the reason that it did not cover the entire field of jurisprudence. Practically, the examiners had conferred upon me the highest degree in their power.

Ribbentropp, who certainly showed his delight more than I did mine, patted me most paternally on the shoulder and whispered: "You did yourself credit. Come and see me to-morrow morning, at eleven. We will talk it up then." There was nothing more to do. I shook each examiner's hand in turn, muttered a few words of thanks, and fled. It seemed as though my head would burst with the pressure, unless I got a breath of fresh air. In a second I was out in the street, inhaling the cool November breeze and paying no heed to the scattering rain-drops. I hurried home, to shuffle off my ball-room costume and have some supper. Not even the successful candidate can live on air after such a trial of his powers of endurance. I felt famished.

But the greatest surprise was still to come. I should mention, by the way, that I was boarding once more with Frau H—, the landlady in whose house I had passed the first two semesters. All my friends and acquaintances knew, of course, that I was a candidate for degrees. But no one had been informed of the day fixed for the examination. That, I supposed, was a profound secret. Frau

H's parlor faced the head of the stairs. Let the reader imagine my bewilderment. As I stepped briskly and softly up the stairway, in the hope of turning down the side-passage and slipping into my room unobserved, the door opened and I was confronted with a blaze of light. The parlor was illuminated! All the candles and lamps in the house had been pressed into the service. The good Frau herself, her face beaming with delight, stood in the doorway. No sooner had I come fairly within reach, than she darted forward and seized both hands— "O, I congratulate you, I congratulate you, *Herr* Doctor. Come in!" Overcome by this unexpected welcome, I suffered myself to be dragged rather than led into the room. On the center-table was a huge cake. The icing bore the inscription of my name, the day, and the year. Around the rim of the cake was a wreath of laurel-leaves. The family were all there in honor of the occasion. Still tongue-tied with emotion, I thanked her as warmly as I could. "But," said I, "how did you know that this was the day?" "Never mind, that is my secret."* "Well then, if you decline to tell me that, perhaps you will inform me how you knew beforehand that I would pass. Suppose I had failed, what would you have done then with your cake and your laurel-wreath?" "*Ach Himmel!* As if any one could sit behind his books so long, only to fall through at last. No, no. We knew better. Besides, Dr. Maxen was sure that you would pass." "So the Doctor has been telling tales, has he?

---

* I suspected the Frau of bribing the beadle.

Well, I can forgive him this time. But just consider, Frau H——, that I haven't had anything to eat for more than six hours, and examination makes one frightfully hungry." So the cake was carefully put away, to be cut in due form the next day, at dinner, and a bountiful supper brought on, that made me feel once more quite at peace with the world.

The reader must suffer me to say a few additional words with reference to the examination as a whole. It impressed me as being throughout eminently fair. The questions were worded carefully, and although searching, and intended to be searching, they did not aim at "tripping" the candidate. The difficulty of the examination did not lie in any one question, but in the immense extent of the ground covered. An occasional slip was not taken into account. What the examiners evidently sought to ascertain was this: Has the candidate before us mastered the subject so as to be able to follow our interrogatories in every line that we may happen to strike? Does he possess a clear survey (*Uebersicht*) over the domain of jurisprudence, an accurate knowledge of general principles and the ability to apply them correctly? Does he hold what he possesses as his own, or is he liable to be disconcerted by any sudden approach? The examiners, as it seemed to me, displayed a high degree of skill in changing the topic as soon as they found that the candidate had his answers ready. In this way they succeeded in running over the entire ground. It was evident that they *knew how to examine.*

A second point to which I desire to call attention is this: <u>the great advantage of keeping cool.</u> An oral examination lasting three hours and more, going into the minutiae of two years' study, and driven at the top of the examiners' speed, is not merely a test of the candidate's knowledge but is a heavy strain upon his physique. The least shade of nervousness, the least touch of headache may lead to disastrous results. One who has his wits about him can, let the worst come to the worst, extricate himself from a predicament by intimating to the examiner that he concedes his ignorance on a certain point, but is ready to be questioned on something else. There is no harm done by this. Examiners are not inquisitors. The candidate must, under all circumstances, be able to give to himself in an instant a clear account of what he is saying. He must never suffer himself to be led from bad to worse. But where he begins to stumble, to talk confusedly, to take back what he has just said, and then repeat it, and then take it back again, he only makes his case hopeless. He forgets what he really knows, and tempts to impatience those who would otherwise treat him with the utmost consideration. Besides, one who is under perfect self-control is rather inspired than depressed by a searching examination. The questions act as a stimulus, developing to a surprising extent latent powers of memory and judgment. A fellow-countryman, who took his degree in medicine at Göttingen, narrated to me the following incident of his examination. After one or two preliminary questions on general physiology, the professor asked him for the chemical composition of the fatty acids. It was a difficult point, and one upon which he had not thought since leaving the chemical laboratory, upwards of two years before. For a moment he was non-plussed. But preserving his coolness and reflecting quietly but rapidly, he felt himself transplanted in imagination to the old lecture-room. He saw the blackboard before him, and upon it the formulae as they had been written out by the lecturer. He had only to read them off, by direct vision, as it were. The precision of his answer gave tone to all the rest of the examination.

But to do this, in fact to pass an examination with any degree of satisfaction and credit, one must be fresh in mind and fresh in body. The candidate who goes into the presence of the examiners tired out with "cramming," runs the risk of killing his chances. I speak on this point with the confidence of one who has been through the ordeal and knows what it is. Although my general health had suffered from excessively rapid preparation, yet on the day of examination itself, thanks to the scrupulous care with which my studies had been tapered down and the complete rest of the preceding twenty-four hours, I was enabled to meet the examiners with as much unconcern as if they had been a dinner-party of friends. No amount of coolness, it is true, will make one know what he does not know. But coolness, and coolness alone, will enable the candidate to show what he does know to the best advantage. At the risk of wearying the reader, I venture to give an illustration of the folly of neglecting the laws of health. Contemporaneous with myself at Göttingen was a law-student by the name of M——, from Bremen. He was unquestionably a remarkable man. His memory was something prodigious, and was surpassed only by his ambition and his capacity for work. He had studied the full term of six semesters, and had set his heart upon obtaining the rare distinction of an *insigniter*. To this end, he had studied with what seemed at times the fanaticism of an idolator. Being on intimate terms with him, I was thoroughly acquainted with his attainments, and set the highest value upon them. He displayed a maturity of mind that was incredible in one only twenty-three or twenty-four years of age. Nothing seemed too minute to escape his attention, too subtle to perplex his powers of comprehension. Taken all in all, he was the ablest student that I have ever met. In comparison with him, I felt that I was but little better than a school-boy. Yet M——, despite advice and remonstrances, simply threw away the prize just as it came within his reach. He was examined exactly one week before myself. Not only did he keep up his twelve and sixteen hours of "cram" from Monday to Friday, but he committed the unpardonable sin of studying all Friday night and all Saturday morning. I met him Saturday afternoon, as he was on his way to the examination. To use a boating-phrase, he was "pumped out" before the race. Deep black rings were around his eyes, the eyes themselves had lost their lustre, his whole manner was painfully nervous. He asked me, in the tone of a dying man catching at a straw, whether I could think of any subject on which he might be unprepared. I suggested one or two *formulae* which had never occurred to him. He made me repeat them until he had got them by heart, and then hurried away. What took place in the examination never transpired. M—— left town the following Monday, without bidding his friends good-bye. He passed with only the second degree, which, to him, was little better than none at all. He was a disappointed man. Yet he had no one but himself to blame. Whoever could have seen him, as I did, only ten minutes before the examination, would not have needed the gift of divination to foretell the result. The examiners, who could only judge by what they saw and heard during the three hours of examination, doubtless regarded the candidate as a young man who had overrated his abilities, who had worked hard, but knew nothing thoroughly and clearly.

In America there is a widely prevalent practice called "reviewing for examination." What it amounts to, every professor knows too well. Students who have neglected their studies from week to week, preparing themselves only when they expected to be called upon to recite, review for examination, by attempting to get up three months' work in as many days. Night and day the suddenly industrious toil over " Trig.," or Greek, or Logic, in the hope of mastering just enough to pass without conditions. The idea of the value of the studies as something to be learned for future use has never occurred to them. Whether the fault lies wholly with the student, or the collegiate system itself is to come in for a share of the blame, is a point open for discussion. Without attempting to settle it in this place, may I take the liberty of submitting at least a query? Can the system which grades the performances of young men down to the per cent and fraction of the per cent, and lays so much stress upon good recitations and good examination-papers, be a happy one? Even assuming that the present method of recitations will be retained, is it necessary that the professor-teacher shall always subordinate instruction to marking?

The candidate who has passed his university examination is not yet a doctor. He is only a *doctorandus*. The ceremony of conferring the diploma is distinct from the examination, and is confined to the dean and the candidate. On the Monday after the examination, I called, by appointment, upon Hofrath Kraut to receive the diploma. This document, printed on parchment-paper and not on parchment, is signed by the dean alone in the name of the faculty, and sealed with the great seal of the university. It is worded, as might be expected, in Latin. It is not my intention to inflict the text upon the reader, especially as it does not differ much in style from the pompous declarations of a like nature issued from our American colleges. But one other document connected with the diploma I must give entire. Before presenting me formally with the diploma, the dean said: "*Herr* Hart, you must first sign this declaration:"

Jus Jurandum a J. U. Doctoribus in Georgia Augusta ante Renunciationem Praestandum.

Ego —— juro atque promitto, me supremos in jure honores mihi nunc conferendos, in nulla alia universitate, ut mihi denuo conferantur, petiturum vel admissurum ; porro, quoties continget, ut vel publice vel privatim sit docendum, scribendum, patrocinandum, judicandum, vel de jure respondendum, me conscientiae, legum, justitiae, veritatis et modestiae summam semper rationem esse habiturum, nec quidquam in his, quod Dei gloriae vel publicae privatorumve saluti adversum sit, commissurum ; de cetero omnia, quae officium, dignitasque doctoralis postulat, sincere optimaque fide peracturum atque praestiturum. Ita me Deus adjuvet et sacrosanctum ejus evangelium.

Abundantly satisfied with the honor of a degree of doctor of laws from the University of Göttingen, and unaware of any intent to pervert my legal attainments to the frustration of divine or human justice, I signed the declaration cheerfully and with a good conscience. The dean informed me that it was a relic of mediaevalism.[*] The object of the first clause was to suppress the practice, once common among candidates, of going about begging the same degree from different universities. The concluding phrase, *et sacrosanctum ejus evangelium*, is altered in cases where the *doctorandus* is a Hebrew.

Within twenty-four hours after my examination, every one in town who knew me at all seemed to have heard of

---

[*] Göttingen is a comparatively modern university ; but in this respect it has adopted the manners and practices of the others.

my success. Even the waiters put on an extra touch of politeness, and greeted me as *Herr Doctor*. Titles have great weight in Germany. Perhaps some of my readers have heard of the German Mrs. Partington, who divides mankind into two classes, the orderly (*ordentlichen*) and the unorderly (*unordentlichen*). The orderly are those who have an *order*, and the unorderly are those who have not. The case is not quite so bad as that. Still there can be no question but that the man who is able to put Doctor, or Professor, or *Rath* before his name is much better off, in the eyes of the community at large, than one who is simply *Herr*. The title is an official recognition that the wearer is a person of some culture and attainments.

The value of university degrees varies greatly with the universities themselves, and even with the several faculties of the same university. In general, the degree of D. D. is not given in course, on examination, but conferred only *honoris causa*, that is, upon men who have distinguished themselves by their published works. With regard to the degree of M. D., the requirements are extensive, and are strictly enforced. The candidate must have studied the full term of four or five years, and offered very satisfactory dissertations, before he is admitted to examination. Jena, I believe, is the only university in Germany that degrades itself by selling its degrees to foreign applicants. The degree of J. U. D. is not often sought after by foreigners, and is even going out of vogue among the Germans themselves. It is not required for admission to the state examination. Ten years ago,

Heidelberg was very liberal in conferring it, while Göttingen was just the reverse. Whereas the philosophical faculty of Göttingen was liberal, and that of Heidelberg not. In general, the Prussian universities were somewhat stricter than the others. Berlin, in particular, pushed its rigor to unwarrantable limits. At one time it was almost impossible to meet the requirements of the Berlin faculty in philosophy. Several universities made, and still make, a practice of excusing the candidate for Ph. D. from the oral examination. This is called taking the degree *in absentia*. The candidate submits his dissertation and goes out of town for a few days. The fiction is, of course, that he is called away by some unexpected and urgent business. To obtain the degree *in absentia*, however, one must prepare a very elaborate dissertation, containing a good deal of original matter. In chemistry, physics, and the like, where the candidate has worked two or three years, perhaps, under the constant supervision of the professors, so that they have had abundant opportunity of testing his knowledge from week to week, this dispensing with the examination is not such an evidence of laxity as it would seem. Upon the whole, the reader may take for granted that a degree is not conferred by a German university except for thorough and bona fide work in that special department of study. Jena, as I have already stated, is the only exception. No German university showers down honorary degrees upon business men and generals, after the fashion of our American colleges.

PART II.

GENERAL REMARKS.

GENERAL REMARKS.

FROM the foregoing personal narrative the reader will probably be able to obtain a glimpse at the mode of life at a German university, to the extent at least of realizing how an American may live and study there. Yet there are certain features of the German method of higher education that can be adequately elucidated only by eliminating the personal element and discussing them in their more general bearings. I have deemed it proper, therefore, to supplement the personal narrative with the following remarks in the way of criticism.

I revisited Germany in 1872–3. In that time I studied at Leipsic, Marburg, and Berlin, and passed a summer at Vienna. Brought thus in contact with professors, students and men of letters in the great German centers of thought, I had ample opportunity of reviewing and modifying early impressions, and of judging the university system as a whole. I venture to offer these remarks, then, as the result of recent comparative investigation.

The first question that suggests itself is naturally this,

I.

What is a University?

To the German mind the collective idea of a university implies a *Zweck*, an object of study, and two *Beding-*

ungen, or conditions. The object is *Wissenschaft;* the conditions are *Lehrfreiheit* and *Lernfreiheit*. By *Wissenschaft* the Germans mean knowledge in the most exalted sense of that term, namely, the ardent, methodical, independent search after truth in any and all of its forms, but wholly irrespective of utilitarian application. *Lehrfreiheit* means that the one who teaches, the professor or *Privatdocent*, is free to teach what he chooses, as he chooses. *Lernfreiheit*, or the freedom of learning, denotes the emancipation of the student from *Schulzwang*, compulsory drill by recitation.

If the object of an institution is anything else than knowledge as above defined, or if either freedom of teaching or freedom of learning is wanting, that institution, no matter how richly endowed, no matter how numerous its students, no matter how imposing its buildings, is not, in the eye of a German, a *university*. On the other hand, a small, out-of-the-way place like Rostock, with only thirty-four professors and docents, and one hundred and thirty-five students, is nevertheless as truly a university as Leipsic, where the numbers are one hundred and fifty and three thousand respectively, because Rostock aims at theoretical knowledge and meets the requirements of free teaching and free study. The difference is one of size, not of species.

If we examine the list of lectures and hours of universities like Leipsic, Berlin, and Vienna, we shall be overwhelmed, at first sight, with the amount and the variety of literary and scientific labor announced. The field seems boundless. All that human ingenuity can suggest is apparently represented. On examining more closely, however, we shall find that this seemingly boundless field has its limits, which are very closely traced and which are not exceeded. Strange as it may sound to the American, who is accustomed to gauge spiritual greatness by big numbers and extravagant pretensions, a German university, even the greatest, perceives what it can do and what it *can not do*.

It is not a place " where any man can study anything." Its elevated character makes it all the more modest. It contents itself with the theoretical, and leaves to other institutions the practical and the technical. The list of studies and hours for Leipsic in the semester 1872-3 fills thirty octavo pages. In all that list we shall discover scarcely one course of work that can be called in strictness practical. A German university has one and only one object: to train thinkers. It does not aim at producing poets, painters, sculptors, engineers, miners, architects, bankers, manufacturers. For these, the places of instruction are the Art Schools of Dresden, Munich, Düsseldorf, the Commercial Schools at Bremen, Hamburg, Berlin, Frankfort, the Polytechnicums at Hanover, Frankenberg, Stuttgart, etc. Even in the professions themselves, theory and practice are carefully distinguished, and the former alone is considered as falling legitimately within the sphere of university instruction. Taking up the four faculties in order: theology, law, medicine,* philosophy, and watching them at work, we shall perceive that the evident tendency of their method is to produce theologians rather than pastors, jurists rather than lawyers, theorizers in medicine rather than practitioners, investigators, scholars, speculative thinkers rather than technologists and school-teachers. Yet every pastor, lawyer, doctor, teacher, botanist, geologist has passed through the university course. What is meant, then, by the assertion that the university gives only theoretical training? Do not the practical men in all the professions receive their professional outfit at the university and can receive it nowhere else? The seeming discrepancy is to be explained only by considering the university as a permanent, self-supporting institution, a world in itself, existing for itself, rather than a mere ladder by which to ascend from a lower to a higher plane. Self-supporting, I mean, of course, in the sense that the university is a detached organism assimilating and growing in accordance with its own laws. In a pecuniary sense, it is wholly or almost wholly dependent upon state subvention. The distinction, subtle as it may appear, is essential in forming a just conception of the character of university work. The university supplies itself with its

---

* Medicine seems to form an exception; the universities do teach the practice of medicine very thoroughly. Yet the exception, which is apparent rather than real, only serves to illustrate the general principle. It is precisely because medicine is so much a matter of empiricism, so little a matter of pure science, that the German universities teach it as they do. Were it possible to establish a *science* of medicine, as distinguished from the mere tentative treatment of disease, we should find the practice thrown into the background of the university course, as is the case in law and theology. Even as it is, the study of medicine is made as theoretical as it well can be.

educational staff exclusively from its own graduate members, who pass their entire lives within its precincts. The professors, assistant-professors, docents whose names one reads in the catalogue of Berlin or Leipsic or Heidelberg are one and all, with scarcely an exception, men who started in life as theoreticians and never made the effort to become practitioners. To them the university was not a mere preparatory school, where they might remain long enough to get their theoretical training, and then turn their backs upon it forever. On the contrary, it was an end, a career in itself. They have always been university men, and never expect to become anything else. In this place I must guard against being misunderstood. The reader would receive a very unfair impression of Göttingen, for instance, if he were to infer, from what has been said, that the Göttingen faculty is made up exclusively of Göttingen graduates. Quite the reverse is the case. Probably two thirds come from elsewhere. As a rule, the young *Privatdocent* receives his first call as professor from a university where he has not been known as a student. There exists in this respect complete parity among the German institutions of learning. The feeling which prompts an American college to prefer its own graduates for professors is something quite unknown in Germany. I leave it to the reader's judgment to decide which of the two systems is better: that of liberal selection, or that of "breeding-in." When I speak of a university as recruiting exclusively from its graduates, I mean neither Berlin nor Leipsic nor Heidelberg in particular, but the twenty

22

universities of the German empire regarded as one body, the members of which are perfectly co-ordinate. Professors and docents, and even students, pass from one to another with a restlessness, we might say, that would be surprising in America, but which is looked upon in Germany as a matter of course. It is the exception, not the rule, when a man passes his entire career as instructor in one place. The key-note of the system is simply this. To those who are connected with the university in any instructional capacity whatever, it is an end and not a means, a life and not a phase of life, a career and not a discipline. The professors are not selected from among the leading lawyers, pastors, doctors, teachers, scientists of the country or province. When a chair already existing becomes vacant, or a new chair is created, and the question of filling it comes up, the Senatus Academicus does not scrutinize the bench or the bar or the gymnasium for an available man. It endeavors to ascertain who is the most promising *Privatdocent*, either in its own midst or at some other seat of learning, the young man who has made his mark by recent publications or discoveries. The newly organized university of Strassburg is a signal instance in point. Within two years after the close of the French war, Strassburg was opened with a full corps of instructors in all the departments. The total number at present is eighty. Yet of these eighty not one, so far as I can ascertain, is what might be called a practitioner. They are all full or half-professors or docents called from other institutions of learning. One who is familiar with the muster-roll of the universities can resolve the Strassburg list into its elements, saying: This man came from Berlin, that one from Vienna, that one from Würzburg, and so on. The reader will probably say: Is not this the case in America also? Are not our college professors all college graduates? To which the answer must be: Not in the same way, not to the same extent. How many of our college professors have been professors, and nothing else? How many have qualified themselves directly for the respective chairs which they occupy, by a life of special study? How many of them formed the resolve while still students, to lead a college life forever, to devote themselves exclusively to instructing others in turn, either at their own Alma Mater or at some other college? I do not have in view such institutions as Yale and Harvard, old, well endowed, fed from the rich soil of New England culture. I mean the typical American college as it exists in the Middle, Southern, and Western States. How many of the professors have been in business, or tried their skill at farming, engineering, journalism? Has or has not the professor of Latin served an apprenticeship as mathematical tutor, or kept a boarding-school for young ladies? How few of the hundreds and thousands of men, from New York to San Francisco, calling themselves professors, can say with a comfortable degree of pride: I selected my specialty in youth, I have pursued it without intermission, without deviation ever since, and I have produced such and such tangible evidences of my industry as a specialist.

No, the reader may rest assured that the character and atmosphere of a German university differ radically from the character and atmosphere of the typical American college. It is a difference of kind, not merely of degree. Comparisons, according to the popular adage, are odious. Yet, even at the risk of giving offense, I take the liberty of drawing a comparison that may serve, perhaps, to throw some light on this vital point. At all events, the comparison shall be a just one. Marburg, in Hesse, has at present 430 students; Princeton, my Alma Mater, has 420. The numbers, then, are almost identical. Each is located in a small country town. Yet Princeton has, all told, not more than 18 professors and tutors; Marburg has 62. Among them are men renowned throughout the world for their original investigations. The same might be said, indeed, of the Princeton faculty, but only with grave restrictions. No one professor at Princeton has the opportunity of working either himself or his students up to his or their full capacity. The instruction goes by routine, each professor contributing his quota to the supposed general development of all the students in a body. At Marburg there is the fourfold division of faculties; there are students pursuing theology, law, medicine, classic philology, modern philology, the natural sciences, history, orientalia. Each instructor has his select band of disciples, upon whom he acts and who re-act upon him. There is the same quiet, scholarly atmosphere, the same disregard for bread-and-butter study, the same breadth of culture, depth of insight, liberality of opinion and freedom of conduct, that one finds in the most favored circles of Leipsic, Berlin, Heidelberg, or Vienna. During every hour of the two months that I passed at Marburg, I was made to feel that a German university, however humble, is a world in and for itself; that its aim is not to turn out clever, pushing, ambitious graduates, but to engender culture.

This condition is both cause and effect. Many of the students who attend the university do so simply with a view to becoming in time professors. The entire *personnel* of the faculty is thus a close corporation, a spiritual order perpetuating itself after the fashion of the Roman Catholic hierarchy. Inasmuch as every professional man and every school-teacher of the higher grades has to pass through the university, it follows that the shaping of the intellectual interests of the country is in the hands of a select few, who are highly educated, perfectly homogeneous in character and sympathies, utterly indifferent to the turmoils and ambitions of the outer-world, who regulate their own lives and mould the dispositions of those dependent upon them according to the principles of abstract truth. The quality of university education, then, is determined by its object, and that object is to train not merely skillful practitioners, *but also future professors.* In fact, the needs of the former class are subordinated to the needs of the latter. In this respect, the faculty acts, unconsciously, in accordance with the promptings of the instinct of self-preservation. If thorough scientific culture is an essential element in national life, it must be maintained at every cost. The slightest flaw in the continuity of spiritual descent would be as dangerous as a break in the apostolic succession of the church. Every inducement, therefore, must be held out to young men to qualify themselves in season for succeeding to their present instructors. The lectures and other instruction must be adapted to train and stimulate *Privat-docenten*, for they are the ones who are to seize and wear the mantles of the translated Elijahs. For every professor dead or removed, there must be one or two instantly ready to fill his place.

This is not the *avowed* object of the university course. One might pass many years in Germany without perceiving it stated so bluntly. Yet I am persuaded that it is at bottom the determining factor in the constitution of university life. It will explain to us many incidental features for which there is elsewhere no analogy; for instance, the sovereign contempt that all German students evince for everything that savors of "bread-and-butter." The students have caught, in this respect, the tone of their instructors. Even such of them as have no intention of becoming *Privat-docenten* pass three and four years of their life in generous devotion to study pure and simple, without casting a single forward glance to future "business." All thought of practical life is kept in abeyance. The future practitioners and the future theoreticians sit side by side on the same bench, fight on the same *Mensur*, drink at the same *Kneipe*, hear the same lectures, use the same books, have every sentiment in common; hence the perfect *rapport* that exists in Germany between the lawyer and the jurist, the pastor and the theologian, the practicing doctor and the speculative pathologist, the gymnasial teacher of Latin and Greek and the professed philologist. Hence the celerity with which innovating ideas spread in Germany. Let a professor in the university of Tübingen, for instance, publish a work on some abstruse, difficult topic, in which he threatens to overturn previous theories and notions. Why is it that in a month or two the book provokes a tempest of assent or dissent from far and near? Simply because every practical man in that line, every lawyer, or doctor, or pastor, as the case may be, has been initiated so far into the theory of his profession as to be able to detect at a glance the full purport of the new departure. Let the book contain but a single mis-statement of an historic fact or an established principle of natural science, and a hundred angry reviewers pounce upon it and hold it up to public condemnation. Whereas, in this country, and even in England also, the grossest blunders pass unchallenged. Our reviewers are either ignorant or indifferent.

To repeat, the university instruction of Germany does not attempt to train successful practical men, unless it be indirectly, by giving its students a profound insight into the principles of the science and then turning them adrift to deduce the practice as well as they can from the carefully inculcated theory. Its chief task, that to which all its energies are directed, is the development of great thinkers, men who will extend the boundaries of knowledge.

Viewed from this point, then, the two conditions, *Lehrfreiheit* and *Lernfreiheit*, are not only natural and proper, but are absolutely essential. Were the object of higher education merely to train "useful and honorable members of society," to use the conventional phrase of the panegyrists of the American system, the German universities might possibly change their character. In place of professors free to impart the choicest results of their investigations, they might substitute pedagogues with text-books and class-books, noting down the relative merits and demerits of daily recitations. In place of students free to attend or to stay away, free to agree with the professor or to differ, free to read what they choose and to study after their own fashion, they might create a set of undergraduates reciting glibly from set lessons and regarding each circumvention of the teacher as so much clear gain. But the Germans know perfectly well wherein the value of their university education lies. They know that speculative thought alone has raised Germany from her former condition of literary and political dependence to the foremost rank among nations. The gain is not without its sacrifice. Many a young man who, under another method, might be drilled into a tolerable alumnus, falls by the way-side through idleness and dissipation. For one who succeeds, two or three fail. Yet the sacrifice is unavoidable. If German thought is to continue in its career of conquest, if the universities are to remain what they are, the training-ground of intellectual giants, the present system of freedom must be maintained.

The professor has but one aim in life: scholarly renown. To effect this, he must have the liberty of selecting his studies and pushing them to their extreme limits. The student has but one desire: to assimilate his instructor's learning, and, if possible, to add to it. He must, therefore, be his own master. He must be free to accept and reject, to judge and prove all things for himself, to train himself step by step for grappling with the great problems of nature and history. Accountable only to himself for his opinions and mode of living, he shakes off spiritual bondage and becomes an independent thinker. He *must* think for himself, for there is no one set over him as spiritual adviser and guide, prescribing the work for each day and each hour, telling him what he is to believe and what to disbelieve, and marking him up or down accordingly.

The universities occupy, then, an impregnable position. Recruiting their tuitional forces (*Lehrkräfte*) from among themselves, they are independent of the outer world. Subjecting all young men of education, the future lawyers, legislators, doctors, statesmen, school-teachers to their own peculiar discipline, infusing into them their own peculiar spirit of freedom, they raise up for themselves allies all over the land. It is not in my power to give the exact statistics either of the present Imperial Parliament of Germany or of any one of the national diets. But I am warranted in saying that a majority of the members of every legislative body in Germany, and three fourths of the higher office-holders, and all the heads of departments are university graduates, or have at least taken a partial university course, enough to catch the university spirit. All the controlling elements of German national life, therefore, have been trained to sympathize with the freedom, intellectual and individual, which is the characteristic of the university method. The nation is devotedly attached to its institutions of learning, and will never suffer their influence or their privileges to be abated an iota. This has been shown repeatedly. No country in Germany can be more arbitrary at times than Prussia. Yet the Prussian government, which has more than once stood in direct conflict with the university of Berlin, has always evinced its good sense by yielding in season. During the dreary period of the reign of Frederick William IV.,* an attempt was made, under the Eichhorn Ministry of Public Instruction, to introduce certain innovations. The number of professors was to be fixed, the students were to be compelled to attend lectures, the new professors themselves were to be selected among the higher public officials. But the university stood firm, and the attempt failed signally. In the "conflict-period" immediately preceding the Austro-Prussian war of 1866, the university of Berlin, notoriously democratic, i. e., anti-squirarchical, in its sympathies, asserted its right of regulating its own

---

* Frederick William IV. was personally a most amiable sovereign, but prejudiced, rather bigoted, and occasionally fanatic. Many of his views were visionary, not to say Quixotic. Ranke, in his *Correspondence between Frederick William IV. and Bunsen*, has vainly endeavored to show the King in a pleasing light.

affairs and refused point blank to take from certain of the professors the *venias docendi* for publicly expressing their disapproval of the acts of the Bismarck ministry. The German mind, with all its painful observance of forms and subservience to powers that be, has an ineradicable love of spiritual freedom. Long after the student has passed into the land of Philistia, becoming there a humdrum deputy tax-collector, or justice of the peace, or road-inspector, or village parson, the casual recollection of his boisterously happy student-days comes over him like the vision of another world. It lifts him out of his dull, plodding round and makes him for the nonce a child of light. You have but to strike the university-chord in the breast of the first squatting Philistine in the first village of Suabia or Thuringia, and he springs up transformed like Lucifer at the touch of the spear of Ithuriel. He is ready to drop his drudgery, to carouse with you all day and all night, to tell of his exploits at the *Kneipe* and the *Mensur*, his fights with peasants and night-watchmen, to listen with rapt attention to all that you may have to relate of the *Georgia-Augusta* or the *Ruperta-Carolina* of golden memory. The German instinct is not always quick, but it is always true. Whatever else the German may learn or unlearn, he will never cease to feel that the university triennium was the one period of his life when he was a free man; he will never fail to perceive that the university itself is the stronghold of the German spirit, its place of refuge from ministerial rescripts and petty police regulations, the only safety-valve for its pent-up energy. We Americans, who live in a surfeit of freedom, as it were, can dispense perhaps with the *libertas academica ;* but the Germans know too well that it is the only phase in the life of the educated classes that prevents that life from becoming an intolerable monotony.

II.

Professors.

The character of the German professor will be best understood by first disposing of the preliminary question: What is he not?

The professor is not a teacher, in the English sense of the term; he is a specialist. He is not responsible for the success of his hearers. He is responsible only for the quality of his instruction. His duty begins and ends with himself.

No man can become a professor in a German university without having given evidence, in one way or another, that he has pursued a certain line of study, and produced results worthy to be called novel and important. In other words, to become a professor, he must first have been a special investigator. Professional chairs are not conferred "on general principles," or because the candidate is "a good teacher," or "well qualified to govern the young." Neither is there such springing about from one department of study to another as we observe in America. Each of the two thousand professors now lecturing in Germany has risen from the ranks, first as gymnasiast, then as student, then as *Privat-docent* in a special branch. As *Privat-docent*, he makes some discovery in botany, or in chemistry, or in anatomy, or publishes some treatise on historical, philological, or theological topics, that attracts attention and elicits favorable comment. The discoverer or the author becomes at once a man of mark, a candidate for the next vacant chair. Living at Bonn, perhaps, or Würzburg, he continues his work. In the course of a year or two, a vacancy occurs at Heidelberg. The Heidelberg faculty, every one of whom has probably read his publications and recognized in him a valuable co-worker, give him a call. This he accepts, removes to his new field of labor, and continues there his investigations. Probably he is at Heidelberg only *ausserordentlicher*. But his fame spreads more and more. A full professorship becomes vacant at Berlin; he is called once more, as *ordentlicher*. During these successive stages, as student, *Privat-docent, ausserordentlicher, ordentlicher Professor*, he has not made a single change in his line of study. He has been throughout an orientalist, a classic-philologist, a mathematician, a chemist, an historian, or a theologian. His time and energies have been devoted exclusively to one limited branch of investigation, with a view to making discoveries. He has not *taught* a single hour. He has simply "read" a course or two of lectures each semester, and has published three or four books. His personal character may be comparatively unknown to the faculty that give him a call. They do not regard in him the man so much as the scholar. It would be fatuitous to assert that personal considerations go for nothing in Germany. Many a man has been put into or kept out of a professorial chair because he had made himself agreeable or obnoxious to one or more of those who held the right of nomination. An instance occurs to me where one of the greatest scholars in Germany, the greatest in his own line, was barred for years from a call to any of the Prussian universities, because he had published a scathing review of a treatise by the leading professor in that department at Berlin. Yet even here the quarrel could scarcely be called personal, inasmuch as the two men had never met. The offender, in particular, was one of the mildest-mannered men in private intercourse. The conflict was not one of men, but rather of views, of principles. Each insisted that he himself was right and the other absurdly wrong. Mere personal favoritism has not much weight in university appointments. The utmost that it can do is to turn the scales where the scholarly merits of competing candidates are balanced, or nearly balanced; but it will not be strong enough to smuggle in a candidate who has not unquestioned abilities.

Professorial life is quiet and uneventful. Once a professor, always a professor. All the *ordentlichen*, and nearly all the *ausserordentlichen*, draw fixed salaries from the university treasury, and receive in addition the fees paid for their lectures. A few of the most celebrated lecturers on law, medicine, and chemistry are in the receipt of incomes that, for Germany, are very good. Vangerow, for instance, who had always one hundred and fifty or two hundred hearers, each one paying not less than $10 a semester, and who derived a large revenue from the sale of his works, in addition to his regular salary, was well off. The same may be said of the leading men in the medical faculties of Berlin and Vienna, who have a large and lucrative professional practice. But in general a professor is a man of very limited means, who has to practice close economy and be content with the plainest housekeeping. Yet the life, which offers so few inducements to the money-seeker, is in the main a pleasant one. The position itself is one of high dignity, especially in the smaller towns, such as Göttingen, Heidelberg, Bonn, Würzburg, and the like. The Germans, it is well known, are sticklers for rank. It is no small matter, then, to a man of cultivated tastes, to feel that, however humble he may seem from a pecuniary point of view, nobody in town can outrank him. The professors and their wives constitute the good society of the place. They can scarcely be said to set the fashion, for the German provincial towns are out of the world of fashion.

The chief attraction in the professorial career, however, is the nature of the work itself. No human lot, it is true, is without its trials. The life of a professor is anything but a bed of roses. It means severe intellectual toil from morning till evening, from manhood to declining years. But there is a freedom about it that is inexpressibly fascinating. The professor is his own master. His time is not wasted in cudgeling the wits of refractory or listless reciters. His temper is not ruffled by the freaks or the downright insults of mutinous youths. He lectures upon his chosen subject, comments upon his favorite Greek or Roman or early German or Sanscrit author, expounds some recently discovered mathematical theorem, discusses one or another of the grave problems of history or morals, and is accountable only to his own conscience of what is true and what is false. He lectures only to those who are willing and able to hear. He is sustained by the consciousness that his words are not scattered by the wayside, but that they fall upon soil prepared to receive them, and will bring forth new fruit in turn. His relation to his hearers is that of one gentleman speaking to another. He is not in perpetual dread of hearing himself nicknamed, of seeing his features caricatured; his domestic repose is not disturbed by midnight serenades. He addresses his pupils as men who know perfectly well what they are about, and whom he must seek to enlighten or convince. To make the method of instruction more evident, we have only to picture to ourselves a man like George Curtius, of Leipsic, "reading" on the Odyssey. He begins probably with a general introduction to the Homeric question, spending perhaps a fortnight in setting forth his views and refuting the views of others. He then gives a detailed description of all the manuscripts of the poem, their comparative merits and deficiencies, and also the best modern critical editions. Then following some generally received text, he translates, either carefully, line by line, or else rapidly, according as the passage may be difficult or easy. As he goes, he makes historical, æsthetical, linguistic excursions. By the end of the semester he has probably finished only a few books. But his hearers, who have listened attentively and with minds prepared by their gymnasial training, have caught the essence of the poem and its relations, and can henceforth study it for themselves. This presupposes of course that the hearers are already good Greek scholars. But how is it where the language is Sanscrit or Persian or Gothic, something which the hearers do not know beforehand, but must commence from the very beginning? Here the professor generally becomes a teacher, yet in a very informal way. He either dictates the grammar from his own manuscript, or takes the class through a printed work, and then sets them to reading. The lessons, if they can be called such, are unmercifully long. Ewald at Göttingen used to rush his Persian class through the phonology and morphology of that language in three or four weeks, and set them to translating two and three pages at a lesson. But, as my informant added, "We could not help learning. We were carried along by the genius of the teacher." I can state, on my own personal knowledge, that Benfey is capable of assigning twenty pages of irregular verbs in Sanscrit at a time. When a German professor teaches after this fashion, his pupils *must* keep up or else drop out. There is no alternative. In the matter of translating, the prac-

*23

tice varies. Some professors let the students read off the original and translate, merely correcting them when they make a mistake; others do the translating themselves, and expect the class to copy down all that is said. However difficult the labor of preparation may be, the pupil has always one consolation. He feels that he is learning; that he is in the hands of a master whose words are those of wisdom and whose enthusiasm is contagious. There is something intoxicating in the consciousness that you are putting forth your best energies; not to get good marks, but to catch the subtle spirit of some difficult language and win the silent approbation of its world-renowned expounder.

As a class, the professors of Germany are hard-workers. One who has never tried the experiment might suppose that it is not so very difficult to lecture eight or ten hours a week. The mere reading-off is perfectly easy; but the labor of preparing a set of lectures that shall be acceptable to a community so fastidious in its tastes, as a university, is immense. The professor being a specialist, it is expected of him that he shall produce something especially good, that he shall be up to the times. There are a few "old fogies," men who live on the reputation that they acquired twenty or thirty years ago. But they form a very small minority. A professor who has any ambition whatever, who is anxious to spare himself the mortification of reading to empty benches, must recast his lectures continually, striking out exploded errors, incorporating new discoveries. The German brain is prolific. The sight of the semi-annual catalogue of new publications in Germany is enough to unhinge the strongest mind. The professor must keep abreast with the swelling tide. He must study each new work in his own department, at least to the extent of knowing what novelties it contains, and how they agree or disagree with his own views. If he does not, if he falls behind, some ambitious rival, some aspiring *Privat-docent*, will overtake and pass him. In this respect, the students are quick-witted and exacting. No sooner do they discover that one professor represents the state of investigation as it was ten or only five years ago, while another gives it as it actually is, than they desert in a body to the younger man. Herein lies the real strength of the German professorial system and the check upon the abuses of *Lehrfreiheit*. A professor is free to lecture upon what topics he chooses; he is not compelled to modify his views. But if he persists in offering stale matter, in selecting topics that have ceased to interest, he does so at the peril of losing his prestige and his hearers.

The pressure upon the professors, accordingly, is heavy and unremitting. But they meet it nobly. There is probably not another body of men in the world so keenly alive to the signs of the times, so thoroughly versed in the current literature of their special departments, so productive of new works. I can think of no more striking instance than the historian Ranke. One might imagine that the *History of the Popes*, and the *History of the Reformation*, published thirty or forty years ago, were enough to entitle the author to rest on his laurels. Yet they were followed by a stately series of additional works: *France in the Seventeenth Century; England in the Seventeenth Century* (each work comprising many volumes); *Wallenstein; Origin of the Seven Years' War; German Powers and the Confederation of Princes in the Eighteenth Century; Correspondence of Frederick William IV. and Bunsen.* Scarcely a semester passes without the announcement of a fresh work from the pen of this venerable giant, now rapidly approaching his eightieth year.

The chief defect in the character of the German professors as a class is one that arises of necessity from their mode of life. Devoted to a narrow range of study, living in comparative seclusion, they are unpractical in many ways and intolerant of dissent. What a German professor teaches, he teaches with an intensity of conviction that leaves no room for doubt or hesitancy. I should be loth to call this trait fanaticism. Certainly it is not the fanaticism of ignorance, or of one-sidedness; the professor, it may be safely assumed, has looked at the question from every side and weighed the evidence. It is rather the intolerance inherent in one who is not troubled with doubts and who fails to understand why another should stumble over what is to him so plain. It springs from want of familiarity with the world, want of appreciation of the complex motives that determine human opinion no less than human action. Man is not a purely intellectual being; the individual status of each one is the resultant of all sorts of forces, prejudices, temptations, inherited sentiments. Yet things are judged in Germany too exclusively by the standard of pure intellect. The Germans neglect the glorious example set them by their national genius, Goethe, and overlook in their criticisms the individuality of the person criticized. Of course there are many bright exceptions, but as a rule German critics judge everything by some exalted, ideal standard of what is absolutely right and absolutely wrong. Does a literary production come up to this standard? Well and good. If it does not,— off with the fellow's head! Hence the sweeping condemnations that one finds in every list of book reviews, the bitter literary feuds that have been waged and are still waged over debatable points where one might expect some degree of charity, some latitude of belief. Not all critics are professors, but all professors are critics. Notices and reviews of publications not purely belletristic or ephemeral in their nature are generally written by professors or docents, who thus give the tone.

The relation between professor and student is, if not positively friendly, at least pleasant. The chief drawback to the lot of a professor in America, namely, police-duty and discipline, does not exist in Germany. The professor, as such, has nothing to do with the university discipline. Unless he happens to be a member of the university court, and this he cannot be unless he is a jurist, or the rector for the time being, he is not called upon to pass sentence upon a student's conduct. He is not obliged to fritter away many hours a week of his valuable time in deciding whether Smith was really suffering from the measles or only shamming, whether Jones ought to be sent home for three months or six months for breaking a tutor's windows. He has nothing to do with the students as a body, does not know more than a tenth of them by sight or by name; his dealings are exclusively with the few who sit in his lecture-room. If the exercises are of a colloquial nature, as for instance in the numerous *practica*, *exegetica*, *seminaria*, and cliniques, he makes naturally an informal estimate of each pupil's capacities. But he keeps no record either of their performances or of their attendance. In consequence, neither professor nor student has any inducement to chicane each the other. They hold the relation of giver and receiver.

A student may pass his entire term of study at the university without coming in personal contact with his professors. He may simply listen from semester to semester, pursue his collateral researches for himself, get his *Anmeldungsbuch* signed, and leave for the state-examination without exchanging a hundred words with all his teachers. In philosophy, mathematics, law, history, this is possible. In medicine, chemistry, and the languages, it is not. But even where it is possible, students generally prefer to adopt another course. They seek the acquaintance of some at least of their instructors. Where they fail, the fault will be found to lie with the professor himself, who is too absorbed in his own researches, too uncongenial in his character, to take any direct, personal interest in his hearers. But many of the professors are more liberal, making it a point to invite students to their houses from time to time. Some indeed have set re-unions, which any one in the course is free to attend. The conversation at these re-unions is not necessarily "shop." George Curtius, the celebrated Greek scholar at Leipsic, holds his re-unions, I believe, with great success. In the first part of the present work, I have spoken at length of the very pleasant relations existing between myself and the *Geheimjustizrath* v. Ribbentropp. Such perfect freedom of intercourse is not usual. Yet something of the sort may be established, by perseverance, in every university. If the student is in earnest, he will in time induce some one of his numerous professors to treat him as a friend and companion.

It may not be superfluous to say a word or two concerning the *ausserordentlichen* professors, as distinguished from the *ordentlichen*. The *ordentlichen* are the full professors; but it would be a grave mistake to suppose that the *ausserordentlichen* are what we style assistant-professors. They are inferior in rank to the full professors, but they are not direct subordinates. The full professor cannot say to the other: "I reserve such and such work for myself. You must teach certain other branches." Each is independent of the other, and each is subject only to the full *Senatus Academicus*. The *ausserordentlicher* does not supplement the work of the *ordentlicher*, but can compete directly with him. These junior professorships are mere rounds in the ladder of ascent; they are not lieutenancies.

III.

Privatdocenten.

In the previous portion of the present work I have indicated briefly my opinion as to the character and functions of the *Privatdocent.* This will not absolve me from the necessity of going into this feature of university instruction more in detail, for here more than anywhere else does the German university differ from other institutions of learning.

In the first place, the docent is not a tutor. He is neither the tutor of England nor the tutor of America. At Oxford and Cambridge, the tutors* are Fellows of the respective colleges, and are the persons who conduct all the official, prescribed college instruction, either by lecture or by recitation. They are in reality college professors, as distinguished from the Regius professors of the university. The reader who wishes to inform himself more fully may consult Mr. Bristed's work. What an American tutor is, we all know. He is, in nine cases out of ten, a very young man without direct preparation for his work and without a university vocation. His qualifications are only general, not special. In this way. Although our college tutors are usually selected among the most promising graduates, yet, inasmuch as the college curriculum aims at imparting general culture and not special training, the most promising graduate is not

---

* Not the so called " private tutors," who may or may not be Fellows.

necessarily qualified for teaching any one branch in particular. His standing is merely one of general average. As a matter of fact, indeed, it happens only too often that a tutorship of mathematics is given to a young graduate whose talents lie in the direction of languages, and vice versa. Furthermore, the tutors are usually recent graduates, who have not yet had time to shake off their undergraduate ways of thinking, and to mature.* But the sorest evil is the circumstance that the tutor has not a *university vocation.* By this I mean that he does not look upon his tutorship as the introduction to a permanent mode of life, the stepping stone to a future professorship. Imperfectly trained as our tutors are when appointed, if they would only remain tutors with a view to becoming professors, the evil would work its own cure. The tutor would develop into a scholar. But, as is well known, the tutorship is usually a mere make-shift. Two or three of the best men, say in this year's class, are straightened in means, or have not yet decided upon their future profession. They accept tutorships, then, not because they regard college-life as their vocation, but because they have nothing better in prospect for the time being. In a year or two, one of them will abandon his books and enter business. Another will leave as soon as he has saved up money enough to carry him through the law school, or the theological seminary, or the medical school. It is easy to see that under such circumstances

---

* Once more, the reader must understand that I have in view the typical American college. At Harvard and Yale the case is somewhat better.

the tutor's heart cannot be in his work. He goes through his daily routine of recitations and draws his salary. Furthermore, he is not his own master, he is not free to decide what he shall teach, how he shall apportion his time. He is merely the executive officer, the lieutenant to carry out the peremptory orders of his superior professor. If we add to all this the personal inconvenience of a tutorship, in which the incumbent has neither the freedom of a student nor the dignity of a professor, but is called upon to do the "dirty work" of college discipline, we need not wonder that so few really able men are willing to serve the apprenticeship.

The *Privat-docent*, on the other hand, moves in an altogether different sphere. In the first place, his work as a student is special, not general. For three or more years he has studied exclusively either law, or theology, or medicine, or philosophy in some one of its numerous ramifications. He has taken his doctoral degree by passing a rigorous examination covering the entire field of his studies, and by presenting one or more dissertations that show his ability to treat certain topics in an independent, manly spirit of research. But, with all this, he is not yet a docent. The university has not yet conferred upon him the right to teach others, the *venias docendi*. To obtain this, he must qualify himself still further; he must habilitate himself (*sich habilitiren*). He waits, therefore, a year or two longer, pursuing his private studies with energy. He then prepares and publishes an elaborate dissertation. In connection with this, he announces ten or twelve theses, or detached propositions, which he is prepared to defend against all comers. The reader will remember the theses affixed by Luther to the door of the church at Wittenberg. The public disputation is held in one of the university rooms. The professors of the candidate's faculty attend. In fact, any one can attend, and, if he sees fit, can take part in the debate. Ordinarily the disputation is a mere ceremony. The candidate stands on the platform, like the knights of the Middle Ages, ready to maintain the merits of his lady-love. His antagonists are his friends, who have been instructed beforehand what to say. After four or five parleys, each lasting a few minutes, the antagonists admit the champion's superiority, and the dean pronounces him a true and worthy knight of science. Occasionally, however, some one of the theses is attacked in earnest, and then the candidate must also defend himself in earnest. In my student-days at Göttingen there was a German-Pole, one B——, a graduate of the university, a rather learned naturalist, who had traveled extensively. This B—— made a practice of attending disputations and bothering the candidates, until he came to be looked upon as a public nuisance. It is needless to say that the disputation is an empty form to which no weight is attached. The real test of the candidate's merit is his dissertation, which has been read in print beforehand by each member of the faculty, and which must be a substantial contribution to knowledge.

In some universities, I believe, the doctorate and the

venias docendi may coincide. As a specimen of an inaugural dissertation, I give one defended by an acquaintance of mine at Marburg, in 1872. It consists of thirty-three pp. octavo, fine print, on the *Evangelium Nicodemi in the Literature of the Occident*. The table of contents runs as follows:

I. The origin of the *evangel. Nicodemi* 1
   Versions A and B 4
II. Diffusion of the *evangel. Nicod.* in the literature of the Occident.
   Anglo-Saxon : Christ's Descent into Hell 12
                   Cynevulf's Christ 12
                   Christ and Satan 12
                   Prose translations 13
   English :   Prose and poetical versions ... 18
                   Langley, Piers Plowman 19
                   Fall and Passion 20
                   Wycliffe 20
                   The Develis Parlament 21
                   Printed editions 22
                   Lyfe of Joseph of Arimathea .. 22
   Celtic :   Gaelic version 22
                   Pascon agan Arluth 23
   French :   Gregory of Tours 23
                   Romance of the Grail 24
                   André de Coutances 25
                   Vincentius Bellovacensis 26
                   Prose translations 27

	Printed editions..............	28
	Romance of Perceforest........	28
Provenzal:	Metrical version..............	29
	Prose translation.............	32
Italian:	Jacobus a Voragine............	32
	Dante.........................	33
	Prose translations............	33
Spanish:	....	33

The following theses were defended:

1. Wright's opinion (Chester Plays, I. 14, note), that the poem, *Harrowing of Hell*, is a controversial poem, is incorrect. *It is a drama.* But there are weightier proofs of this than the proofs cited by Mall (The Harrowing of Hell, Breslau, 1871).

2. The codex Bodl. Digby, 86, fol. 119, contains the best ancient text of the *Harrowing of Hell*. This manuscript, and not the Brit. Museum, Harl. 2,253, should have been taken by Mall as the basis for his edition.

3. Mall's view that the *Extractio Animarum ab Inferno* of the Townely Mysteries and the *Descent into Hell* of the Coventry Plays are borrowed from or are modifications of the *Harrowing of Hell*, is untenable.

4. The more recent MS. of the Old-English poem, *The Owl and the Nightingale*, Jesus Coll. Ox., Arch. I, 29, affords a text approximating more to the original structure of the poem than the older MS. Brit. Mus. Cott. Calig., A. IX.

5. Verses 153–187 of *The Owl and the Nightingale* are to be assigned to the Nightingale and not to the Owl.

6. Germanic *ă* has retained its integrity in Anglo-Saxon only in open syllables.

7. It cannot be proved that Joseph of Arimathea was honored in England as a national saint prior to the Norman Conquest. The *saga* that Joseph preached Christianity to the English is, therefore, not of Celtic nor of Anglo-Saxon origin.

8. The Latin text of Q. Curtius Rufus *De gestis Alexandri Magni* was just as fragmentary at the end of the twelfth century as it is now.

9. Alexander de Bernay betrays, in his share of the *Romance of Alexander*, traces of the influence of the Arthurian romances.

10. General interest in the Alexander *saga* could have been awakened only by the crusades.

11. Alliteration had not gone out of use in England in the thirteenth and at the beginning of the fourteenth century. The poets of the so called Germanic reaction found it still in existence, and merely purified and improved it.

12. The discrepancy between secular and spiritual life, between the real and the ideal, which disorganized the Middle Ages, was also one of the principal causes of the decay of mediaeval literature.

The university, in conferring upon one of its graduates the *venias docendi*, puts itself under no obligation to him. It neither gives him a salary nor guarantees him hearers. It merely authorizes him to announce lectures in the university catalogue, and to use the university rooms for such classes as he may succeed in bringing together. His lectures are entered by his hearers in their *Anmeldungsbücher*, and received as full equivalents in the university and state *curriculum vitae*. The university has proclaimed to the world that the docent is fully qualified to teach. The only restriction laid upon him is that he shall not charge less for a course of lectures than the amount fixed by the professors for a like course on the same subject. The object of this is to prevent ignoble under-bidding. With the discipline of the university he has no more to do than the professors have. He is simply a candidate for a professorship, and shapes his life to suit his own views and purposes.

No words of mine, I fear, will do full justice to the part played in the university by the *Privatdocenten*. They are the life-blood of the institution. Young men in the vigor of manhood, ranging in age from twenty-five to thirty-five, thoroughly educated, purged of the folly and the aimless bravado of studenthood, awakened to a sense of life's responsibilities but not crushed by them, neither set in their ways like the older professors, they are most delightful companions. You will find them ready to converse with you on any and every topic, and equally ready to join you in a walk or a drive or a *Kneipe*. They can roll *Kegel* and talk Gnostic philosophy in the same breath, startle you with their knowledge of Sanscrit roots and their familiarity with university slang, but all with a quiet, unassuming, gentlemanly air, a deference to your views, and a liberality of culture that are fascinating to the last degree. The flush of manhood is in them, the stirring consciousness that they are on the high road to scholarly fame. But they are not so far ahead that they look upon the rest of the world with disdain or indifference. Their days pass in a quiet round of study. While their means are usually quite limited, their desires are simple and easily gratified. It matters little how a man may live or what he may do, provided his work be agreeable and his surroundings congenial. The *Privatdocent* has nearly all that goes to making life pleasant. The professors treat him with deference, the students look up to him with respect. He is already becoming, in a quiet way, an authority in the university world. He has for his next-door neighbor or his vis-a-vis a brother docent, a co-worker in the same line of thought, with whom he can hold familiar intercourse in a spirit of generous rivalry. The reader who wishes to view this phase of life in its refreshing simplicity cannot do better than study the charming tableau presented by Gustav Freytag in his *Lost Manuscript*.

I should give the reader a very unfair impression of professors and docents by suffering him to infer that they all injure themselves with overwork. On the contrary, the first thing that puzzles the newly fledged student from America is the leisurely, *dolce far niente* way in which his instructors seem to live. Not a few labor unremittingly, but the majority, I am persuaded, indulge in a good deal of recreation. On any fine day, from spring to autumn, one can see professors with their families out for an airing. They do not fail to attend concerts, balls, and the theatre. As for the *Privatdocenten*, one stumbles upon them everywhere and at all times. The secret of success in study is, in the first place, to be well trained, in the next place, to limit the field of study, and finally to work by rule. These three elements are combined in Germany to perfection. A German works about as he fights; he tries to keep cool and to avoid overshooting the mark. What cannot be done to-day, may be done to-morrow, provided one is on the right course and does not desist altogether. A rest of half a day or even a whole day does good rather than harm. The German university men accomplish a prodigious amount of work, but they do it by planning intelligently, by carefully forecasting ways and means, by availing themselves of the countless side-helps that each man can get from his co-workers in a land where labor is so minutely subdivided, and by adding here a little, there a little, until the whole becomes symmetrical and complete in all its parts. Viewed from day to day, the progress may seem slow. But if you only have the patience to wait six months or a year, you will find something grand in its proportions and original in its conception.

The office of the *Privatdocent*, whatever it may be in theory, is in practice twofold. He mediates between professor and student. He stimulates and helps his student-friends by advising them in their choice of lectures and books, and by mapping out their studies for them.

He gives them hints as to examination, or the best way of approaching professors, and also private instruction. On the other hand, he keeps the professors up to the mark by competition. What should we say if the senior professor of mathematics in some American college contented himself with the Calculus, while his aspiring tutor announced in the college catalogue a special course in Quaternions? We should say that it looked as though the tutor were trying to steal the professor's thunder, and that it could not be tolerated because subversive of order. Yet this is what every *Privatdocent* does, or tries to do. His sole aim in life is to cause himself to be regarded as one who knows quite as much as, if not more than, the nominal professor. No one will assert, of course, that a young man of thirty or thirty-five is likely to be better informed than a professor who has had the start by twenty years and more. Yet the mere effort to compete does credit to the *Privatdocent*. It quickens his faculties, it gives point to his studies. It does credit also to the German system. Under that system, no professor, however celebrated, has a right to rest from his labors, to say: My work is done, there is nothing more to learn. The university can be imagined as arguing in this wise: We shall become a dead body, if new ideas be not set forth in our lecture-rooms as fast as they arise. If the professor is not equal to the task, here is Dr. So and So, who is evidently a man of the times. Let us leave the professor to vegetate in harmless indolence, and make the Dr. his colleague, else we shall lose our students.

IV.

Students.

How shall one portray successfully in words the lineaments of that unique variety of the human species known as the German student? Although myself a student for over three years, associating more or less intimately with my fellow-students, I must plead inability to do better than sketch a very imperfect silhouette. The difficulty lies in the circumstance that there is no analogy between the German student and the American undergraduate, nothing that can help both the reader and the writer to make a fair comparison. The American collegian is — pardon me the expression — simply a school-boy of larger growth. He may be old enough to luxuriate in a moustache, muscular enough to row in the Saratoga regatta, eloquent enough to carry off some gold medal, studious enough to be regarded by his associates as a prodigy of learning. But, with all that, he is none the less a schoolboy. From the day of his matriculation to the day of his graduation, he is under surveillance more or less intrusive, he pursues a prescribed routine of study, his attendance is noted down, his performances are graded, his conduct is taken into the account, his parents or guardians receive monthly or term reports. In other words, during the entire period of four years the collegian is made to feel that he is looked upon as one incapable of judging and acting for himself. His college life is a mere continuation of his school life. The sphere is a trifle larger, it is true, the teachers are abler men, there is a greater variety of character among his associates, yet, in all substantial respects, he is still a school-boy, he learns set tasks. Whereas the German student is the direct opposite. When the young *Primaner* receives from the gymnasium his certificate of " ripeness " for the university, he knows that his school-boy days are over, that he has done forever with lessons, marks, grades, surveillance, courses of instruction. He is a young man free to select his studies, his professors, his rooms, his hours of work, to regulate the entire course of his life, to be what his own energy and talents may make him. Possibly he is not any older than the Freshman, possibly not any better prepared than if he had just left Andover or Exeter or the Boston Latin school. Nevertheless he is an altogether different creature. The shaping of his destiny lies in his hands, *and his alone*, and he feels it. If he succeeds, the merit is due to himself; if he fails, he has no one but himself to blame. He knows that neither rector nor dean nor professors will trouble themselves about him, will care whether he attends regularly or "cuts" regularly, whether he improves or wastes his time, whether he has a *Mensur* every week, whether he goes to bed sober or intoxicated. He is a young man, and can look after himself. Should he make himself obnoxious by a breach of public order and decency, he will be summoned before the university court, tried as every culprit is tried, according to the forms of justice, and punished impartially, without favor and without shedding of tears.

It will be impossible to understand the character of the German student without making this element of moral freedom and direct personal responsibility the starting-point in our investigations. In no other way shall we be able to account for such extremes of lawlessness on the one hand, such models of industry on the other. Both idleness and industry display an intensity, so to speak, that we shall look for in vain in an American college. The "rowers" do nothing but row, the industrious do nothing but study. Young *Graf von*, whose position in life is fixed, whose allowance is ample, feels that he is not sent to the university to study, but to while away his minority. What does it matter to him, whether the professors are dull or interesting, whether the Pandects were the work of Justinian or of Julius Caesar? The *Graf* is a man of some education, perhaps. A goodly amount of Latin and Greek and mathematics has been drummed into him at the gymnasium or the *Ritter-akademie*. But he does his best to shake off the burden and to enjoy life, after his fashion, with other like-minded young scions. He becomes reckless, and would degenerate into a bully but for one wholesome check. He has to fight. Side by side with the son of the nobleman is the son of the bourgeois, aping the follies of the upper classes, wasting his father's hard-earned gains, committing all sorts of extravagances, yet sturdy, clear-headed, and hard-fisted. Not more than one *Mensur* is needed to teach the nobleman that he is no match for the plebeian in fighting. It is the old story, re-told, of the Cavaliers and the Roundheads.

Nearly all the good *Schläger* in Göttingen came from the middle and lower classes. The very best one, I believe, was the son of a country parson. University life has certainly this one merit: it puts all its members on a footing of perfect equality.* Distinctions of rank vanish on the *Mensur* and in the lecture-room. The university court, in its praise be it said, knows no respect of persons. The son of the humblest barber or shop-keeper will get nothing less than justice, the son of the count or baron nothing more.

I have said that the "rowers" do nothing but row, the industrious do nothing but study. This is a blunt way of putting the antithesis, and needs some qualifications and restrictions. Those who idle away their time do so without fear and without restraint. Their attendance at lectures is merely nominal. In most instances, the habit of idleness, once acquired, is not shaken off. But in very many instances, it is. To understand this point fully, it will be necessary to look more closely into the student's antecedents. As a general thing, the young *Fuchs* enters the university overworked. He has been kept at school for eight or ten years, drilled unmercifully, watched sharply, and held in strict subordination. He cannot obtain his certificate of "ripeness" until he has complied with all the school requirements. The final examination is conducted under the supervision of state officials. All at once the pressure is removed, he is free

---

* The reader cannot do better than study, in Freytag's *Lost Manuscript*, the spirited description of the Crown Prince's duel, the causes that led to it, and the results.

to enter the university, becomes his own master. The first effect of this newly acquired freedom is to unsettle him. He changes his place of residence, forms new associations, is brought in contact with unwonted temptations. A new life has dawned upon him. He hardly knows which way to turn his steps, every prospect seems so fair. He joins probably some *Corps* or *Verbindung*, thereby subjecting himself to the direct influence of men more experienced than himself. It becomes his ambition to rival them in all that they undertake. His new friends are so agreeable, the new life is so fascinating in its freedom, that he glides along in a round of pleasure and excitement. He is undergoing the process called in German *ausrasen*, by us, "sowing wild oats." But if there is in him the making of a man, the dream will not last forever. By the end of the first semester perhaps, and certainly by the end of the second, an awakening will come. The *Fuchs* is no longer a *Fuchs*, but a *Bursch*. He perceives that what was once pleasure has begun to pall, that he has wasted valuable time and opportunities. Yet his case is not hopeless. Energy and self-denial will make the loss good. He therefore limits his *Kneipen* to one evening a week, discards *Frühschoppen*, attends lectures diligently, turns a deaf ear to invitations for a walk or a drive, keeps as much as possible out of the way of a challenge, brushes the cobwebs from his books, and begins his studies in earnest. His previous dissipation has served to sharpen his wits and to give his character a somewhat firmer set.

Some few students lose no time at the university. They pass from their preliminary to their special training without a break. Yet they are less numerous than one might suppose, and they do not always make the best workers in the long run. Taking the German method of education just as it is, we may be tempted to regard *Ausrasen* as after all not an unmixed evil. The admission need not imply sympathy with dueling and inordinate drinking. The question can be put in this shape. Is it not desirable that the boy who has been subjected to severe and protracted schooling should take a year or a half-year for rest? As *Secundaner* and *Primaner* he has been worked up to his full capacity. He has had scarcely a day outside of the brief vacations, that he could call his own. Before taking up in seriousness his life-study, is it not well in him to let his mind lie fallow a while? The shiftlessness, the bravado that prevail among German *Füchse* are, I am persuaded, nothing more than the misdirection of this healthful instinct to snatch a brief respite, to look around and enjoy life during the interval between spells of severe labor. The roll of professors and docents of any German university will be found, on examination, to contain the name of many a man who was a wild student in his first and second semester. The professions will reveal even a larger percentage. No less a man than Prince Bismarck himself was among the wildest of the wild at Göttingen thirty years ago.

The German students exhibit such varieties of character that it would be useless to attempt to reduce them to one category and label them thus and so. They have only one trait in common: individuality of thought and freedom of action. Such a sentiment as "class-feeling" does not exist among them. In America, where the same set of young men recite side by side in the same recitation-rooms for four years, it is perhaps only natural that the feeling of class unity should exist as it does. It is not in itself an evil, although liable to grave perversion. Three fourths of the public disorder in our colleges are due to it in one or another shape. In Germany, it simply does not exist. There are no courses of study, no classes. Even those who are pursuing the same general studies do not take the same lectures in the same order. Among those who attended Herrmann's lectures on Church Law with myself were men who had heard the Pandects at Heidelberg, with Vangerow, or at Munich, with Windscheid, or at Leipsic, with Wächter. Nearly every German student changes his university once, many of them more than once. Comparatively few pass their entire triennium or quadrennium in the same place. This is not mere vagrancy. It arises from the laudable desire to hear the best men in each department. Its effect is also beneficial. It gives breadth and variety of culture. The South German, by removing to Göttingen or Bonn or Berlin, shakes off his superfluity of broad good-nature, becomes less garrulous and more earnest. The Prussian or Hanoverian at Heidelberg or Tübingen, on the other hand, is toned down and softened by the charms of southern *Gemüthlichkeit*.

The student lives by himself and selects his companions according to his own taste. Even if he is not a member of a *Corps* or a *Verbindung*, he belongs to some less formal association that holds its meetings regularly. The members are not necessarily of the same faculty; one may be a chemist, another a philologian, another a jurist. The only bond of union is that of congeniality. There are no literary clubs,* no debating societies among the students. Reunions are for social pleasure, not for work; still less for mere displays of questionable eloquence. Study is something that each man is supposed to attend to in the seclusion of his own room. When he meets his friends, he lays aside "shop." Politics, in the English and American use of the word, are unknown in the German university. The time when the students were political conspirators has gone by, the time when they may take a part in the liberal discussion of political questions of the day has not yet arrived. Perhaps it will never arrive. What prompted the conspiracies and insurrections among the students during the period of the Reaction was a sense of the gross injustice and glaring incompetency of the Metternichian era, rather than a deep-seated preference for a republican form of government or a clear perception of the ways and means of reform. The Germans as a nation do not take an absorbing interest in political questions. Now that the petty *misère* of the old Confederation has been swept away, and

---

* There were literary clubs at one time, e. g., the celebrated Göttingen *Hainbund*, but they seem to have gone out of fashion.

the country placed under the control of one permanent dynasty, the Germans are satisfied to let well enough alone. The only subject that is in the least degree likely to arouse them is the conflict between Church and State. Yet even this important issue cannot be said to have agitated the students, and for a very obvious reason. They all think alike on the point. The students, Catholic no less than Protestant, are liberals. The Ultramontanes do not attend the universities, even the paritetic and purely Catholic universities, in numbers, for they feel that the general tendency of higher education is against them. The reader will remember that the leaders of the Old-Catholic movement in South Germany are the members of the theological faculty of Munich. The priests of the Catholic church are, at least have been until now, educated at the so called *convicta* and seminaries, rather than at the gymnasiums and universities. Indeed, the express object of the recently adopted Church Laws in Prussia is to force all candidates for orders into the gymnasium and university. Those laws provide that henceforth no one shall be admitted to orders or receive a parochial charge who has not passed through the full gymnasial and university course. The influence of university life is so liberalizing that the Ultramontane party meets with little favor from students, even from those of the Catholic faith. The young man who is made to feel every day for upwards of three years of his life that he must weigh all things and judge for himself, will not be apt to fall on his knees before the dogma of infallibility.

I have heard the most conflicting opinions expressed by Americans as to the intellectual ability of German students. It is not, under any circumstances, an easy matter to gauge with exactness the capacities of a class of young men numbering many thousands. One is liable to blunder by attempting to generalize from the imperfect data furnished by the very few with whom one may come in direct contact. The difficulty is increased, moreover, by the circumstance that the German mode of study affords so few opportunities for testing merit. Under the American system, where each student recites in public from day to day for years, both his fellow-students and his professors know perfectly well what he is capable of. Whereas, in Germany, the most promising scholars may pass unnoticed amid the crowd of listeners. There is absolutely but one way of eliciting information, namely, through personal intercourse, and that way is, from its very nature, limited and imperfect.

In the first place, the German student is older than the American. The average age of admission of this year's graduating class at Yale was eighteen. This is for America a high average. The German rarely attends the university before his twentieth year. Many students are even older. In the next place, the German is much more thoroughly trained. On this point, I must beg the reader to dismiss all prejudice and look the facts full in the face. That we have a few good schools, is a truism which nobody will deny. But that we have not any thing like a school-system, by virtue of which all young men, wherever they may live, can be trained for their higher education, is equally true. I except the eastern part of Massachusetts, where wealth and intelligence are so diffused that almost every district has an excellent preparatory school. But where, I venture to ask, outside of the eastern part of Massachusetts shall we find the match for a German gymnasium? Is there in the entire State of New York a single school, public or private, that can show a programme like the following:

Religion: a. Catholic. Martin's Manual, The Church and Her History. b. Protestant. Bek's Exposition of the Book of Acts.

Latin: Cicero's Catiline Orations, 1–4, pro Milone, pro Ligario; Virgil's Æneid, Books 3, 5 and 6, and parts of 9 and 10; Cicero's Tusculan Disput.; Tacitus, Book 3, and parts of 2 and 4; Horace, Odes, Books 3 and 4; Epistles, Book 1; Satires, Book 1.

Greek: Xenophon's Anabasis, Book 7; Herodotus, Schnitzer's Chrestomathy; Homer, Odyssey, 1, 2, 15, 16, 17, 18, parts of 20, 21, 22; Sophocles, Antigone; Demosthenes, 1–3 Olynthiacs; Philippics, 1; Iliad, 7, 9, 21, 22, 24; Plato's Apology and Crito.

Hebrew: Grammar, Mezger's Exercises; Gesenius' Syntax; Psalms; Isaiah.

French: Syntax, according to Eisenmann; Grauer's Chrestomathy.

English: Gantler's Chrestomathy; Shakespeare's Julius Caesar.

German: History of Old and Mediæval Literature,

with Scholl's Specimens; Nibelungenlied; Grammar of Middle High German; Schiller's Wallenstein read and explained.

History: Pütz, Roman History; Pütz, Middle Ages.

Physical Geography.

Chemistry: Metalloids and Metals.

Physics: Brettner's Manual.

Natural History: Mineralogy and Geology; Somatology and Anthropology.

Mathematics: Quadratic Equations; Diaphantic Equations; Arithmetical and Geometrical Progression; Geometry.

Archæology: Homerica; Greek and Roman Antiquities.

Mythology: Stoll's Greek and Roman Mythology.

Philosophy: Psychology and Logic.

Perhaps the reader thinks that this must be some "crack" school in Berlin or Leipsic. Not at all. It is the programme for the gymnasium of a town of which he has, in all probability, never heard. If he consults his Gazetteer, he will find that Ellwangen is a small town in Württemberg, forty-five miles N. E. of Stuttgart. Population, in 1857, 3,000. At the present day, probably 5,000. Yet we find this obscure Franconian town, off the highroad of commerce and culture, giving its children the best of training. I have quoted the programme only for the upper classes of the gymnasium proper, and have omitted the *Realclassen.*

As an offset, let me submit the following programme

from North Germany. As Prussia is the centre of Germany, so Brandenburg is the centre of Prussia. In the *Prima* of the *Ritter-Akademie* of Brandenburg were pursued, during the year ending Easter, 1872, the following studies.

Religion, 2 hours a week. Gospel of St. John, in the original. History of the Mediæval Church. Epistle to the Galatians, in the original. History of the Modern Churches.

German, 3 h. Themes. Résumé of German national literature from Opitz to Lessing. Also, reading of Richard II. and Macbeth. Exercises in Logic.

Latin, 8 h. Cicero pro Plancio. (In private, Quintilian X). Tacitus, Annal. XII–XV. Exercises and Themes. Extemporalia. Horace, Odes Bk. II. and III. Selected Satires and Epistles. 10–12 Odes memorized.

Greek, 6 h. Sophocles, Electra. Thucydides II, 1–64. (In private, Homer). Plato, Protagoras. (In private, Thucydides, IV). Exercises and extemporalia.

Hebrew, 2 h. Selections from Psalms and Samuel. Hebrew doctrine of forms, entire, according to Gesenius. Selections from the Snytax.

French, 3 h. Review of Grammar. Oral translations into French, from Ploetz' Exercises. Bazancourt's Crimean Expedition read.

History, 3 h. Review of Ancient History. History of the World from 1715–1789.

Mathematics, 4 h. Trigonometry and Stereometry.

Physics, 2 h. Mechanics. Electricity, and Magnetism.

The final examination at the gymnasium consists of oral and written reviews (the examination proper), and of themes prepared at home. I give specimens of the themes set by the *Ritter-Akademie.*

German. What are the permanent merits of Klopstock in German Literature?

Latin. Quam fuerit funestum cum ceteris Graeciae civitatibus tum Atheniensibus bellum Peloponnesiacum argumentis comprobetur.

Mathematics. By revolving an isosceles triangle and the inscribed circle, you produce a cone and a sphere. What are the proportions of the two bodies in respect to their superficial area and their solid contents?

A few words of explanation are needed. Hebrew is obligatory only upon those who intend to study theology. By *extemporalia* are meant extempore translations made during the school-hour. The teacher reads aloud from some German work, and the pupils translate as well as they can into Latin, without the aid of grammar or dictionary.

By *privatim* reading is meant this. The teacher assigns to the pupil portions of a certain classic author, to be read at home but not recited upon in school.

Neither the gymnasium at Ellwangen nor the *Ritter-Akademie* of Brandenburg can be regarded as occupying the foremost rank among German schools. The gymnasiums at Berlin, Cologne, Leipsic, Frankfort, and the other large cities, and the celebrated institution at Schulpforta are superior in the quality of their teachers and their pupils. The *Ritter-Akademie*, as the catalogue shows, is a school for the Brandenburg nobility.

In 1863, when the population of Prussia (before the annexation of Hanover and Hesse-Cassel) was 18,000,000, *i. e.*, less than half the German Empire, there were 172 gymnasiums in Prussia, giving instruction to 45,000 pupils, and 83 *Realschulen*, giving instruction to 20,000 pupils. The difference between the gymnasium and the *Realschule* is that the latter teaches less Latin and comparatively little Greek, but goes deeper into history, modern languages, mathematics, and the natural sciences. I have no recent statistics in my possession, but I shall probably not go very wide of the mark in stating that in the German Empire of to-day there are between five and six hundred schools of the first order, instructing nearly 150,000 pupils on what Matthew Arnold has called so happily "the higher plane" of education.

At Ellwangen there were forty-five pupils pursuing the studies that I have mentioned. These pupils were taught by eight instructors. In the *Prima* of the *Ritter-Akademie* there were nineteen pupils taught by five instructors. These figures show clearly that the German system is one of small classes, where the instruction can be brought home to the pupil.

Finally, there is an additional feature in the German school system which has been overlooked even by so careful an observer as Matthew Arnold. I allude to the circumstance that a German seldom changes his school. He is kept at the same institution from his tenth or even his eighth year to his twentieth. He has a chance to master one set of text-books thoroughly, to advance regularly, year by year, in carefully measured progression. He wastes no time by sudden changes either of books or of teachers. Besides, even should a boy be transferred from one gymnasium to another, he would find in his new school the same quality of instruction and a similar corps of instructors.

It does not come within the scope of this work to exhaust the subject of German schools. The reader who wishes to inform himself more thoroughly may consult Matthew Arnold's treatise. I touch upon the schools only as they influence the universities, in the endeavor to make the reader appreciate more accurately the difference between the American undergraduate and the German student. It is perfectly true that no amount of system will atone for want of brains. Many a young man who has been pushed through the gymnasium by the aid of persistent and kindly disposed teachers will drop as soon as the momentum is spent. Sluggish, inert in himself, he becomes at the university a mere dawdler. His thin plating of knowledge wears off little by little, until the ignoble metal beneath appears in all its worthlessness, and you wonder how any such fellow could ever have been pronounced fit for a university. Yet is Germany the only country in the world that exhibits this phenomenon of running to seed? Does not every American college graduate men who know actually less than they did on entering?

The only just way of comparing two systems is to take them at points widely apart. The idler of Germany, I am confident, has forgotten twice as much as the idler of America, the industrious student knows twice as much as the industrious undergraduate, and the future scholar of Germany is a man of whom we in America have no conception. He is a man who could not exist under our system, he would be choked by recitations and grades. What he studies, he studies with the devotion of a poet and the trained skill of a scientist. The idea of competing, of putting forth all his energies in a trial of skill after the fashion of the English university examination, has never occurred to him. He studies to learn, to master what has been done before him, and to contribute if possible to the growth of knowledge. He reads with a view to permanent results, not to examinations. To justify these assertions, it will be necessary to define more precisely what I mean by "knowledge." Life in Germany is not so free as in America. It presents fewer elements of excitement, moves rather in a prescribed routine. It does not exhibit a like frantic haste after fame and wealth. The newspaper press, vegetating rather than flourishing under humdrum circumstances, is deficient in everything that we call enterprise. Any one of our great dailies gives its readers more and better reading than the entire press of Berlin. The Germans do not look upon their newspapers as daily pabulum. The German boy, although well informed, grows up in comparative ignorance of the great social and political movements around him. He knows much less of the world, his mind is not stocked with scraps of news gathered from papers and magazines. The American boy, to use an Americanism, is much more wide-awake. He can tell you what has happened yesterday in China or Africa, what is likely to happen to-morrow in South America. Yet we can scarcely call this knowledge, in the highest sense of the term. It is rather *allotria*, the unsifted, unarranged, undigested materials of knowledge. What the German gymnasiast knows at all, he knows well, because he knows it as an item of general training, and in its relations to other things. For instance, although Germany and France are next-door neighbors, the gymnasiast does not watch from day to day, from month to month, the political convulsions at Paris and Versailles. Yet he has probably read with a good deal of care the history of France from its origin, and is in a position to form a correct judgment as to what these convulsions really betoken. If you lay before him the events as they transpire from time to time, he will *understand* them, because he will view them as the present out-cropping of forces which he has traced in their operation for centuries.

By way of presenting the average German student more in the concrete, I take the liberty of drawing the portrait of the one whom I knew best. He came from a small town in the Hartz mountains, a town almost identical in size and general character with Ellwangen. My friend H ——, who was my teacher in German and also for a while in Latin and Greek, was a young man of twenty-three or twenty-four, tall, large of frame but not muscular, and in excellent health. His spirits were invariably good. He was a thorough Latin and Greek scholar. I was particularly struck with his proficiency in writing Greek. He wrote it very rapidly, in an easy, current hand, using abbreviations not unlike the ligatures in the editions of the sixteenth century. In short, he had a Greek *hand*, and did not print each letter separately as an American does. He filled in the accents after writing, as an American or Englishman crosses his *t*'s and dots his *i*'s. He seemed to have the entire Greek grammar as well as the Latin at his tongue's end, he was never at a loss for rule and exception. He had studied Hebrew enough at the gymnasium to be able to read the Old Testament with the vowel points. He had also studied Sanscrit under Benfey at the university, and could read the epic poetry with fluency. In addition to this, he was a fair scholar in mediæval German, and was well versed in ancient and mediæval history. To crown all, he was an excellent pianist, sang well, and could drink his five *Schoppen* of beer every evening and rise to his work the next morning as fresh as though he had gone to bed fasting. He was by no means a book-worm, but enjoyed life as it passed. For the subject of his doctoral dissertation he selected the Greek of Euripedes. As the classic student will know, the texts of this author have come to us in a very corrupt state. My friend, not content with studying the texts themselves, employed his leisure time for an entire semester in collating stray fragments of the great dramatist scattered through the writings of other authors, and especially the quotations contained in patristic Greek. Although not competent to venture an opinion on such a subject, I have no doubt that H —— made a very exhaustive and scholarly dissertation. Yet he was not a "first-rate." I have known more than one student who was decidedly his superior in breadth of learning and grasp of intellect. Graded after the American fashion, he would have ranked as tenth in a class of one hundred. He was a man, not of genius, but of talent and industry, one who has profited by his opportunities without foregoing the minor pleasures of society. From this class of students Germany recruits her gymnasium teachers.

Perhaps the reader would like to know what I mean by a "first-rate." In my third semester I became acquainted with a young Dr. B ——, who had been out of the university three years. He was then barely in his twenty-sixth year. In addition to his uncommon attainments in Greek and Latin, he had passed a year in France, and two years in England. He spoke English and French with perfect fluency and precision, and could maintain a conversation in Italian and Spanish. He was a favorite pupil of Ewald in Persian, Hebrew and Arabic, and, as Benfey assured me, was the most promising young Sanscrit scholar of Germany. Soon after I made his acquaintance, he was appointed professor of Oriental Languages at Queen's College, Bombay, through the influence of Max Müller. In less than a year after entering upon the duties of his professorship, he inaugurated the publication of a long and carefully edited series of valuable Sanscrit texts. He was, in all respects, what we call a "driver," a man who knows no rest.

If opinions differ concerning the intellectual ability of German students, they differ even more widely concerning their manners. On this point, I am disposed to accuse my countrymen of a touch of prejudice. Disappointed in not finding the German student the exact counterpart of themselves, they are averse to associating with him freely. They overlook the circumstance that student-life is emphatically the period of fermentation, that the scum and froth now on the surface will soon disappear, leaving the clear, sparkling wine. German ways are not our ways. Many things that we look upon as indispensable in the deportment of a gentleman are secondary matters to a German, while he on the other hand views with disfavor much that we regard as permissible. Intercourse between the German and the American becomes, then, a question of mutual forbearance. Each party has to make some concession, and the German — to his credit be it confessed — is the readier of the two to waive a portion at least of his prejudices.

For one, I never had any trouble in dealing with my fellow-students. If, in returning to my room in the evening, I was met by a party of "rowers" bent on picking a quarrel, I had only to intimate my nationality to pass unmolested. In fact, even that was not usually necessary. In a small university town, like Göttingen, foreigners become known as such. Not infrequently I have heard one man soberer than his companions say: "O, pshaw! That's an American. What's the use of wasting words on him." Yet that was German student-life at his worst. In the ordinary intercourse at public dining tables and in the lecture-rooms, I have always found the same ceremonial politeness that men of the world show to one another. The men with whom I read the Institutes of Gaius and of Justinian were *Corps* students; my associates in Dr. Maxen's *Exegeticum* were *Wilde*. The one set was fully as agreeable as the other. In fact, the *Corps* students were a trifle more easy and genial in their manners. One who is desirous of making acquaintances will have no difficulty. He will find many bright young fellows, well educated, limited in their means, thoroughly in earnest with their studies, but affable and entertaining, out-spoken in their opinions, somewhat positive, but not apt to give or to take offense. In one respect they differ from young Americans. They do not indulge in sportive demonstrations of familiarity. Even *Dutzbrüder* do not slap one another on the back. The student, indeed the German in general, seems to have adopted the motto, *Noli me tangere*. Even one who is brusque in his manner, not to say uncouth, will never presume upon personal liberties. This, I suspect, is the result of the individuality engendered by culture. However intimate men may be, each seeks to maintain his individuality. Much that we regard as "fun" would be looked upon by the German as an unpardonable want of dignity and self-respect. The student wishes to be just what he is, and will not give up an iota of his idiosyncracies for the dearest friend on earth. You may argue earnestly, even heatedly with him; that is only manly. But you cannot venture to ridicule him, for that would be assuming superiority and treating him as a boy.

The cardinal sin of the students is excess in drinking. They all drink, and nearly all drink too much. Yet it should be borne in mind that this vice is not confined to the students. Germany is preëminently a land of free living. Everybody drinks as a matter of course. The students merely push the custom to an extreme, by their *Saufcomment*. On the other hand, what they drink is much less injurious to health than the gin and whisky of America. Although beer and wine produce temporary intoxication, they do not waste the tissues and nervous energy. Many a man who has kneiped persistently through his university course, and barely passed the state-examination, settles down into an orderly, sober citizen. Germany is a land of drinking, but, paradoxical as it may seem, it is not a land of drunkards. The average American village can exhibit more hopeless sots, men saturated to the core and reeking with alcoholic fumes, than are to be found in a large German city, like Hanover or Leipsic.

Much, if not all, that is crude, chaotic, absurd, repellant in the student's composition will disappear in the course of time. I rest this belief upon the teachings of history. Not farther back than fifty or sixty years, the student was indeed a lawless creature. Who has not heard of the madcap revelries, the follies and Reign of Terror of the Jenensians? Greatly as the dukes of Weimar loved and favored their university, they were forced to put down more than one outbreak at the point of the bayonet and sabre. In the last century, the students of Jena not infrequently fought their duels in the open air, on a platform in the market place in front of the townhall. Intoxicated students reeled through the streets at all hours, insulting peasants and women, lording it over the Philistine. The history of the universities throughout the eighteenth, seventeenth, sixteenth and fifteenth centuries is a record of violence, bloodshed, and debauch. The country itself was in a state of transition. The Reformation had emancipated the German spirit from the shackles of tradition, the Thirty Years' War turned brother against brother, land against land. The dreary epoch of *Pennalismus*, an elaborate system of fagging, set in. Letters and breeding seemed to have passed from the memory of men. From 1648 to 1749, the year of Goethe's birth, the country lay prostrate, exhausted, as one dead. When the revival came under Bodmer and Breitinger, Lessing, Goethe, Herder and Schiller, there came with it the French Revolution, the Storm and Stress period, and later still the era of Romanticism and the Reaction. The nation revived, but not without many a racking birth-throe. It had no peace, either in politics or in philosophy. System after system rose and fell, Leibnitz, Thomasius, Spinoza, Kant, Schelling, Hegel, Fichte swept across the German mind, as the Swedes, French, Croats, Russians, Cossacks, Italians, English swept over the country. It was not until the July Revolution and the death of Goethe, in round numbers the year 1830, that Germany caught the first glimmerings of the dawn of material prosperity and national stability. Is it surprising, then, that the students should have been in sympathy with the state of their country, should have exhibited in their action and sentiments every phase from imbecile pedantry to heaven-defying Titanism? The student of to-day, as I have said on a previous occasion, is not the student of 1830, or of 1800; neither is he the student of 1900. With increase of wealth and the consciousness of belonging to the foremost political power in Europe, will also come a keener appreciation of the axiom, *noblesse oblige*. Many things tolerable, permissible in the subjects of a second-rate power struggling for acknowledgment, will appear incompatible with membership in a great nation. Foremost among the subduing, repressive agencies of the future, I am disposed to rate the compulsory military service. Until very recently, none but Prussian students had to serve their term; students in the other German states could purchase exemption. Now all have to serve alike for one year, as *einjährige Freiwillige*. Viewed on one side, this is a cruel waste of time; on the other, it will undoubtedly teach the students habits of subordination, and cure them of many of their present vagaries. The man who has drilled and mounted guard for a twelve-month is apt to take a soberer view of life. The Prussian universities are a proof of this; the dueling at them was never so bad as it was at the non-Prussian. We should do the German student great injustice by ignoring his antecedents. His virtues are mainly his own, his vices are mainly inherited; they are the relics of a by-gone age, and cannot be shaken off by a single generation, much less by arbitrary enactments emanating from those in authority. They must disappear of themselves, one by one.

As one who has enjoyed to the full and in a thankful spirit the privileges of the *libertas academica*, I should regard the diminution of that freedom by the smallest tittle as a disaster to Germany and to the world at large. Fortunately there is no danger of such a blunder. The Germans are too strongly attached to their system of school and university to tamper with either, too deeply conscious of the services rendered by both school-master and professor to suffer the one to interfere with the other. At the same time I cherish the hope that the day will come, and that right speedily, when the *Saufcomment* and the *Mensur* shall have disappeared save as traditions, when the student shall have been toned down to conformity with the rules of ordinary society, and shall cease to look upon himself as aught but a free man pursuing liberal studies. Hitherto the ideal and the real have seldom been blended in German life. Side by side with the highest spiritual culture, are still to be found only too often slovenliness of garb and awkwardness — shall I call it uncouthness? — of manner. The students are not alone in this respect. The same defect may be observed, although less frequently and in a less degree, in professors and men of letters. How often is the traveler in Germany pained at the want of congruity between the soul and the man, how often forced to regret that the *entire* being, to use the threadbare expression of Matthew Arnold, is not yet pervaded by sweetness and light. It is not for Americans to find fault with German students or professors. We are too deeply in their debt to speak of their sterling qualities in a tone of flippancy. It behooves us to admire and respect them. Yet the friend who rejoices in their prosperity may be permitted to wish for them a trifle more of ease and grace of manner, a character just a shade less positive and a shade more winsome.

V.

Discipline.

After endeavoring so strenuously to represent the German university as an institution that affords the utmost intellectual and social freedom, it may seem inconsistent in me to devote a special section of the present work to the subject of discipline. How can there be such a thing as discipline at Berlin, or Leipsic, or Göttingen? What hold has the university, as a body, a corporation, upon the individual student? To which I answer: a very strong hold, much stronger indeed than the arbitrary sway of our American faculty-meetings. When the university makes its authority felt, it does so with the precision, the dignity, and the inflexibility of a legal tribunal.

The administration of discipline is entrusted to the university court. The composition of this body varies with the different universities. The principal members, however, are the Rector and the University Judge (*Universitätsrichter*). This latter, who may be a member of the legal faculty and who must be a jurist, is a government official. He represents directly the head of the nation. The Rector,* if not himself a jurist, associates with him some member of the legal faculty as adviser. In grave emergencies, *e. g.*, in case of a student-insurrection, the Senatus Academicus would be convened. But ordinarily the administration of justice is in the hands of the two men above mentioned. The beadles are the university police, empowered to make arrests and summon delinquents. The proceedings before the university court are strictly legal in their character, the form of procedure being prescribed by royal mandate. The court is responsible, directly and personally, to the Ministry of Public Instruction. It has the power of compelling the attendance of those subject to its jurisdiction, and of compelling testimony under oath, if necessary.

The jurisdiction of the court is strictly defined. So also are the punishments that it can inflict. These consist of fines, imprisonment, damages, and suspension or

---

* The rectorship is not a permanent office, but rotates from year to year among the four faculties.

expulsion. (The ordinary punishment is imprisonment in the university *Carcer* for a term varying from one day to two weeks. The offender is permitted to attend lectures, on parole, but otherwise is kept in close, and usually solitary, confinement. His meals are served in his cell, by the beadle. He has to pay for them at fixed rates. He can have in his cell such books as he may need for pursuing his studies, and he is permitted, I believe, to smoke. The beadle will also furnish beer, to a limited extent, "on the sly." Incarceration, therefore, does not interfere with one's studies; it merely restricts one's freedom of movement for the while. It is scarcely a hardship to be locked up after this fashion for a fortnight. Yet it is a monstrous bore, and looked upon as such by those who have had occasion to experience its sobering influence.

Fines are imposed occasionally for breaches of public order. Damages occur chiefly in connection with alimentation suits. In general, whatever has to do with the money-matters of the student is under the exclusive control of the academic court. Nearly every university has its *Credit-edict*, a legal enactment prescribing with minuteness the amount to which and the objects for which shop-keepers may give credit. Civil suits for goods sold and delivered, services performed, room-rent, and the like, must be brought in the academic court. They will not be received by the ordinary civil courts. If the claimant has not complied with the terms of the *Credit-edict*, his claim is barred, and cannot be brought even after the student has left the university. The exception, like that arising from our usury laws, runs *in perpetuo*. The object of the *Credit-edict* is to protect students, who are proverbially thoughtless, from being overreached, and to break up the pernicious system of unlimited credit which prevails among the shop-keepers in university towns.

The reader will perceive that the university court has nothing to do with the manners and morals of the student, except so far as they may be violations of positive law. But the moment the student transgresses the limits of public order and decency, he is promptly arraigned and promptly punished. He is tried as offenders are tried in our police courts, *i. e.*, for a specific offense, proved by witnesses, and punished by fine or imprisonment. The notion of reforming the delinquent, of reducing him to a more or less lachrymose state and exhorting him to mend his ways, is not one that influences the *Universitätsrichter*. His business, like that of every other judge, is to punish.

The leniency with which dueling is treated may seem to conflict with this view of the university court as the guardian of public order. Although I have already discussed the subject of dueling, I take the liberty of reverting to it, by way of adding a final word. According to the German theory, dueling is not strictly an infringement upon public order. When two men quarrel in the street and come to blows, they commit a breach of the peace for which both are to be punished. But if, instead of this, one man challenges the other, and the challenge is accepted, the duel which ensues is something of a different nature; the elements of agreement and secrecy come in to change its character. The duel is punishable, but not as a breach of the peace. I do not say that the theory is a correct one. I merely give it as it has been set forth to me repeatedly by Germans. It will explain to us why street-fighting is of such rare occurrence in Germany, and why dueling is comparatively so common. Let us suppose the case of two students becoming involved in a personal altercation. One of them considers himself insulted by the other. He has his choice of redress. He can either challenge, or he can lay the matter before the university court and demand a formal apology and declaration of honor (*Ehrenerklärung*). The court is bound by the terms of its constitution to listen to his complaint, to examine the evidence, and to compel the offending party to retract, under penalty of expulsion. It is not a question of what the judge may or may not think best, it is a question of legal right on the part of the complainant, and is to be settled according to the evidence. But if the student sees fit to waive his legal privileges and to resort to arms, he takes, as I have said before, his chances. The university judge, seeing himself ignored, is certainly not going out of his way to investigate the affair, about which he knows nothing. All that he does know is that the practice of dueling prevails among students, and that any attempt on his part to put a sudden stop to it would bring a nest of hornets about his ears. The beadles cannot watch the movements of seven hundred or a thousand young men carefully enough to prevent more than one duel in ten. Occasionally they succeed in making a capture. The offenders are then tried summarily and imprisoned for a fortnight. It is only when the dueling threatens to become too frequent, that the university judge considers it necessary to whip up his myrmidons to extra zeal and activity.

But dueling aside, the reader can rest assured that public order is strictly maintained. The student may idle away his time unchecked, he may amuse himself in a variety of questionable ways, he may befuddle himself every day in the week, for in doing so he injures only himself, and the university does not consider itself a reformatory school. But he must not do aught to interfere with the comfort of peaceable citizens. Boisterous singing in the streets, breaking lamps, stealing signboards, abusing night-watchmen, and a dozen other playful diversions of the kind, against which the American faculty is comparatively helpless, are certain to call down the wrath of the judge. The offenses are committed, but then they are always punished. Each successive generation of students learns by its own experience the sad truth embodied in the following parody on Schiller's *Song of the Bell*, inscribed in charcoal on the walls of the Göttingen *Carcer*:

> *Gefährlich ist's den Pudel wecken,*
> *Verderblich ist des Profax' Zahn,*
> *Jedoch der schrecklichste der Schrecken,*
> *Das ist der Wolff in seinem Wahn.*

Wolff was at the time judge. *Profax*, corresponding to our term "Prex," is the cant name for Prorector.

To give an idea of the strictness of the principles upon which university justice is administered, I narrate the following incident. It was the only occasion on which I came in contact with the court. One afternoon in August, during the long vacation, I called at the room of a friend, bringing with me an Italian, a young man not connected in any way with the university but engaged in special work in the library. My friend stepped into his sleeping-room to change his coat preparatory to joining us in a walk. While we were waiting for him, the Italian amused himself by throwing an empty soda-water bottle at a dog in the public square below. It was a thoughtless, boyish freak, committed on the spur of the moment, and did no harm, not even to the dog. Nevertheless, glass is not a substance to be trifled with. The bottle fell upon the unpaved earth and did not break. One of the beadles, who happened to pass by at the moment, made a note of the house and the room. No sooner had the university re-opened in October, and the university court resumed its sessions, than my friend was cited to appear. I accompanied him as a witness. But my testimony was not even received. The judge addressed my friend:

J. Herr ——, you are charged with having thrown a bottle from the window of your room on such and such a day last August. Did you commit the offense?

A. I did not. I knew nothing of the affair until it was over.

J. But the bottle was thrown from your room?

A. Yes. But it was thrown by somebody else, without my knowledge and consent.

J. Who threw it, then?

A. An acquaintance, named ——.

J. Can you produce him in court?

A. No. He has left Göttingen, and, I suppose, will not return. I do not know where he is at present.

J. Very well. Then I shall have to hold you responsible. The occupant of a room is liable for all that takes place in his room. You are fined twenty silver groschen (fifty cents). I cannot tolerate any such dangerous practice as throwing bottles upon public ground, where people are passing continually. If you cannot produce the real offender, you must suffer yourself.

Such a system operates to promote a healthy tone among the students. One rarely if ever hears them speak of their professors in words of disrespect. A student may look upon some one professor as an old-fogy, or *langweilig*, and his lectures as a bore. But in all this there is no personal hostility, no grudge. Furthermore, one does not hear from the students complaints of injustice. Every man who has "sat out" his term in the *Carcer* knows full well that he was legally tried, and legally punished. He would no more think of complaining of unfair treatment than would the habitués of Jefferson Market. He knows that his sentence was inflicted, not for the violation of an ill defined and fluctuating code of morals and etiquette, but for the violation of laws and regulations emanating from the State itself and administered by a State official who is personally responsible for neglect and maladministration.

VI.

Comparison with English Universities

I approach this part of the subject with reluctance. Not having visited either Oxford or Cambridge, my knowledge of the English university system is at best only second-hand, and confessedly imperfect. English scholarship ranks high in America. We are apt to regard the best men of Oxford and Cambridge as prodigies in their respective departments. Without intending to speak in disparagement of the English universities, I venture to put in a word of dissent from the indiscriminate praise that is heaped upon them in Mr. Bristed's work. One has only to study attentively Matthew Arnold's report on the educational system of Germany, above all to read between the lines and detect what the author thinks but dares not express, to gain the conviction that higher education in England labors under many and grave evils.

The chief objections that may be urged against the English system, so far as I can formulate them, are as follows. The education afforded by Oxford and Cambridge is illiberal, is expensive, and is comparatively unproductive of results.

It is illiberal both in its quantity and its quality. All told, the number of students at Oxford and Cambridge is between 3,000 and 4,000. Leipsic alone has almost as many. In the German Empire, the matriculated students (according to the University Calendar for the present summer) are in round numbers 16,000. This includes twenty universities, but not the Catholic Academy of Münster. It does not include non-matriculating attendants at lectures, of whom there are 1,816 at Berlin alone, nor does it include the Austrian universities. In other words, there are five men pursuing a higher education in Germany for one in the United Kingdom. To this it may be objected that the comparison takes no note of institutions like the universities of Edinburgh and Glasgow, Trinity College (Dublin), and others of a more limited nature in the city of London. But do Edinburgh, Glasgow, or Trinity rank with Oxford and Cambridge? I put the question as a foreigner, one who is free from petty local prejudices or jealousies. Are not the students who set the tone better prepared at Oxford and Cambridge than elsewhere? Is not the instruction, as a whole, of a higher order? Do not Oxford and Cambridge claim to be the seats of learning by eminence? When an English writer speaks of "university men," does he not mean, as a matter of course, Oxons and Cantabs? Regarding the amount of study accomplished, the scope of the curriculum, prestige, wealth of endowment, social and political influence, we shall be constrained to place Oxford and Cambridge by themselves, as the best that the English system can exhibit. This will not hinder us from admitting the personal superiority of many Edinburgh and Glasgow graduates.

As the best, then, that the United Kingdom can exhibit, I must pronounce Oxford and Cambridge illiberal in comparison with the stately list of universities that begins with Berlin and ends with Würzburg. Oxford and Cambridge do not represent the entire Kingdom, do not train the men from all classes of society and for all the professions. The German university is national property, the English is not. It is a private corporation, pursuing objects of its own selection and heeding public clamor only when that clamor becomes too loud, too unmistakable to be longer neglected. It is sectarian in its character and in its tendency, aristocratic in its atmosphere, and — severe as the expression may sound — bigoted in its mode of instruction. It is sectarian because it is a Church of England institution. Now the Church of England is as liberal as any church well can be. The very circumstance that it is broken up into so many factions or cliques only proves as much. Yet broad and generous as it may be, it is still narrow in mind and heart as compared with mankind at large. Is it not strange, then, well nigh intolerable, that a country like England, claiming to have shaken off all the fetters of spiritual and political bondage, should tolerate such exclusivism in letters? Dissenters, Catholics, and Jews, it is true, can now pursue their studies at Oxford and Cambridge, and are admitted to competition for university prizes. But since how long? And even now, can the Dissenter, the Catholic, or the Jew look upon Oxford or Cambridge as his university, are any of the professors his professors, is any part of the curriculum shaped with reference to his tenets? In Germany, the Catholics have their own universities, or, in Protestant countries, their paritetic faculties. Among the professors are not a few Jews, men of the widest reputation. Every German, irrespective of creed, of sectional jealousy, feels that any German university can be his, that wherever conflict of religious opinion comes in, allowances are made for his peculiarities. The consequence is that all the German universities are knit together by the strongest of spiritual bonds. Students pass freely from one to the other, without so much as dreaming of jealousy or of drawing invidious comparisons. The 16,000 young men now attending the twenty German universities are put on a footing of the most absolute equality as to rights and obligations. Nor is this all. These universities meet the intellectual wants of the entire nation. Not only is no man excluded from them, either theoretically or practically, but every man of literary, scientific, or political aspirations must attend them. They are the only avenues through which one can hope to enter the professions. They are shaped so as to furnish instruction of the highest order in every branch. One can scarcely mention a subject of investigation that is not taught at every German university by one, or ten, or perhaps twenty men of ability. The universities are State institutions, open to all citizens as a matter of right. They are under the control of the Ministry of Public Instruction, they are the Corinthian capital of the national system of education. They are just as much national property as the public schools, the courts, the post-office.

What is the contrast presented by Oxford and Cambridge? Young men are compelled to wear an absurd mediæval garb, one that might afford a good question for our debating societies, namely, whether it was intended by nature for ornament or for use. Young men are compelled to attend the religious services of a church which does not represent the entire nation, are compelled to live by routine, to keep hours. And finally, they are compelled to follow prescribed courses of study. Everywhere compulsion, nowhere the freedom that the German is taught to regard as the prime element in study. The instruction at Oxford and Cambridge is excellent in its way, but it runs in too narrow grooves, it has too much the character of training for a boat-race, and too little the character of "science." Those who compete for fellowships and prizes are hampered in many ways, being forced to acquire a certain amount of superficial familiarity with branches outside of their chosen department. The classical men are bored with mathematics, the mathematical men are bored with the classics. It is only within twenty or thirty years that the "natural-science" men have had any chance whatever. We shall scarcely find a more apt illustration of the weakness, the want of liberality in the English system, than Mr. Bristed's description of Dr. Whewell's advent to power, as Master of Trinity College, Cambridge. Mr. Bristed writes (p. 119), "By these and similar proceedings he made himself very unpopular with the mass of students, and the classical men were particularly annoyed at an avowed intention of changing the plan on which scholarships had been given. It was semi-officially announced through the various tutors and other college officers (the Master is not supposed to hold any *personal* communication with the undergraduates in his official capacity), that a certain modicum of Mathematics — I forget how many marks, but certainly more than many of the classical men had been in the habit of aspiring to — would be absolutely insisted upon, and the classical papers of those who did not come up to this standard would not be looked at. * * * The classical men found the University Tripos regulations which required them to go out in Mathematical Honors before they could sit for Classical, exceedingly oppressive, but they endured them as sturdily as their elders do the taxes; it was some compensation and consolation to be able to do without the much disliked study at Trinity, and to get Scholarships and Fellowships by dint of Classics alone. For Trinity scholars had been so utterly unmathematical as to go out among the πολλοὶ, and yet were elected Fellows after it. The cases were not very common, to be sure, but they were numerous enough for a precedent. To introduce into the college examinations any restrictions like those which embarrassed the university ones, was invading the votaries of classical lore in their very citadel." The reader must bear in mind the distinction between the college and the university. Trinity College is the seat of classic learning, yet the University of Cambridge, as a whole, is mathematical in its proclivities. The college favors a certain set of studies, the university another. A new Master is appointed for the college, who threatens to change its character. Those students who had entered Trinity College in good faith, supposing that no more than a limited amount of work in mathematics would be exacted from them, find their prospects of college preferment suddenly overcast. With them it was not merely a point of honor, but a question of pecuniary loss. They were cut off from the chances of a Fellowship. Can anything be imagined more arbitrary, more spasmodic? One man is to have the right of setting and upsetting. Education, which should be planned in accordance with definite principles, is to be made a matter of individual caprice.

Neither Oxford nor Cambridge is a university in the true sense of the term. It is a congeries of colleges. Each college has its own organization, its own administration, its own body of students and instructors. The university has but a nominal share in the instruction and the discipline. The most that it does is to set the requirements for the Tripos. In Germany there are no colleges. The faculties of the university are co-ordinated. The rectorship passes year by year from one faculty to another. The student is responsible to his faculty for the quality of his work, but the discipline is administered by the university at large. The theologian, the jurist, the classical philologist, the mathematician, the student of medicine, the historian, the geologist, are co-equal. No one can claim precedence over the other. Merit is not gauged according to preconceived opinions as to the respective superiority of classics over mathematics, or vice versa, or of the two over the sciences of nature. Each student has his own branch of study, and ranks as good or bad according to his performances in that branch alone.

To make this perfectly clear, I should place side by side, in tabular array, the list of hours and studies of Oxford, for instance, and of some German university, say Leipsic. But the space is wanting. I give in a subsequent place the list for Leipsic alone. The reader who wishes to inform himself more fully, need only contrast it with the Oxford calendar. After making the comparison, he will scarcely be tempted to rank the two institutions as equals.

The secret of the German university instruction is this. It rests upon a broad basis of well graded public schools. How England stands in this respect, has been abundantly shown by Matthew Arnold. The English have no schools that correspond to the German gymnasiums. Both Oxford and Cambridge, with all their pretensions, have to make good the defects of even such schools as Eton, Rugby, Harrow and Winchester. I have cited in another place the courses, in whole or in part, of two gymnasiums selected at random as representatives of their class. They show that the public schools of Germany teach all that a man need master in the way of general discipline. The classics are well taught, but so are mathematics, the modern languages, the natural sciences, history, and belles lettres. The *Primaner* who gets his *Maturitätszeugniss* (certificate of ripeness) is fully the peer of the best sixth-form boy of Rugby in classics — even Mr. Arnold admits that — and, what Mr. Arnold passes over in silence without expressly admitting, he is superior in everything else. He knows all that can be expected of a well educated man in the way of general information on general topics. For his special training, and for this alone, there remains the university.

An additional defect of the English universities is their practice of testing scholarship by close competitive examinations. The Honor-men of Oxford and Cambridge, the Scholars and Fellows, are undoubtedly men of superior attainments. They have done a prodigious amount of work in a very short time. The question is, whether the work is of the right kind, and whether it is done in the right way. After reading attentively Mr. Bristed's work, and others, I am forced to the conclusion — shared moreover by the leading scholars of Germany — that competitive examinations are not the proper test of scientific study. Speed, knack, what the English call "pace," is unduly exalted at the expense of thoroughness and originality. The candidate for honors reads certain works and authors because he has every reason for believing that they will be "set," he neglects others because he knows that they are not "set." In other words, he subjects his individual preferences to the conventionalisms of the examiners. Term after term, year after year, he is kept on the stretch. He asks himself repeatedly the question: Can I afford to do this? Will it not be safer to do that? He has not the opportunity of branching off into some unexplored field of study and producing novel, independent results. Questions which the English Honor-man passes over, on the plea that they will probably "not pay," are precisely the ones which the German student takes up with patience and energy, in the hope of achieving reputation as an original thinker. Besides, the strain involved in preparing for a competitive examination is too severe. It exhausts the mind and the body. Success is too dearly bought, failure is disheartening. The soundest thinkers of England, I believe, are slowly awaking to the consciousness that the prize-examinations of Oxford and Cambridge do not answer their purpose satisfactorily.

In the next place, the instruction at Oxford and Cambridge costs too much. Compared with Germany, England is an expensive country. Yet the cost of living at an English university is largely in excess of what it should be, even for England. The reason is that prices are arbitrary, and the style of living is conventional. The tone is set by the many wealthy young men, noblemen and parvenus, who have more money than they know how to spend properly, and who launch accordingly into all sorts of extravagance. What with "tigers," horses, dogs, boating-clubs, elaborate dinners and suppers, they make an ostentation of wealth that either throws the poorer students completely into the shade, or forces them into ruinous competition. This can scarcely be said of the German universities. The wealthy students of Berlin or Bonn or Leipsic do not exercise a like influence over their fellows, for the reason that they do not come in such close personal contact with them. In England, a student has the same associates for three or four years, lives with them in the same quadrangle, recites in the same classes, attends the same chapel and church, sits at the same Commons. In Germany, each man lives by himself, selects his rooms and his dining-place according as his means may permit, and associates only with men who are personally congenial. If he has had the ill luck to make the acquaintance of a "fast" set in his first semester, it is an easy matter to reform by cutting them in the second. If the worst comes to the worst, he has only to try a change of air by removing to another university. It was a common saying in my day, that the Heidelberg idlers came to Göttingen, after a semester or two, to do their studying.

Not only are the expenses of living at Oxford and Cambridge out of all proportion to the benefit received, but the atmosphere of both places, particularly of Oxford, is thoroughly aristocratic. I do not condemn this unqualifiedly as a fault. If England sees fit to maintain her aristocratic institutions, it is not for the foreigner to take her to task therefor. Yet this concession should not prevent us from looking the facts full in the face and estimating their bearing and probable results. The higher education of England is in the exclusive possession of the higher, say rather the highest classes. Not that all the students come from the nobility and the *bourgeoisie parvenue*. The real study at both Oxford and Cambridge is done by the sons of toiling barristers, country clergymen of the Church of England, and other persons of limited means. Yet even these students are under the influence of the aristocratic element. They themselves are aristocrats in disguise, they represent the side lines of the nobility. Most certainly they are not democratic. The popular element in England is excluded *de facto* from participation in the real or supposed benefits of Oxford and Cambridge. If we examine, on the other hand, the mass of students in any German university, we shall find that it is composed of representatives of every class, from the highest nobility, perhaps the royal family itself, to the lowliest shop-keeper and district tax-collector. From this results the happy equality that characterizes the German seats of learning. They are neither aristocratic nor democratic in the political or the social sense, but they are what they should be,—national. They exist for the entire nation, they are supported by contributions from the national purse, and they supply the nation in turn with all its clergymen, physicians, lawyers, teachers, men of science. Hence the respect, I may say the enthusiastic affection, the unbounded pride that the nation as a whole takes in its universities. It is not pride in any one university, in Berlin or Leipsic, nor in any one professor or set of professors, but in the system as a system, that affords to all an equal chance of first-rate education at the lowest possible price. Now much as we respect Oxford and Cambridge, great as may be our veneration for the names and associations that cluster around them, we cannot in fairness regard them as in this sense national. They are English, intensely English; they could not exist outside the factitious atmosphere that envelops English "society." Yet they do not represent the entire nation, only its governing classes. We do well to think with admiration of the great scholars that have lived and died on the banks of the Isis and the Cam. But we shall do better to judge them also by what they have failed to accomplish. What have they done for the *diffusion* of science and of culture in England? Have they not, by their exclusiveness, their prejudice, helped, unconsciously perhaps yet not the less directly, to make the English folk what it is, the most benighted, the most illiterate, the most helpless, the most brutal among all the nations that call themselves civilized? Oxford and Cambridge are at this day not seats of learning pure and simple, they are the trysting places of the nobility and the *bourgeoisie parvenue*. The noblemen are in need of money to preserve and round off ancestral acres, the wealthy seek after titles. At the university, then, are laid the foundations of future alliances political and matrimonial. Probably half the students who go to Oxford and Cambridge, do so not to study but to "form connections." And the possible results? It is not for me to predict coming events. Yet should the fourth estate succeed in sending a certain number of representatives to parliament, enough to form a majority with the Dissenters and the Catholics,—such a conjuncture is anything but impossible,—what position would the English universities occupy? Could they make any reply to the searching demand: What have you done for us? Of what good to us are your scholarships, your fellowships, your Regius professors? Why should we refrain from reconstructing you from top to bottom?

Finally, the English university system is comparatively unproductive of results. It may seem presumptuous in any one man to break thus the rod of judgment over the backs of so many hundreds older, wiser, more renowned than himself. Yet surely any one claiming to be a scholar has the right to judge other men's scholarship by what it accomplishes. Personally acquainted with not one of the many professors and fellows of Oxford and Cambridge, I can estimate them only by what they do and by what they fail to do. Regarding science and scholarship in the aggregate, then, I venture to assert that there are only two departments in which the English are at the present time prominent, viz., pure mathematics and natural history. In all the others, they play a subordinate part. And in these two departments themselves, the universities have but a small share. Such men as

Tyndall, Huxley, and Darwin, move outside the university sphere. It may be doubted even whether they meet with as hearty support and encouragement in their own country as they do in Germany and in France. In the departments of law, history, speculative philosophy, philology, orientalia, theology, the English universities produce scarcely anything that can be called first-rate. Let us take up some of them in order. As for law, neither Oxford nor Cambridge pretends to give a legal education. Oxford looks upon its honorary degree of D. C. L. as the choicest gift in its power to confer. Yet Oxford is incapable of teaching the Pandects. Were an Oxford fellow, I do not say an undergraduate, to undertake the study of the Civil Law, what help could he obtain from the university? The very first thing that he would have to do would be to learn German and French, because in those languages alone would he find available text-books. Even in the English Common Law, Oxford and Cambridge do nothing. The lawyer pursues his studies at the Temple, and at the Westminster Courts. Should he be foolhardy enough to venture upon the history of the Common Law, where will he find any aid and encouragement, any professors who can guide him in his researches, can tell him what to read and how to read it? He must work by himself, must spend years of toil in forming mere preliminary judgments, such as the German student picks up in his first semester. In other words, there is not in all England a school of legal history or legal philosophy. Nor are the English better off in the matter of political history. The leading historians of the present generation are Freeman, Froude, Trollope and Lingard. As to Froude's merits, the reader may consult the stinging reviews of him in the *Historische Zeitschrift*. With regard to the others, can any one compare them for a single sober moment with men like Ranke, Waitz, Wattenbach Droysen, Jaffé, and von Sybel? Is there any spot in England, inside or outside the universities, where history is taught as an independent branch of science? The English do something for the history of their own country, but not much more than the Germans are doing for them. Whereas they do nothing for the history of Germany, next to nothing for the history of France, Italy and Spain. The most that they do is to appropriate the hard-won researches of continental scholars and serve them up to the public in the shape of palatable magazine articles. Still worse is the case with philology. One might suppose that the shades of Bentley and Porson would rise from the dust and castigate their degenerate successors. The only philologist of general reputation connected with the English Universities is Max Müller a German! It would be superfluous to call off in this place the long array of names of men who have made Germany famous in this department, all the Grimms and Bopps, and Schleichers. What have the English to set up against them? When the student of philology begins his investigations into the origin of language, into the relations of the Indo-Germanic, the Semitic, the Ugric families of languages, what English authorities and text-books does he consult? Even in the field where, above all others, we have reason to expect much of English scholarship, namely, the very limited department of *English* philology, the state of things is, to speak mildly, humiliating. The only scientific, rational grammars of the English language are the works of two Germans, Koch and Mätzner. The only critical edition of the body of Anglo-Saxon poetry is by a German, Grein. And that same German is obliged to suspend his edition of the body of Anglo-Saxon prose because he discovers that the English text-editions upon which he relied are untrustworthy! No Englishman thinks it worth the while to go out of his way to study the *Hildebrandslied* or the *Nibelungenlied* or *Parzival*, yet he suffers the German to invade him in his home and instruct him upon Beovulf, Cynevulf, and Aelfric.

It is needless to push the comparison farther. While the Germans, restless, enterprising, thoroughly trained, have ransacked the libraries of all Europe, making themselves at home in the political and literary history of every country, editing rare works in old French, old Spanish, Italian, Slavonic, Norse, inventing new theories and processes and bringing them within the reach of every student, the English have rested on their labors, in insular exclusiveness. They have trod their round of Tripos and Little-Go, they have written clever verses in Latin and made smooth translations and "floored" papers, but they have not produced their share of scholars. They are laggards in the great international handicap, because they are overweighted with routine and with narrow-minded devotion to certain studies. Is it because the English spirit has lost its quondam energy of initiative? For one, I am loth to believe it. I have not lost faith in the brain-power of the Anglo-Saxon race. What that race needs is emancipation from the thraldom of caste in education. Should the fourth estate do nothing worse than reconstruct Oxford and Cambridge, Eton, Harrow, Rugby, and the entire system from top to bottom, its advent to power might be hailed as a blessing.

VII.

Comparison with American Colleges.

To enter into an elaborate comparison of the German and the American systems of higher education, feature by feature, would not only swell the present work beyond reasonable limits, but would expose the one making it to the charge of being unpractical, unpatriotic, radical, aggressive, *doctrinaire*. The time has not yet arrived when the real friends of educational reform can look for a fair, rational discussion. Passion and prejudice run too high, there is too much dogmatism on the part of both conservative and innovator. The argument of the advocates of the existing regime might be framed somewhat in this wise. The American system is American, it has grown out of the needs of the country, it is adapted to the formation of national character, it gives our young men what they require for playing their part in public life. Moreover, we are here, strongly entrenched. Beside us there is none else, we cannot be dispossessed of our vantage ground, what are you going to do about it?

Now there is not one of the above propositions that is not susceptible of being overhauled and corrected, or at least modified. But the time for doing it is not yet at hand. The American public is still indifferent, as a public. It is not aroused to the vital connection between the State and education in all its stages, highest as well as lowest. The explanation of the signal failure of the movement in behalf of Civil Service Reform is to be found in the circumstance that the public is apathetic. The nation at large does not care whether it has better office-holders or not. It secretly approves, rather than disapproves, of the principle of succession in office. After a man has been post-master or revenue-collector for four years, it is only fair — argues the American mind — that he give some one else "a chance." Such is public opinion, and it is idle to quarrel with it. A similar view is taken of education. We do not need highly educated men. So long as our graduates can spell with tolerable accuracy, have a modicum of the classics and mathematics, can write and declaim with fluency, what more do you expect of them? They must become "practical," must learn the theory through the practice, and rough it with the others. Right or wrong, this is the average estimate set upon the value of college education. The public does not perceive the importance of any thing higher and more systematic. Indeed, I am tempted at times to believe that the colleges have exceeded, on some points, the demands of their friends. They give more than is expected of them. There are symptoms of a desire to react from the progress made during the past fifteen years. In making this assertion, I have in view, not so much Yale and Harvard as the colleges in the Middle and Western States. Urged on by a spirit of rivalry which is in itself deserving only of praise, these latter have made their curriculum more extensive and have also enforced its requirements more strictly. In doing this, they have gone a step too far, they have outrun the capacities of the preparatory schools. Up to the outbreak of the Civil War, the American college was an easy-going institution, where one was not forced beyond his natural gait, but had leisure to follow his inclinations, and especially to read. This has been changed. New professorships in the natural sciences have been created, and the chairs have been filled with energetic young men, enthusiastic in their vocation, and — I trust they will pardon the bluntness of the expression — rather intolerant towards those who do not keep pace with them. Many of the professors in the older departments are also young men who have studied abroad, are equally enthusiastic, and equally intolerant. The result is that we are called upon to witness a curious phenomenon, one that must act as a disturbing element in every system of education, to wit, a *direct conflict of studies*. Our undergraduates have at the present day too many studies, and are hurried through difficult and disconnected subjects at too rapid a rate. The new professors in the classics and the new professors in the natural sciences threaten to tear the child asunder between them, and there is no Solomon at hand to decide upon the true alma mater. Viewed in this light, the assertion now going the rounds of the press and attributed variously to Mr. Beecher and Mr. Fields, namely, that our colleges have not succeeded in producing one first-rate man in any department since 1855, will perhaps receive its explanation. Whatever the college of by-gone days may have failed to do, it certainly gave its pupil a better opportunity than his successor now enjoys, of maturing in conformity to the laws of individual being.

The present remarks will be confined to three points: the want of connection between College and State, the question of economy, and the question of discipline.

The College, unlike the German University, rests upon nothing and ends in nothing. We shall not obtain a just conception of the University unless we view it in its twofold bearing. It is, on the one hand, the key-stone of the arch of public-school education in Germany. Everything in that system leads up to the university by a series of carefully graduated steps. The gymnasium rests upon the *Volksschule*, the university rests upon the gymnasium. The whole cannot subsist without each one of the parts. On the other hand, the University is the door of approach to all the professions and also to public office. Whoever is not content with trade and commerce must submit to its liberalizing discipline. Without the public

*29

schools as a basis, and state-service or the professions as a goal, the University would speedily lose its right of being.

It will be needless to dwell upon the contrast presented by the college. I have said that it rests upon nothing and ends in nothing. By this is meant that the college is wholly dissevered from the state. It does not rest upon the system of public schools, neither is it the place where candidates prepare themselves for state-service. Massachusetts excepted, there is not a state where public schools attempt to fit young men for college. The needful preparation can be obtained only at academies and private schools which are exempt from state control and which pursue each the plan that seems to it best. However excellent these schools may be, they do not constitute a well organized, uniform system. The college ends in nothing, because its curriculum is not enforced as the condition precedent to civil and professional appointment.

Dropping abstract terms, I put the case of real "national education" before the reader in the shape of an imaginary example. Let us suppose the state of New York to enact a statute to the following effect: "As soon as may be practicable, the academies of this state shall be reconstituted as public schools of the first grade. The teachers now in office shall be required to pass an examination equivalent to that for B. A. or B. S. in some one of the acknowledged colleges of the state. Future applicants for the position of teacher in the academies and grammar schools must have passed through the full public school course, beginning with the grammar school and finishing with the college, and received the degree of B. A. or B. S. The colleges shall be placed under the supervision of the State Board of Education. The trustees of a college shall have the right to propose nominations for professorships, but the governor of the state shall exercise his discretion in rejecting unsuitable nominees. No college shall be considered as a state institution or entitled to recognition as an institution of learning, that does not submit to the regulations of the state authorities. As soon as the provisions of this act shall have been carried out, no one shall be admitted to the bar or bench of this state, or be permitted to practice medicine in the state, or be employed as teacher in the public schools, who shall not have received the degree of B. A., M. D. or B. S. from some state college acknowledged as such. Furthermore, no one shall be eligible for appointment or election to state-office without such degree. Finally, all private schools wishing to be placed on an equality with the state academies or grammar schools must conform in all respects to the curriculum of the academy or the grammar school, and must submit to the state requirements in the matter of holding examinations and appointing teachers."

Such an ideal enactment, imperfectly sketched as it is, will nevertheless, I trust, bring the case home to the reader. It is of course impracticable. Yet I venture to say that until we are prepared to introduce and maintain something of the sort, it will be useless to talk of Civil Service Reform and University Education. Our officeholders may be improved somewhat in quality, our colleges may give a higher grade of instruction, but we shall not have a body of trained officials, neither shall we have a system of universities. Our colleges teach already all that can be demanded of institutions that receive no official recognition from the state, and that are viewed with indifference, not to say skepticism, by the leaders in mercantile and political life. Let the reader extol our college system to the best of his ability, I still maintain that so long as three fourths of our national and state representatives, nine tenths of our office-holders, and the majority of the teachers in our public schools are nongraduates, it is the most extravagant optimism to regard the colleges as playing any acknowledged part in *national* life. The famous Simmons case proves this beyond controversy. If there be any city in America that has just reason to be proud of its public-school education, it is Boston. If there be any college in America that has done more than another for the promotion of learning and culture, and that is merely waiting for the word to constitute itself into a bona fide university, it is Harvard. Yet Boston and Cambridge combined were unable to prevent the appointment of a man notoriously incompetent, a man whose mere nomination, under a system like that of Germany, would have been an impossibility.

It would not be difficult to show that in point of economy also our colleges have much to learn from Germany. The reader's most careful attention is invited to the tabular statement of income and expenditure for the university of Leipsic, presented elsewhere. Two of our colleges, Harvard and Yale, have each — if I mistake not — as large an income as that of Leipsic. If smaller, the difference is certainly inconsiderable. Yet both Harvard and Yale would be slow in provoking a comparison between themselves and Leipsic. To what, then, must we look for the explanation of this disproportion in America between the outlay and the results effected? In part, but only in a small part, to the relatively higher figures of professors' salaries in America. Each one of the full professors at Harvard receives $4,000 a year, I believe. At Yale, the salaries are very nearly as high. No one will have the shabbiness to assert that the pay is too high. As a class, American professors are insufficiently recompensed. After years of toil and annoyance, they can be thankful if they are able to keep themselves and their families out of debt. Were the salary of every professor doubled, the increase would be nothing more than justice. It is difficult to understand why professors, who are men of ability and culture, who devote themselves unselfishly to the best interests of the nation, should not be paid as liberally as our best lawyers and physicians, why the guardians of the spiritual interests of men should fare worse than those who look merely after their bodies and estates. It is not more than six years ago that the president of Harvard was forced to admit in public that his senior professor received less than the chief cook of the Parker House! Things have been bettered since then, but they have not been radically cured.

Now for this state of affairs the party chief in responsibility is the college itself. Not Harvard, nor Yale, nor Princeton, nor Cornell alone, but the spirit of our college system. We have been misled by rivalry into copying after England in the feature that is least worthy of imitation. I mean — buildings! Had the money which has been sunk in brick and stone and mortar during the past twenty years been judiciously invested, the salary of every professor in America might be doubled at this moment. If this assertion sounds extravagant, the reader has only to scrutinize carefully the condition of any one of our colleges, to note the amount of money expended upon costly edifices, and then to judge for himself whether that amount, if placed at interest, would not add at least fifty per cent to the annual income. What are the buildings necessary for keeping up a college? Those which contain the libraries and apparatus, and the rooms suitable for lectures and recitations. Whatever goes beyond this, is superfluous. We may derive some wholesome lessons on the point from examining into the conduct of the German government in re-establishing the university of Strassburg. Although barely three years have elapsed since the annexation of Alsace, the university has a full staff of eighty professors, and a body of six hundred students. Yet the university of Strassburg has not at this day *a single building that it can properly call its own*. To estimate such a policy of organization with due regard to its extraordinary singleness of view, we must bear in mind that it was not induced by stint of funds. Prince Bismarck, as Chancellor of the Empire and Administrator of the Imperial Provinces, had *carte blanche*. Probably no man since the days of Cardinal Wolsey enjoyed a like opportunity of immortalizing himself in stained glass and stone. The French indemnity money was pouring into the German coffers in a steady stream, Germany was wild over its sudden accession to wealth. It would have cost but a word from the Prince to divert a paltry fraction, say twenty of the thousand millions, to the glory of German architects and the greater glory of the unificator of his country. But the Prince knew too well what he was undertaking. He knew that the strength of a university does not consist in its array of dead buildings, but in its force of live men, that the ultimate test of the capacity of a university is its ability to pay professors. So the Prince quietly let the twenty millions take their natural course into the imperial treasury, and contented himself with organizing the Strassburg university after the model of all the others, to wit, as an unobtrusive congregation of eminent men in the receipt of good salaries. For the mere appliances and paraphernalia of learning, for permanent laboratories, library buildings, botanical gardens and the like, he trusted to the future, and to the general principle that, given the skilled artisan, the workshop will follow of itself.

Will it be necessary to descant upon the painful contrast afforded by our colleges, to show, instance by instance, how we have spent our money upon the workshop, until we have none left wherewith to pay the workman? The city of Philadelphia expended two millions of dollars upon Girard College. It succeeded in erecting a Grecian temple that is the wonder of the tourist and the terror of the teacher. After years of tinkering and patching, the rooms are even now scarcely suited to the purposes of instruction, and the instructors themselves are scantily paid.

Instead of scattering my remarks over a number of colleges, permit me to concentrate them upon that one with which I am most familiar, namely, Cornell. Much has been bruited about of late as to Mr. Cornell's dishonesty. It is needless to say that the charges were completely disproved by the Committee of Investigation in their report, but it may not be surperfluous to add that nobody connected with the university put the slightest faith in the charges. On the contrary, it was a matter of almost public notoriety in Ithaca that Mr. Cornell was at one time rather embarrassed in his finances, in consequence of the obligations into which he had entered gratuitously for the benefit of the university. There is not the shadow of a doubt but that the intentions of Mr. Cornell have always been strictly honorable. Yet it is not the less evident that the affairs of the university have been badly managed from the outset. Instead of beginning on a modest scale, and developing the field of operation gradually, keeping pace with the growth of resources, the managers of the university started it in extravagance and then conducted it with the most humiliating parsimony. There was but one object for which money seemed to be forthcoming, and that object was ostentatious architecture. The Cascadilla was completed and the North and South Universities were erected at an expense of not less than $250,000. Ample accommodation for lectures and recitations — which was all that was needed — could have been had for $75,000. Furthermore, instead of locating the university in the town of Ithaca, where it would have been comparatively accessible, it was pitched upon the crest of a hill four hundred feet high and exposed to the inclemency of the weather. By dint of lavish expenditure in planting trees, it is possible that the buildings may be sheltered, in the course of a generation, from the searching east winds. But nothing can ever screen them from the furious northerly and westerly gales that sweep across the lake every winter and spring. Only one who has himself struggled for half a mile through the snow against a cutting north-wester, and reached his lecture-room half blinded and benumbed, scarcely able to collect his thoughts or to keep his teeth from chattering in the presence of the class, will appreciate the trials of our model American university furnished with " all the modern improvements." The casual visitor, who views the grounds on a pleasant day in June or October, knows nothing of all this. He perceives only the beauty of the landscape, and congratulates the university on its admirable location! The expression, as I have heard it again and again, always sounded like the cruelest of friendly mockeries. A fine view on a fine day is but a sorry atonement for months of wearing toil and exposure. How shall we explain this mania, peculiar to America, of locating public institutions on hill-tops? Is it that the whole world may see what feats of architecture we are capable of, crude conglomerations of bald, unrelieved lines, distorted chimneys, unsymmetrical windows, or do we desire the votaries of knowledge to look upon her temple as an Alpine " station? "

Had Mr. McGraw, Mr. Sage, and the other donors given, not buildings, but the money expended on buildings, had the university husbanded its resources and lived year by year within its income, had it refrained from luxuries, such as high-priced lectures from outsiders, and the purchase of questionable libraries; in short, had the university patterned in only this one respect of economy after the German universities that it professes to regard as its beau ideal, its available capital would be greater than it now is by the round sum of one million dollars.

Cornell University is not the only institution that has made the mistake. Every college in the land can tell the same story with variations. Harvard, Yale, Amherst, Dartmouth, Princeton and the others have received during the past ten years many handsome donations, but these donations have come usually in the shape of buildings. Few of the donors appear to have stumbled upon the patent fact that what a college needs in the first place is money, in the second place money, in the last place money, or upon the equally patent fact that every building entails upon the college additional expenses. A chapel costing $70,000 forces the college to an annual outlay of $1,000 to $2,000 for repairs, heating and attendance. Let us consider the most common form of donation. A friend of —— college, we may say, wishes to bestow the handsome sum of $200,000. Instead of endowing four or five professorships, thereby directly relieving the college from so much pressure on its general income, he erects a handsome dormitory, capable of holding fifty students. Each student pays for his suite of rooms $250 per annum, an excessive amount for the forty academic weeks. The aggregate rental would be $12,500. From this are to be deducted the expenses for insurance, repairs, heating, and servants' wages, say $3,000. The net yield to the college, then, is only $9,500. Whereas the original fund, if judiciously invested, would have yielded $14,000. There is a waste, accordingly, of $4,500, to say nothing of the extra burden of worry and responsibility imposed upon the college authorities.

Is it surprising that the expense of collegiate life should have increased so rapidly within five years? Our colleges have grown rich in appearance, but in reality they are little better off than they were fifteen years ago. They have added one stately building after another, they have surrounded their students with objects that incite to extravagance, they have encouraged, directly or indirectly, an almost luxurious style of living, yet they are not a whit more independent of student support.* In fact, they have been forced to raise their tuition-charges. The Senatus Academicus of Leipsic could dismiss five hundred students at a blow, without curtailing the regular official salary of any one of its professors by so much as a penny. I doubt whether the American college can be found that would venture to send away twenty of its students, and *keep them away*. The truth is that the salaries of the professors depend too much upon the tuition-fees paid by the students. This the students themselves have found out, and they are prepared to act upon it. They know that dormitories, chapels, libraries, laboratories, by whomsoever erected in the first place, are supported by the tuition-fees that come from them. They hold the purse-strings, and they have already begun to assert their so called rights.

Intimately connected with this matter of economy is the further one of discipline. The German university court, whenever it does interfere, is inflexible; it can afford to be. Conscious that the university is a state institution, and that the government is pledged directly to its support, it is not diverted from the strictest administration of justice by the dread of diminishing the income derived from students. The vacillating policy, the alternate spasms of laxity and strictness that mark the course of discipline in an American college, on the

---

*The average yearly expenditure of the class of 1874 at Yale is stated at over $1,000.

other hand, are too well known to require more than a mention. Those of us who have passed or are passing through college know that such a thing as strict, even-handed justice does not exist for students. Private failings are punished with too much severity, public disorder with too little, and in general there is a want of fixity of purpose. The quality of the discipline varies from term to term, even from week to week. I remember the instance where two students, room-mates, arraigned for precisely the same offense, were punished, one by suspension for three months, the other by suspension for six. The secret of the difference was that they were *not trie at the same faculty meeting.* Not one of those professors who voted for the respective sentences perceived the gross injustice of the discrimination until attention was directed to it by myself, as registering clerk of the faculty. It is not my object to discuss the grave question of public disorder and the proper way of meeting it, for I believe that there is only one way, not attainable at present, and that way lies in the absolute monetary independence of the college itself. Until professors' salaries can be secured by better means than precarious student-support, we have no right to expect a thorough reform. Professors are after all only men. Situated as they are, they cannot afford to be stricter, they must temporize, must yield here and there to student clamor and to inveterate traditions and prejudices. At the same time, I cherish the belief that it is possible to effect at least a partial reform, by changing the mode of administering discipline. The change would consist in abolishing the present cumbersome faculty-meetings and in lodging the entire control in the hands of the president and say two advisers. A college faculty, to speak the plain, unvarnished truth, is a body without a soul, without a sense of responsibility, for the simple reason that the individual is lost in the multitude. It is impossible to obtain from an aggregation of twenty or thirty men anything like uniformity of action. The whole is broken up into groups, or cliques, which do not act in concert, and according as one or the other of such cliques may be present on a given occasion, the voting will be decided one way or the other. Furthermore, college professors, as a class, have loose notions as to what is really evidence, and what is not. Although sitting as judges, they have not received a legal training. They are determined in their opinions only too often by hearsay, vague rumors, and general reputation. Finally, their functions are too heterogeneous. They are in direct conflict with the cardinal principle of Anglo-Saxon justice, to wit, the separation of legislative powers and judicial.

The college faculty enacts laws and regulations, and then proceeds to carry them out, not infrequently legislating *ex post facto*. It seems to me that this evil might be remedied by diminishing the number of faculty-meetings to one a month, and by restricting the action of the faculty to the discussion and adoption of general measures. The carrying out of those measures could be intrusted to a select Executive Committee, consisting of the president and two professors (chosen with regard to their legal attainments) and responsible directly to the trustees. Without claiming for such a tribunal infallibility, I am confident that it would have at least the following merits. It would expedite matters wonderfully. None but the members of a college faculty can estimate the amount of time wasted in mere parley. Three men will accomplish as much in an hour as twenty men in an entire afternoon. In the next place, the rulings of a tribunal of three would be uniform. Each member would be bound inflexibly by his previous action. And in the third place, there would be personal responsibility; students, parents, trustees, and outsiders would know whom to hold accountable. Under the present system, the burden of responsibility is shifted from man to man, and the student who may feel himself aggrieved is never at a loss for pretexts for raising the cry of injustice. There is no risk run in impugning the decisions of a faculty of twenty, but to attack a committee of three is a step from which the ordinary student would shrink. The establishment of an Executive Committee, as indicated above, would introduce a healthier tone of feeling between faculty and students, and would rid the professorial vocation of many trials and annoyances.

VIII.

Statistics of the German Universities.

The following table will show the respective ages of the universities of Germany:

Prague	1348	[Helmstädt	1576]
Vienna	1356	[Altdorf	1578]
Heidelberg	1386	[Herborn	1584]
[Cologne	1388]	Graz	1586
[Erfurt	1392]	Giessen	1607
Wurzburg	1402	[Paderborn	1616]
Leipsic	1409	[Rintelin	1621]
Rostock	1418	Salzburg	1622
[Trier	1454]	[Osnabrück	1632]
Greifswald	1456	[Bamberg	1649]
Freiburg (in Baden)	1456	[Duisburg	1655]
Ingolstadt	1472	Kiel	1665
Tubingen	1477	Innsbruck	1677
[Menz	1477]	Halle	1694
[Wittenberg	1502]	Breslau	1702
[Frankfort-on-the-Oder	1506]	Göttingen	1734
Marburg	1527	[Fulda	1734]
Strassburg	1538	Erlangen	1743
Königsberg	1544	[Stuttgart	1781]
[Dillingen	1549]	Bonn	1786
Jena	1558	Berlin	1809
[Olmütz	1567]	Munich	1826

The names inclosed thus [ ] designate universities that no longer exist. By "Germany" is meant the old German-Roman Empire of the Middle Ages, embracing parts of Switzerland, Eastern France, Bohemia, and the Austrian duchies. A glance at the above list will reveal the striking preponderance of South Germany over North Germany in culture and in educational facilities, until comparatively recent times. Since the middle of the eighteenth century, the seat of intellectual activity has been transferred. We see following one another in rapid succession the renowned series: Breslau, Göttingen, Erlangen, Bonn, Berlin. Catholic Germany has been distanced by Protestant. Another point of interest is the number of universities that have gone under: no less than eighteen. This tendency to slough off the sicklier, effete members, and to concentrate the resources of higher education still exists, but not in an active form. It is among the possibilities that Giessen and Marburg may be fused into one; also Rostock and Greifswald. Now that railroad communication has facilitated travel, and Germany is consolidated into a compact realm under one system of imperial administration, the petty German princes can no longer aspire to have each his own *Landesuniversität*.

The following tables show the respective numbers, first, of the faculties, next, of the students, at the existing universities. The figures are taken from the *Universitäts-Kalender* for the summer of 1874.

FACULTY.	Prof. ordin.	Prof. extraord.	Prof. honor.	Privatdoc., etc.	Instructors, Fencing masters, etc.	Total.
I. *German Empire.*						
Berlin	57	55	4	57	5	178
Bonn	56	25	1	16	1	99
Breslau	50	20	3	25	8	106
Erlangen	34	12	1	2	5	54
Freiburg (Baden)	38	4	1	6	3	52
Giessen	35	12	1	6	4	58
Göttingen	57	24	1	19	7	108
Greifswald	36	10	....	7	3	56
Halle	45	22	....	21	5	93
Heidelberg	40	25	2	26	14	107
Jena	30	13	8	12	4	67
Kiel	38	5	....	13	4	60
Königsberg	46	8	....	16	7	77
Leipsic	56	49	2	31	3	141
Marburg	40	8	....	14	2	64
Munich	66	9	12	21	5	113
Rostock	26	2	....	6	....	34
Strassburg	53	19	1	6	4	83
Tübingen	44	14	....	17	5	80
Würzburg	38	7	....	14	3	62
II. *German Austria.*						
Graz	44	10	....	10	3	67
Innsbruck	41	6	....	10	2	59
Prague	56	26	....	35	5	122
Vienna	82	38	....	100	6	226

STATISTICS OF GERMAN UNIVERSITIES.

STUDENTS. (Winter 1873-4.)	THEOLOGY.		Jurispr., Cameralia, etc.	Medicine, Pharmacy.	Philosophy.	Total matriculated.	Non-matric. attendants at Lectures.	Grand total.
	Protestant.	Catholic.						
I. German Empire.								
Berlin	173	....	560	333	691	1757	1816	3573
Bonn	57	110	243	137	266	813	35	848
Breslau	65	94	337	168	423	1087	19	1106
Erlangen	178	....	41	156	70	445	....	445
Freiburg	....	86	48	105	45	284	5	289
Giessen	11	....	99	86	142	338	27	365
Göttingen	101	....	286	154	459	1000	18	1018
Greifswald	28	....	75	287	138	528	12	540
Halle	219	...	159	146	494	1018	22	1040
Heidelberg	26	....	273	82	204	585	55	640
Jena	79	....	73	74	132	358	18	376
Kiel	53	....	19	57	40	169	36	205
Königsberg	59	....	202	161	185	607	10	617
Leipsic	399	....	1012	559	906	2876	64	2940
Marburg	54	...	51	145	168	418	15	433
Munich	....	74	258	402	409	1143	17	1160
Rostock	36	....	38	30	31	135	....	135
Strassburg	48	....	156	165	195	564	36	600
Tübingen	253	132	171	177	81	814	9	823
Wurzburg	....	143	104	499	126	872	...	872
II. German Austria.								
Graz	....	63	347	296	189	895	80	975
Innsbruck	....	166	116	102	179	563	78	641
Prague	....	141	822	472	336	1771	40	1811
Vienna	....	165	1442	997	703	3307	506	3813

The following list, taken from the official catalogue of Leipsic for the winter of 1873-4, gives the analysis of the body of students of that university.

	Theology.	Jurisprudence.	Medicine.	Pharmacy.	Nat. Science.	Philosophy.	Pedagogics.	Philology.	Mathematics.	Agriculture.	Cameralia.	Total.
I. *German Empire.*												
Anhalt............	5	5	8	1	3	2	..	6	..	2	1	33
Baden.............	1	7	..	1	1	..	..	2	..	..	3	15
Bavaria...........	18	9	8	..	1	1	1	4	1	1	1	45
Brunswick.........	4	8	6	..	1	2	..	8	1	5	..	35
Bremen............	1	3	1	..	..	2	..	1	1	..	1	10
Bückeburg.........	..	1	..	..	..	..	..	1	..	..	1	3
Alsace-Lorraine....	2	..	..	..	..	1	..	..	..	1	..	4
Hamburg...........	4	10	4	2	2	2	..	5	..	1	2	32
Hesse-Darmstadt...	2	7	..	..	3	..	..	3	1	2	1	19
Lauenburg.........	1	..	..	..	..	..	..	.	..	..	..	1
Lippe	..	3	3	..	1	..	..	2	..	1	1	11
Lübeck............	..	2	..	..	..	1	..	2	..	..	..	5
Meckle'g-Schwerin,	17	14	6	.	..	5	..	8	3	7	..	60
Meckle'g-Strelitz...	4	5	3	..	..	1	..	2	..	..	..	15
Oldenburg.........	4	4	7	1	..	..	..	3	2	1	..	22
Prussia	154	420	156	66	64	44	3	139	33	43	18	1140
Reuss	5	10	1	..	..	..	1	2	..	1	..	20
Saxony (Kingdom).	114	333	141	44	56	20	60	73	32	24	11	908
Saxe-Altenburg....	9	12	2	2	3	..	3	4	..	..	..	35
Saxe-Coburg-Gotha	1	6	1	1	1	..	..	4	..	..	1	15
Saxe-Meiningen....	8	8	2	3	1	..	..	7	3	..	..	32
Saxe-Weimar.......	1	14	3	1	..	1	5	5	1	1	..	32
Schwarzburg.......	3	7	1	3	2	2	1	5	..	..	..	24
Waldeck...........	2	..	..	..	..	..	..	..	..	..	..	2
Würtemburg.......	2	10	17	..	2	..	..	1	..	1	..	33
	362	898	370	125	141	84	74	287	78	97	41	2551

STATISTICS OF GERMAN UNIVERSITIES. 361

	Theology.	Jurisprudence.	Medicine.	Pharmacy.	Nat. Science.	Philosophy.	Pedagogics.	Philology.	Mathematics.	Agriculture.	Cameralia.	Total.
II. *Other European States.*												
Denmark..........	..	..	..	..	..	..	1	..	..	..	..	1
France............	..	..	..	..	1	1	..	..	..	..	..	2
Greece............	..	2	2	..	..	3	.	..	..	..	..	7
Great Britain......	9	..	1	..	2	2	..	1	..	..	..	15
Italy	1	..	..	..	3	..	..	1	..	1	1	7
Holland...........	..	2	..	..	2	..	..	1	..	..	..	5
Austria............	13	17	18	1	5	13	1	12	..	15	1	96
Roumania.........	..	7	2	..	..	2	..	1	..	..	..	12
Russia	1	12	12	2	4	15	1	9	..	7	8	71
Sweden, Norway ..	..	..	..	..	1	..	..	..	..	1	..	2
Switzerland	1	12	11	2	2	5	2	4	1	4	1	45
Turkey............	2	2	1	..	1	..	..	3	..	1	..	10
	27	54	47	5	21	41	5	32	1	29	11	273
III. *Non-European States.*												
North America.....	8	7	8	..	4	11	..	6	1	..	..	45
Brazil	..	..	1	..	..	..	..	..	..	..	..	1
Venezuela	..	..	1	..	..	..	..	..	..	..	..	1
Japan	..	1	..	..	..	..	..	..	..	..	..	1
Africa.............	2	..	2	..	..	..	..	..	..	..	..	4
	10	8	12	..	4	11	..	6	1	..	..	52
Recapitulation.												
I. German Empire	362	898	370	125	141	84	74	287	78	91	41	2551
II. Oth. Euro. Stat.	27	54	47	5	21	41	5	32	1	29	11	273
III. Non-Euro. Stat.	10	8	12	..	4	11	..	6	1	..	..	52
	399	960	429	130	166	136	79	325	80	120	52	2876

The Leipsic catalogue for the winter of 1872-3 announced the following schedule of studies. The figures in ( ) denote the number of hours per week.

I. Theology.

1. *Full Professors.*

Fr. Delitsch — Biblical Theology of the O. T. (4 h.); Interpretation of the Minor Prophets (4 h.); Grammar of Biblical Chaldee (2 h.); *Hebraicum* (1 h.).

Kahnis — History of Dogma (6 h.); Eccles. Hist. of the Later Middle Ages (2 h.); Symbolic (4 h.); Practical Exercises of Theol. Soc'y (3 h.).

Luthardt — Dogmatics (6 h.); Interpret. of St. John's Gospel (4 h.); Introd. to Dogmatics (2 h.); Exercises of the Soc'y for Dogmatics (2 h.).

Lechler — Church History since Gregory VII. (6 h.); Interpretation of Ep. of St. Peter (2 h.); Practical Exerc. in Church History (2 h.).

Fricke — Life of Christ accord. to Four Gospels, with Prefatory Criticism of the Gospels (4 h.); Interpret. of the Messianic Proph. of O. T. (3 h.); Interpret. of Paul to Galatians (2 h.); Soc'y for Exegesis of O. T. and N. T. (2 h.).

Tischendorf — Interpret. of Epistle to Romans (4 h.); Interpret. of the Parenetic Parts of Ep. to Romans (2 h.).

Baur — Practical Theology (1 h.); German Lit. from Klopstock to Present Day, in its Relations to Religion and the Church (3 h.); Exercises of Homiletic *Seminar* (2 h.).

Hofmann — Practical Theology (6 h.); Evangelical Pedagogic and its History (4 h.); Exerc. of *Seminar* for Catechetic and Pedagogic.

Hölemann — Interpret. of Job (4 h.); Soc'y for Exegesis of O. T. and N. T., Disputations, etc., in Latin (2 h.).

2. *Assistant-Professors.*

W. Schmidt — Interpret. of I. and II. Corinth. (4 h.); Hermeneutics of N. T. (2 h.); Soc'y for Catechetic (2 h.).

Cl. Brockhaus — Archæology of Christian Art (2 h.).

3. *Privatdocenten.*

Schürer — Life and Teachings of St. Paul (2 h.).

Joh. Delitsch — History of the Doctrine concerning the Person of Christ (2 h.).

II. JURISPRUDENCE.

1. *Full Professors.*

Müller — Common and Statute Law of Saxony (10 h.); *Practicum* for Saxon Law (2 h.); *Exegeticum* (2 h.).

Wächter — Pandects (10 h.); Theory of Possession (2 h.).

Hänel — Sources of the Roman Law (2 h.); Criminal Procedure accord. to R. L. (2 h.).

Osterloh — Civil Procedure acc. to Comm. Law of Germany and Saxony (10 h.); *Practicum* in Procedure (2 h.); *Relatorium* (2 h.).

Heinze—German Crim. Law (7 h.); History and System of Legal Philos. (4 h.); Internat. Law (2 h.); *Seminar* for Crim. Law Practice (2 h.).

A. Schmidt—Pandects (12 h.); Institutes and Hist. of Rom. Law (6 h.).

Friedberg—Hist. of German Law (4 h.); German Const. Law (4 h.); Commercial Law (3 h.).

Kuntze—History of Rom. Law (6 h.); Commercial Law (incl. Insurance) (4 h.); Exegesis of Passages from Digest (2 h.).

Stobbe—German Common Law, excl. of Commercial Law (7 h.); Eccles. Law (4 h.); Exercises in Germ. Law (2 h.).

Schletter—Crim. Procedure accord. to Comm. Law of Germany and Saxony (4 h.); Law relating to Public Officials (4 h.).

2. *Assistant-Professors.*

Weiske—Mining Law.

Höck—History of German Const. Law (6 h.); Commercial Law (6 h.); Obligations, accord. to Germ. Law (2 h.).

Götz—Commercial Law (2 h.); Property Law (2 h.).

Voigt—Institutes and Hist. of Rom. Law (10 h.); Encyclopaedy of Law (3 h.).

Nissen—*Practicum* for Civil Procedure (2 h.); for Crim. Procedure (3 h.).

Lueder—Criminal Law (7 h.); Agricult. Law (3 h.).

III. Medicine.

1. *Full Professors.*

Radius — Pharmacy (4 h.); Public and Private Hygiene (2 h.).

Weber — Organs of Hearing in the Amphibia (3 h.).

Wunderlich — Medical Clinic (9 h.); Pathol. and Therap. of Acute Constit. Diseases (4 h.).

Credé — Gynecological and Obstetrical Clinic (7 h.); Practical Exercises in Obstetrics, with Manikin (4 h.); Obstetrical Demonstrations (2 h.).

Wagner — Spec. Pathol. Anatomy (7 1-2 h.) : Pathologic-histological Exercises (5 h.); Exerc. in Pathol. Institute (4 h. daily); Medical Polyclinic (5 h.).

Ludwig — Physiol. of Organs of Sensation and Locomotion (5 h.); Physiol. Consultat. (2 h.); Exercises in Physiol. for Advanced Students.

Thiersch — Surgical Clinic (9 h.); Surgery (4 h.).

Coccius — Ophthalm. Clinic (6 h.); Pathol. Optics (2 h.); Internal Inflam. of Eye (2 h.).

His — Systemat. Human Anat. (10 h.); Dissecting (8 h. daily).

Braune — Army Practice (2 h.); Operations (4 h.); Dissecting (for those attending Clinics) (4 h. daily); Topograph. Anatomy (2 h.).

Czermak — Introduction to Physiology (Public Lecture)

*31

2. Assistant-Professors.

Bock — Diagnostic Phenomenology.

Sonnenkalb — *Practicum* for those entering State Service (3 h.); Medical Jurisprudence (4 h.).

Carus — Comparat. Anatomy of Vertebrates (4 h.); Comparat. Osteology (2 h.); Comparat. Anat. and Physiol. of Domest. Animals (4 h.).

Germann — Diseases of Women (2 h.).

Hennig — *Examinatorium* in Obstetrics (6 h.); Pediatric Clinic (2 h.).

Reclam — Med. Jurispr. (2 h.); Alimentary Substances (2 h.); Exercises in Hygienic Investigations (2 h.).

Merkel — Physiol. of Human Voice (principally for Philologists) (2 h.); Laryngiatric Polyclinic (3 h.).

B. Schmidt — Surgical Polyclinic (6 h.); Vivisection (2 h.); Hernia (1 h.).

Thomas — Exercises in Physical Diagnosis (2 h.); Polyclinic (3 h.).

Schwalbe — Use of Microscope (1 h.); Anat. of Brain and Spine (2 h.); Exercises with Microscope (courses of 6 h. each)

3. Privatdocenten.

Meissner — Obstetrics with Reference to Jurisprudence (2 h.); Pract. Exerc. in Obstetrics.

Haake — Exercises in Obstetrics, with Manikin (3 h.); Intra-uterine Therapeut. (1 h.).

Naumann — Pharmaco-dynamics (2 h.); Medical Baths (1 h.).

Hagen— Otiatric Polyclinic (12 h.); Laryngoscopy, Pharyngoscopy, and Rhinoscopy (2 h.); Galvanism Applied to the Ear (2 h.).

Wendt— Polyclinic for Diseases of Ear (9 h.).

Friedlander— Constitut. Diseases (4 h.).

Kormann— *Examinatorium* for Obstetrics (courses of 36 hours each).

Wenzel— *Repetitorium* for Human Anatomy (6 h.); Anatomy for Non-medical Students (2 h.).

Siegel— Public Hygiene (2 h.); Medical Jurisprud. (2 h.).

Heubner— Clinical Propædeutics (3 h.); Special Pathology and Therap. (6 h.); Electro-diagnosis and Electrotherapeut. (2 h.).

Hüfner— Physiol. Chemistry (2 h.); Analysis of Animal Tissues and Humors.

L. Fürst— Diseases of Children (2 h.); Propædeutics of Obstetrics (1 h.); Pediatric Polyclinic (3 h.).

IV. PHILOSOPHY.

1. *Full Professors.*

Overbeck— Greek Mythology in Art (5 h.); Explanation of Select Spec. of Antique Art (3 h.); Exerc. of Archæol. Soc'y.

Drobisch— Psychology (5 h.); Outlines of Perception (3 h.).

Fechner— The Interrelations of Body and Soul (2 h.).

Fleischer— Interpret. of the Koran (2 h.); Introd. to Study of Mod. Arabic Periodicals (2 h.); Interpret. of the Behâristan of Djâmî (2 h.); Turkish Syntax (2 h.); Exerc. of the Arabic Soc'y.

Roscher — Polit. Economy (4 h.); Finance (3 h.); Nat. Economy and Statistics (2 h.).

Brockhaus — Interpretation of Epic Passages in the Râmâyana (2 h.); Interpret. of Select Hymns from the Rigveda (4 h.).

Wuttke — Hist. of French Revol. (4 h.); Histor. *Seminar;* Exam. of Essays, and Review of Sources for Hist of Saxon Dynasty (3 h.).

Hankel — Magnetism, Electr., Heat (6 h.); Terrestrial Magnetism (2 h.).

Zarncke — Grammar and Lit. Hist. of Old Norse (4 h.); Interpret. of Nibelungenlied (6 h.); Exerc. of Germanistic Soc'y.

Ahrens — Logic (4 h.); Fundam. Doctr. of Ethics (2 h.); Theories of State and Administr. (4 h.); Exerc. of Soc'y for Study of Government.

Curtius — Greek Grammar (4 h.); Grammat. Soc'y (2 h.); Exerc. of Philol. *Seminar* in Interpret. of Odyssey, etc. (2 h.).

Masius — Hist. of Pedagogic (4 h.); Schools and School Regul. of 16th and 17th Cent. (1 h.); Pedag. *Seminar* (2 h.).

Ebert — Introd. to Compar. Philol. of Romance Lang. (3 h.); Provenzal Gram. and Interpret. of Bartsch's Chrest. Prov. (2 h.).

Ritschl — Greek and Roman Metres, Hist. of Greek Lyric Poetry (4 h.); Interpret. of Æschylus (in Latin), in

Philol. *Seminar* (2 h.); Interpret. of Terence, and Lat. Disput. in Philol. Soc'y (2 h.).

Kolbe — Organic Chemistry (4 h.); Laborat. Practice (7 h. daily).

G. Voigt — History of German Empire from Charlemagne to Downfall of the Hohenstaufen (4 h.); Age of Luther and Charles V. (2 h.); Histor. Soc'y.

Scheibner — Functions of the Ellipse (5 h.); Differ. and Integral Calc. (4 h.).

Schenk — Botan. Physiol. (3 h.); Fossil Plants (2 h.); Laborat. Practice.

Bruhns — Comets and Determ. of Courses (3 h.); Spher. Trig. and Progr. in Applic. to Astron. (2 h.).

Neumann — Electrodynamics (4 h.); Discuss. of Mathem. Exerc. (1 h.).

Leuckart — Compar. Anat. (6 h.); Zoology of Vertebrates and Origin of Species (4 h.); Labor. Practice (daily).

Blomeyer — Agriculture (4 h.); Plants of Commerce (2 h.); Law of Farming (1 h.).

Zirkel — Chem. Geology (1 h.); Mineralogy (6 h.); Laborat. Practice.

Wiedemann — Inorgan. Chem. (6 h.); Laborat. Practice.

Lange — Legal Antiq. of Greece (4 h.); *Seminar*, Interpret. of Epistles of Horace, Lat. Disputat. (2 h.); Roman Archæol. Soc'y (2 h.).

Peschel — Physical Geography (4 h.).

Zöllner — Astron. Physics (4 h.); Principles of Perception in their Relations to Nat. Sciences (2 h.).

Krehl — Encyclopædy of Semitic Philol. (4 h.); Interpret. of Arnold's Arabic Chrestom. (2 h.).

Strümpell — Logic (4 h.); Problems of Relig. Phil. (2 h.); Pedagog. Exercises.

2. *Assistant-Professors.*

Nobbe — Odes of Horace (2 h.); Lat. Disputat. (2 h.).

Marbach — Geom. and Trigonom. (4 h.).

Jacobi — Agriculture (2 h.); *Cameralia* (1 h.); Discuss. of Geogr. and Topograph. Nomenclature (1 h.).

Wenck — Hist. of Germany from Westphalian Peace to Accession of Frederick the Great (4 h.); Hist. of Germany from Accession of Rudolph of Habsburg to End of 14th Cent. (2 h.).

Fritzsche — Frogs of Aristophanes (2 h.); Latin Style (2 h.); Greek Soc'y (Aristotle's Metaphysics); Lat. and Greek Disputat.

Hermann — Introd. to Phil. and Logic (4 h.); Aesthetics (4 h.); Criticism of Leading Mod. Systems of Philosophy (2 h.).

Knop — Agricul. Chem. (4 h.); Labor, Practice.

Minckwitz — Origin and Developm't of German Lyric Poetry (2 h.); Origin of Homer. Poems (2 h.).

Ziller — Psychology (4 h.); Phil. of Religion (2 h.); Pedagog. *Seminar.*

Eckstein — Odes of Horace explained in Latin (3 h.); pedagog. *Seminar.*

Brandes — Hist. of Central Europe in Reformation (2 h.); Hist of France (2 h.); Germanistic Soc'y. (1 h.).

Biedermann — German Hist. (1806-1871) (2 h.); Hist. of Germ. Lit. in 18th and 19th Cent. (4 h.); Nature and Hist. of Drama (2 h.).

Hirzel — Pharmacy of Inorganic Preparat. (2 h.).

Seydel — Hist. of Mod. Philos. (4 h.); Relations of Philos. and Religion, especially since Kant (2 h.); Philosoph. Soc'y.

Pöckert — Saxon Hist. (2 h.); German Hist. since Westphalian Peace (2 h.).

Birnbaum — Cattle-Raising (3 h.); Administr. of Estates (5 h.); Import. Questions of the Day (2 h.).

Hildebrand — Germ. Lit. of the 18th Cent. (4 h.); Interpretation of M. H. G. poem *Meier Helmbrecht* (2 h.).

Knapp — Labor Question in England, France, Germany (4 h.); Pract. Exerc. in Statistics (2 h.).

Lipsius — Thucydides, Bk II. (4 h.); Exerc. of Greek Archaeol. Soc'y. (2 h.).

Ebers — Old Egypt. Grammar (3 h.); Interpret. of Passages in Genesis and Exodus relating to Egypt. (2 h.).

Leskien — Grammar of Church Slavonic (4 h.); Hist. of Serbic-Croatic Lang. (2 h.).

Credner — General Geology (5 h.); Labor. Practice (2 h.).

Stohmann — Chem. Technology (3 h.).

Mayer — Analyt. Geom. (4 h.); Mathem. Exerc. (1 h.)

Zürn — Anatomy of the Horse (2 h.); Veterinary Surgery (4 h.); Hygiene of Domestic Animals (1 h.).

3. *Privatdocenten.*

Weiske — Meteorology (2 h.).

O. Delitsch — Methodology of Geogr. Instruction (2 h.); *Relatorium* in Geography (2 h.).

Paul — Musical Art of Greek Drama (2 h.); Harmonics of Mod. Music, etc. (2 h.).

Frank — Natural History of Fungi (2 h.); Seeds in Agriculture (2 h.).

Mühll — Theory of Elasticity (4 h.); Potential and Conic Functions (2 h.); Mathem. Exerc.

Loth — Persian (2 h.); Encyclopaedy of Arabic (2 h.).

Carstanjen — Analyt. Chem. (4 h.).

Schuchardt — Span. Grammar (3 h.); Ariosto (1 h.).

Englemann — Planetary Orbits (2 h.); Mechanical Quadrature (1 h.).

Nitsche — Nat. Hist. and Palæontol. of Molluscs (2 h.); Developm't. of Invertebrates (2 h.).

Philippi — Thucydides (3 h.); Hist. of Athens (1 h.).

Hirzel — Hist. of Greek Philos. (4 h.); Interpret. of Plato's Phaedrus; Pract. Exerc. in Aristotle's Ethics.

Sachsse — General Agricult. Chem. (4 h.); *Repetitorium* for Analyt. Chem. (1 h.).

Luerssen — Morphology, Physiology of Algae, Fungi, etc. (3 h.).

Schuster — Hist. of Greek Phil. down to Aristotle; Interpret. of Plato's Gorgias.

Fürst — (since deceased) Isaiah (3 h.); Pirke-Aboth (1 h.).

Langer — General Theory of Music (2 h.); Varieties of Musical Composit. (2 h.).

I have selected Leipsic because it is, beyond question, the leading German university at the present day. The number of its matriculated students exceeds that of Berlin by one thousand, and falls short of that of Vienna by only a few hundred. Vienna owes its large numbers to two circumstances. First, it is the only seat of learning for an immense district measured by a radius of one hundred and fifty miles, whereas Leipsic is in the heart of Germany, and has for its next-door neighbors Halle, Jena, Berlin and Breslau. Next, the medical school and the hospitals of Vienna are the most renowned in the world. If we deduct the excess of medical students of Vienna over Leipsic, we shall find that in the other departments the latter leads the former. For breadth and variety of learning, and for activity, the Leipsic faculty is unrivaled. The reader who is in any degree familiar with the great movements of thought will have no difficulty in recognizing in the above list of professors men pre-eminent in every branch.

Berlin has been outstripped in the last ten years. This decline of the university that was once foremost has been made the subject of much discussion, both as to its causes and its possible cure. The most obvious cause is the enhanced expense of living. In 1863, only eleven years ago, the cost of living was moderate. A very good room could be obtained for eight or ten thalers a month. This was more than the rates at Göttingen, yet not much more than the rates at Heidelberg and Bonn. Other items of living, such as meals and clothing, were no higher than they were elsewhere. Now, one can not obtain a tolerable room under twenty-five to thirty thalers a month, table-board has doubled in price, clothing also, and the general tone of the city has changed. One is victimized at every turn. So long as Berlin remained the capital of the obscure kingdom of Prussia, it was a quiet, *gemüthliche* city. But in becoming the seat of the North German Confederation, and later still of the German Empire, it lost its former simplicity without acquiring the large-mindedness of a world-centre like London or Paris. The French milliards have launched the Berlinese upon a career of wild extravagance. The university plays no longer the same important part that it did in city life. Both students and professors feel that they are pushed to the wall by the herds of *nouveaux riches*, by stock-brokers, contractors, house-builders, and adventurers. Yet the rise in prices is not the only cause of the decline of the university. The faculty itself is in part to blame. Like not a few other institutions, it has lived too much on its past reputation. Its most distinguished professors are men extremely advanced in life, many of them are crotchety, opinionated, illiberal, set in their ways, and unsympathetic. They hold too much aloof from the spirit of the times. The university needs an infusion of new blood. Yet it will be difficult to obtain such an infusion. The rising celebrities find it more advantageous to accept a call to Leipsic or Munich or Strassburg, where the salaries, nominally no greater, are in reality adequate to the style of living, and where they can exert more influence. I doubt whether Berlin will ever overtake Leipsic. The Saxon government, relieved from the responsibilities of political action, seems to be devoting its energies and its resources to the promotion of more spiritual interests. The King and his Ministers have now little else to do than to take this indirect and laudable revenge upon Prussia. With plenty of money at their command, they can, to use a mercantile phrase, go into the market and buy up whatever is best. Leipsic is slowly but surely drawing to itself the young men of promise.

To complete the picture of the Leipsic university, I give the following tabular statement of expenditure and income for 1873. The figures were graciously furnished at my request by Professor Zarncke (Rector in 1872), through the mediation of my friend Dr. Felix Flügel.

Private Income of the University.

1. From buildings and rents (shops in the city)............................	57,811
2. From Endowments and the Faculty Fiscus	36,942
3. Matriculation and other Fees............	8,100
	102,853

Expenditures.

1. Sinking Fund......................	15,904
2. Expenses in carrying out terms of special bequests.........................	672
Carried forward....................	16,576

Brought forward		16,576
3. Salaries of Employees		18,618
4. Salaries of Professors,		
Theological Faculty	18,180	
Legal	28,308	
Medical	27,896	
Philosophical	83,479	157,863
5. Apparatus of Instruction (Laboratory, Library, etc.)		99,773
6. General Expenses, Printing, Pensions, etc.		9,582
7. Student Stipends		2,270
8. At the disposal of the Ministry (Contingent Fund)		10,000
Thalers		314,682

Deducting the 102,853 of private income, there is an annual deficit of 211,829 thalers, met by appropriations from the state treasury. Of the total expenditures, 275,454 go for salaries and the apparatus of instruction, say *ninety per cent of the whole*. Even deducting the 18,618 paid to employees would leave the percentage at almost eighty-five.

The above statement, be it also observed, takes no account of lecture-fees. These fees, although paid in first instance to the university treasurer, are not entered in the general fund, but are transferred directly to the respective professors. So little are they regarded as an item of university income, that my informant has not even thought it necessary to give them. I am constrained, therefore, to make a computation based upon mere conjecture. Assuming that there are 3,000 students, in round numbers, and that each one pays only twenty-five thalers a year,— a low average, and one that makes ample allowance for such poor students as obtain a remission or abatement of their fees,— we get the sum of 75,000, which sum is to be added of course to the 157,863 of official salaries. It is an interesting feature, and one that reveals in the strongest light the radical difference between Germany and America, that what we regard as the main source of support for our colleges, their life-blood, is not even entered by the university of Leipsic in the official statement of its income.

Leipsic is one of the few universities that have property of their own. The others are Heidelberg and Greifswald. I do not know of any besides these three. Leipsic is by far the wealthiest. The other universities are dependent altogether upon state appropriations. This is undoubtedly the case with Göttingen (formerly Hanoverian) and the Prussian universities.

With regard to the salaries of the Leipsic professors, I take the liberty of quoting Professor Zarncke's own words: "The highest salary is about 3,500 thalers, but some of the professors are in receipt of gratuities (*Zuschüsse*) in addition. Thus the *ordinarius* of the law-faculty has an addition of at least 1,000, the directors of the hospitals have about 600 in addition, and so on.

*32

This does not include lecture-fees, which, in many cases, must amount to 2,000 or 3,000. Accordingly our best paid man can not be in receipt of less than 7,000. But this, to be sure, is a highly favored position (*eine glänzende Ausnahmestellung*). The minimum for an *ordinarius* is, at present, about 1,000. Most of the *ordinarii* receive 1,800 to 2,000. The average income of the *ordinarii* would be 2,500. As to the *extra-ordinarii*, no fixed rule prevails. A few receive no salary, others receive only 500, others again 1,000. One, if I mistake not, receives 1,200."

These salaries will appear, at first sight, decidedly meagre. Yet it should be borne in mind that money is only a relative notion. Whether a person in receipt of a fixed sum is well off or poorly off, depends upon the purchasing power represented by that sum. I should rather take my chances as *Ausserordentlicher* of the Leipsic faculty with 500 thalers a year, than as an American assistant-professor with $1,000. The Leipsic man has one decided advantage over his American colleague. His official duties are light, and lie altogether in the direction of his chosen studies. He is not called upon to give instruction to classes for twelve, fifteen, or even twenty hours a week, nor is his time frittered away in enforcing general discipline. One course of lectures (four or five hours a week) is his quantum of work. Whatever exceeds this, is a matter of personal ambition. If he is successful enough to establish two or three courses, the lecture-fees are his private gain.

His time is almost wholly his own. His salary enables him to live. To make this point clear, I shall endeavor to show as fully as possible the purchasing power of money in a town like Leipsic. The estimate will be of interest to those of my readers who may wish to know what to expect in Germany. I passed two months in Leipsic in the summer of 1872. Being pressed for time, I took the first apartment that I could find, without stopping to advertise or to bargain. It consisted of a study, with two windows facing on the main street, and a sleeping room with one window. Both rooms were commodious, perfectly clean, and well furnished. The furniture was, for Germany, almost elegant. I paid ten thalers a month. The same quarters could not be obtained in New York for less than $10 a week. Breakfast, consisting of two cups of coffee, bread and butter, and eggs, served in my room, cost five thalers a month. My dinner at Müller's restaurant, one of the best in town, cost, including a glass of beer, twelve thalers. Supper, a substantial warm meal, averaged about ten thalers. The aggregate of my expenses for living, then, was thirty-seven thalers a month. I venture to say that for this trifling sum I lived better, that is, more at my ease, feeling that I got more for my money, than I have ever succeeded in doing, under like circumstances, in America. As it was, I paid too much. I was a stranger, in a hurry, and unable to take the time for devising ways of economy. One located permanently in Leipsic could live fully as well for three fourths of the amount. Many a good room can be had, by hunting after it, for six thalers a month. The incidental expenses of life in Germany are nothing, as compared with those in America. An excellent suit of clothes can be purchased for twenty-five or thirty thalers, a pair of shoes for five or six thalers. Amusements are also very cheap. By purchasing a season ticket for the *Schützenhaus*, the great concert garden of the city, the price of admission is reduced to three cents an evening. For this trifling sum, one has the entrée to a large and beautifully illuminated garden; the music, lasting from eight to eleven o'clock, is furnished by two large bands that play alternately in different sections of the garden. In addition to the music, there is a display of acrobatics. The best reserved seats at the opera and theatre cost only one thaler. But subscription-seats can be obtained at less than half the price.* There are numerous reading-rooms, where one can have access to all the periodicals, magazines and reviews, for a mere pittance, not to speak of the newspapers taken in the cafés.

During my stay in Leipsic I was too much absorbed in my private studies to take very careful note of the world around me. Besides, it was the long vacation for the greater part of the time. But in 1873, on my return home from Vienna, I stopped for a few days to make some purchases. Having complete disposal of my time, I employed it in studying the outward manifestations of

---

* It would be ungrateful in me to fail to mention the delightful motets delivered gratuitously every Saturday afternoon in the Church of St. Thomas.

intellectual activity. At certain hours of the day the streets of the inner city, in the neighborhood of the university building, were thronged with students on their way to and from lecture. More particularly was this noticeable at one o'clock, when the midday pause comes in. The arched ways and courts of the quondam Dominican cloister, with all the avenues of approach, resembled a huge swarming ant-heap. Hundreds, thousands of young men, *Mappe* in hand, were hastening away to their rooms and their dining-places. Although there was no disorder, none of the turbulence and boisterous demonstrations that distinguish an American class let loose, it was almost impossible to make one's way against the surging mass of humanity. On one occasion I amused myself, while enjoying an after-dinner cup of coffee in the Café Français, by studying the motley composition of my neighbors. The upper rooms of the Café are given up to smokers, and at this hour of the day nearly all the guests are students. To my left sat a party of Poles sibilating to their hearts' content over a game of draughts. To my right, a sedate party of Greeks, men of thirty or thirty-five, puffing cigarettes and conversing in an undertone. Directly in front, Germans boisterous over "Scat." In the adjoining billiard-room, three or four of my countrymen still more boisterous over pool, "damning scratches" and taking for granted, with the license that prevails among Americans on the Continent, that no one could understand them. The whole world seemed to be represented in that post-prandial reunion in the smoking-room of the Café Français. Coming fresh from the scenes of the Vienna Exhibition, I thought to myself that Leipsic too was a World's Fair, a standing parliament of the nations. The quiet Saxon town had made the world its tributary. Among its students were men who had played the role of professor at home, men well on in the thirties and even forties, who had saved up a few hundreds and had come from the four quarters of the earth, had crossed mountains and continents and oceans, in quest of the fountain of knowledge.

The reader has before him the materials with which to construct an image of the great university in its magnitude and its variety. Let him add thereto the city gymnasiums, with their numerous staff of highly educated teachers, the celebrated Conservatory of Music, the many scientific and literary institutions, the bureaus of the countless perodicals that have their headquarters here, the great publishing houses of Brockhaus, Teubner, Tauchnitz and others scarcely less renowned, each one of which has its *personnel* of critical proof-readers, editors, and literary advisers, and finally the many authors themselves residing here permanently. The aggregation of talent and culture is startling. The city throbs with the pulsations of intense and sustained intellectual effort. Leipsic is the head-centre for the culture of the most productive nation of the present day. Only London, Paris and Berlin, I am persuaded, surpass it in the number of men of learning, while in proportion to its population — barely 100,000 — it is without a peer.

IX.

Practical Hints.

It was part of my original purpose to sketch the prominent features of the six or eight leading universities of Germany, and to enumerate the most celebrated professors in each department. But aside from the difficulty, not to say the impossibility of doing justice to the claims of all and each, I was deterred by the further consideration, that such a comparison, with all the care that might be put upon it, would have no permanent value. The universities are shifting in their nature. One rises, the other falls; a few professors die or remove, new ones come in their place, and the character of the university is modified. Within my own experience I can recall a striking instance of this shifting. Ten years ago, Göttingen stood slightly in the background, while Heidelberg was, if not the largest, certainly the most conspicuous of all the universities. But Vangerow and Mittermaier have since died, and the number of Heidelberg students has fallen to five hundred, while Göttingen, stimulated by the accession of new men, has raised its numbers to a thousand. The two universities have changed positions. The resuscitation of the university of Strassburg has drawn off many of the best scholars from the older seats of learning. The smaller towns, in particular, such as Marburg, Würzburg, Tübingen, have suffered severely. Professors die and remove in America also, but their coming and going does not affect so directly the general status of the college. The undergraduate is sent to one college rather than to another, because the outline of study meets the views of his parents, or because they wish him to be reared under the influence of the religious denomination controlling that college, or because his family is traditionally identified with it. Each college in America draws its supply of teachers and students from its own especial sources, represents certain fixed interests, and moves therefore in an orbit of its own. I doubt whether one undergraduate in a hundred is determined in his selection of an alma mater by the circumstance that a certain professor or certain professors are enrolled in its faculty. Indeed, so long as the professor himself is hindered from displaying his talents to their full extent, is limited to a share in the prescribed curriculum, the student is forced to disregard individual merits and to estimate the college only in its totality. In Germany, on the other hand, where the organization is uniform and all the universities rest on the same basis and are administered in accordance with the same principle, the character of each one at a given epoch is determined solely by the professors composing the faculty. If they are men of progress, the university itself will flourish; but if they represent rather the ideas and methods that are passing away, the university will be on the wane.

The reader will understand, then, that I do not attempt to furnish the data by which he can decide for himself which one of the twenty universities may be best suited to his needs. On this, as on every other point, the advice and opinion of friends who have lived in Germany, and are in a position to judge men and institutions by the light of their own personal experience, will be far more to the purpose than any mere remarks from me. All that I can do is to throw out a few practical suggestions of a general nature.

The first is that every one who thinks of entering upon German university life should decide beforehand upon his specialty. The object of the university is not to afford general culture, but special training. Everything is made subservient to minuteness and thoroughness of research. Hence the American who should matriculate at Leipsic in the expectation of finding merely a Yale or a Harvard on a more generous scale, would find himself grievously disappointed. He may study any one subject he chooses, but he must study it to the exclusion of all others.

To make a proper selection, one must have finished his preliminary training, i. e., must have taken his American degree of B. A. or B. S. The American college goes little beyond the gymnasium, and, moreover, is not so thorough in its method. The American graduate is somewhat older and considerably more worldly-wise than the newly matriculated *Fuchs*, but I take the liberty of doubting whether he is equal in solid attainments, or in capacity for work. His education is marred by many flaws, it is not sufficiently symmetrical. Composition, oratory, and *miscellanea* have been cultivated at the expense of more difficult acquisitions. One who enters the university without the preparation afforded either by the gymnasium or the college, commits the grave blunder of building on too narrow a foundation. He runs the risk of making his studies hasty and superficial. The German is not permitted to make such a mistake; he is kept back, even against his will, until he has "ripened." The American is not under the same restraint, there is nothing to hinder him from entering a German university at the age of seventeen or eighteen, quite unprepared. Yet not many do so. The danger most to be apprehended comes in the shape of the temptation to expedite matters by breaking off one's college course in the Junior or even in the Sophomore year. Not a few of the Americans now studying in the universities of Germany are young men whose impatience has thus outrun their discernment. The mistake is fraught with serious consequences. Whoever commits it is neither one thing nor the other; he has not secured the benefit of gymnasial training, nor has he made his mark, so to speak, at home. If my words are to have any weight, I feel it to be my duty to impress upon the young reader the importance of completing his college studies before embarking upon the ocean of university life. To say this, one does not need to be blindly enamored of the American college system. That system has many and grievous faults. Yet taken as it is, for better and for worse, it is our system, the die that stamps its mark upon our culture. The man who has not received that impress must resign himself to passing at a discount. College training, imperfect as it undoubtedly is from the point of view of pure theory, has nevertheless practical advantages that must not be disregarded. It prepares young men for the sudden crises, the contingencies and irregularities of American life. It does not afford, I regret to say, the highest instruction in any one department of knowledge. He who seeks after such instruction must go abroad for it. Yet the college is the place where one can best fit himself for playing his part as an American, the place where one can form useful connections and enroll himself in the brotherhood of American thinkers and men of action.

These remarks concerning the colleges will apply with equal force to the schools of science and of medicine. After consulting with friends, and joining their opinions to the results of my own observation, I feel warranted in asserting that the surest way of reaping the full benefit of the advantages afforded in Europe is to prepare for them by taking a full course of study at home. Study abroad is like travel abroad; one brings back only what one took away with him. That is to say, one must prepare himself for the mission, by acquiring an ample stock of ideas and principles, and a practical familiarity with methods and processes. Otherwise, the phases of foreign life and thought slip from the mind like the evanescent kaleidoscopic impressions made by a moving panorama. Although entertained for the while, one is left in reality no wiser than before.

We can even go farther, and hold that the American

student should not only have completed his general education, but that he should have mastered the rudiments of his specialty, before matriculating in a German university. It is the first step, as we all know, that costs. The German passes direct from the gymnasium to the university. But then he is at home, he has parents and friends near at hand, who can advise him from time to time. The American is thrown more upon his own resources. He has not only to learn the language, but he has to familiarize himself with novel ways of living. However high-spirited and self-confident, he will be overcome at times by a feeling of helplessness, the consciousness of having to learn everything at once. The struggle is then too intense, too wearing. It will be materially lightened, if the student has already taken a start, if, while working amid strange surroundings and against the odds of foreign nomenclature, he is still working according to methods with which he is to some extent familiar. Let us take the study of chemistry for the purposes of illustration. To attempt to learn at once German and chemistry from the very beginning is too difficult. It can be done; indeed, it has been done repeatedly. Yet success is bought at too great a cost. Six months' practice in an American laboratory would reduce the labor by at least one half.

Furthermore, there is a practical consideration which has been too often overlooked. It is this. The American does not live to study; he rather studies to live. Were life merely a pleasant sojourn in the secluded haunts of literature and science, one could afford to take up his abode early in a German university and linger there year after year in the delightful pursuit of abstract knowledge. But to the American mind, study presents itself as the means to an end, and that end is position, salary, whatever we may choose to call it. Much that is taught in a German university is proper enough in itself, and conducive to the highest interests of culture, but is not available, not yet at least, in America. One who wishes to prosper on his return home, should have the faculty of selecting, should be able to seize upon the essential, the practical, and disregard the unessential. But this ability presupposes experience, a knowledge of what the home-public will receive with favor. Hence it is that the men who have first initiated themselves into their vocation at home, serving their time as tutors or assistants, maturing, growing with the needs of the community whom they serve, will succeed in turning even the briefest course in a German university to such good account, while others, who hastened abroad and prolonged their stay, return confused in their notions and blundering in their aims.

The parents who place their children at school in Germany, in the expectation of giving them the benefits of a "thorough continental education," commit a grave error. It is not an easy matter to get an American boy into a really good German school. Our boys stand in marked disfavor with the school-authorities. Teachers and directors have learned by painful experience that young

*33

Americans are prone to be idle and mutinous, exerting an evil influence over their associates. Nothing short of the strongest testimonials, backed by explicit guarantees from resident citizens, will open the doors of the gymnasium. The private schools that make a practice of admitting Americans and English are, to say the least, questionable in their character and in the quality of their instruction. They are unquestionably inferior to the best of our own schools. Besides, conceding even that the American boy is placed at the gymnasium in his fifteenth or sixteenth year, pursues successfully the studies of *Secunda* and *Prima*, and enters the university, in what respect is he better off than his countryman who has just arrived from over the water? He is more thoroughly trained in Latin and Greek, in mathematics, and in history, and he speaks German with the fluency and precision of a native. A great gain, no doubt, but obtained at a terrible price. The youth is completely denationalized! He is no longer an American, he has no sympathy with American life and character, he fails to appreciate American modes of thought and sentiment. Unless he has had the good fortune to reside with his own family, the probability is that his proficiency in German has cost him the total, in any case the partial loss of his mother-tongue. He is unable to write a letter or a composition in English, without committing the most absurd blunders in style, in grammar, and in orthography. Let him pass three years additional at the university. He will return to his native country, a young man of twenty-three, highly educated, no doubt, but helpless, unpractical, ignorant of the ways of his countrymen. He will be almost as much a foreigner as any one of the hundred immigrants landed to-day at Castle Garden.

Of all cruel delusions that have played havoc with education, this one of "the languages" has been the most baneful. Parents do not seem to perceive that their first duty to their children is to make them Americans. What is in itself only a means, they look upon as an end. It is perfectly true that a knowledge of French and German is not only useful, but is necessary in all or nearly all the professions. The man who has not command over the resources of these two languages labors under great disadvantage. Yet it is advisable that we should meet and answer fairly the question: What is meant by *knowing a language?* If by knowing a language is meant simply the ability to maintain a conversation or write a letter, let us be candid and admit that the accomplishment is a mere superficial varnish, a something that is not worth the acquisition. The small-talk of the ordinary letter and the drawing-room is no better and no worse in one language than in another. Where is the gain in keeping a boy or a girl for years in a *Pension*, far away from the refining influences of home, merely that he or she may be able to rattle off bilingual platitudes? How many of the hundreds and thousands of young men and women who have been reared at great expense in France and Germany, and who pride themselves on their glibness of conversation, have made or are likely to make their mark as authors and thinkers? If French is worth learning at all,— and this applies to German and every other language,— it is worth learning, not as a " beggarly account of empty boxes " with pretty gilt labels, but as a vast storehouse of thought and culture. To know French in the sense of being able to say, Good Morning, How D'ye Do, and to order one's dinner and berate the waiter, is a superfluous accomplishment. But French as the vehicle used by Racine, Pascal, Moliére, by the great writers of France, to convey their thoughts and ideas, is an object worth striving after. The man or the woman who is able to read French works with an understanding of their relative merits, with a clear insight into their development and into the special phase of national life that each one represents, has just reason to be proud. French language is one thing, French literature is another. The latter is a final object of study, the former is not. But to know French literature as the body of French thought, one must look upon the language as preliminary, the mere avenue of approach. And to become a good scholar in French literature, one must be in the first place a good scholar in English. One must be reared at home, must receive the best training that his own country can afford, and must place himself in accord with whatever is distinctively American and English. In no other way can one *compare* the literature in French with the literature in English, and do justice to each. The two Americans whose names are most strongly associated with foreign culture are

Longfellow and Lowell. They have won for themselves imperishable fame as genial mediators between the Old World and the New. Yet neither Longfellow nor Lowell, I am confident, looks upon his knowledge of French, or German, or Italian as anything more than the key with which to unlock the treasure-houses of European thought. They were both sound English scholars, graduates of American colleges, before they embarked upon their foreign tours of exploration. They went abroad knowing what to look for, prepared to accept or reject, to assimilate, and to reproduce.

It is time that protest should be raised against this pernicious practice of placing our boys and girls at European schools. These schools are excellent, better indeed than our own, in many respects. But they are not planned for Americans, and they can never fit their pupils for the peculiar duties and responsibilities of American life. The higher education of the German universities is the best in the world. Yet Americans should beware of entering upon it before they are fully ripe, before they know what to take and what to leave.

In speaking of the universities of Leipsic and Berlin, I have already mentioned the rates of the chief items of expenditure. It will be needful to add in this place, therefore, only a brief comparison of Leipsic with the smaller university towns. At Marburg, my room cost exactly one half the Leipsic price, but was much inferior in every respect. Indeed, by reason of the wretched style of building that has prevailed at Marburg, it is difficult to obtain a good room at any price. I may say, in general, that a good room may be had at Tübingen, Halle, Würzburg, Jena, and the other towns, except Bonn and Heidelberg, for six or seven thalers a month. Table d'hôte will be somewhat less than at Leipsic, the other meals will differ but slightly. Whoever has at his command $500 per annum, in gold, will be able to live in comfort, to have good rooms and excellent fare, to add twenty or thirty volumes each semester to his library, and to travel for a fortnight each vacation. There is many a German student who would be thankful to receive as much as $300 per annum. The only universities that can be called expensive are Berlin and Vienna. For these two places, $800 to $1,000 will scarcely be too much.

What particular subject shall be studied, is of course a question that must be settled by each one for himself, according to his predilection and his opportunities. As a matter of fact, the majority of the Americans who study in Germany pursue chemistry and medicine. Next in point of numbers are the students of the classics. After them come the theologians. Very few take up the subject of Roman jurisprudence. So long as the law is looked upon in America as a bread-and-butter study, I see no reason to expect a change in this respect. To use the current phrase, "it will not pay" to spend two or three years over the Institutes and the Pandects. Yet I cannot refrain from expressing my regret that so few of our young lawyers should think it worth the while to make at least the effort to emulate the great Chancellor Kent, and to develop themselves not merely into clever practitioners but into accomplished jurists. A knowledge of the principles of the Roman Law is the foundation of study in international jurisprudence, and is also indispensable to a full understanding of the movements recorded in Continental history. If by history we mean in sincerity the formation of national character and habits, and not merely the chronicle of battles and court intrigues, we cannot escape the conclusion that to study the history of a nation one must examine into its system of laws. For the laws of a nation are the permanent expression of the nation's habits, its views concerning property, the marriage relation, the rights and duties of parents and children, the connection between church and state. The political and social constitutions of France, Germany, Italy, and Spain, rest, to a large extent, upon the system of rules and maxims bequeathed to them or imposed upon them by the Romans and confirmed by the mediæval church. The first step, then, toward the knowledge of continental history is the study of the general principles embodied in the *corpus juris.* In support of this position, I refer to the practice of the German universities, that place the Institutes and History of Roman Law among the requirements for the degree in history.

Although loth to say aught that may have the appearance of an attempt to influence others in the selection of their vocations, I make one, and only one suggestion. Should any one of my readers be desirous of testing for himself the boasted superiority of the German university system, and should he be wholly undecided in his choice of a subject, why may he not take up history, and more especially the history of Germany? Not only is the field inviting in itself, but it is one in which he need fear no rivals. The balance of power in Europe has been shifted over night, the veterans of Austria and France have gone down before the charge of the Prussian citizen-soldier, the first have become last, and the last first, but we have still to learn how this wonderful change has been effected. We count our German citizens, adopted and native, by the million, yet no one has told us in our own language what the change means, how it came to pass, what were its conditions and its remote origin, what it portends in the history of European civilization. We are left to the dreary platitudes of the English press and the incoherent Jeremiads of the French. Will not some one of our future scholars write for us the history of Germany, based upon German authorities but conceived from the American point of view? The harvest is there, awaiting the harvester. Let him show how the German race, foremost in the Middle Ages, misdirected by the inordinate ambition of the Hohenstaufen and the Habsburgs, bewildered by the Reformation, crushed by the Thirty Years' War, crazed by the Revolution, has nevertheless, by virtue of its marvelous vitality, regenerated itself, reconstituted itself from crown to sole, regained its former ascendency through the one great revival on record. The labor, I am aware, is immense, but the reward will be commensurate. The initiatory discipline can be acquired only at a German university.

I conclude with a practical hint. Most Americans who visit Germany for the purpose of study leave home at the close of the so called commencement season. But many of them travel during the summer months, instead of proceeding direct to Germany and locating themselves permanently. This is a mistake. As a student, one has abundant opportunities for travel during the regular vacations. One's first aim should be to acquire some familiarity with the language. By leaving at the end of June, one can reach almost any city or town in Germany by the middle of July. From this date to the middle of October, the commencement of the winter semester, is a period of three months, which can be devoted exclusively to the study of the language. If this time is put to account, there will be very little difficulty in attending lectures in October. The Christmas vacation will afford ample time for visiting Berlin and Dresden, the spring vacation can be taken for the Rhine, and the succeeding summer for South Germany and the Alps. There can scarcely be a better adjustment of study and travel for the first year. One loses no time in going to work, and has the additional gain of traveling when he is already familiar with the language of the country, the coins, and also the ways of living. It will not be necessary, perhaps not advisable, to spend the three months above mentioned in a university town Any place where the language is correct and living economical will answer. Hanover, in itself considered, would be perhaps the best place. But it is somewhat expensive, and is overrun with English and American families. Brunswick is a handsome city and offers many inducements. Next to it in desirability come Gotha, Weimar, and the other towns of Thuringia. From Leipsic eastward, and Cassel southward, the German loses in purity and elegance. But wherever one may go, one point should never be overlooked, namely, to secure good letters of introduction from Americans and Germans to their personal friends in Germany. Mere general letters will not be of much avail. The letters should emanate from men of some distinction in America, and should be addressed to their personal acquaintances abroad. One such letter may secure the bearer a kind reception and a home at the start, and will certainly save him weeks of vexatious search after lodgings and the other incidentals of life. Even if the addressee can do nothing in the way of direct assistance, he can always advise, and to a foreigner, young and inexperienced, the smallest grain of advice is worth many a pound of self-bought wisdom.

www.ingramcontent.com/pod-product-compliance
Lightning Source LLC
Chambersburg PA
CBHW022118290426
44112CB00008B/717